WOMEN WHO STAY

WOMEN WHO STAY

Seafaring and Subjectification in an Ilocos Town

RODERICK G. GALAM

Ateneo de Manila University Press

ATENEO DE MANILA UNIVERSITY PRESS
Bellarmine Hall, Katipunan Avenue
Loyola Heights, Quezon City, P.O. Box 154
1099 Manila, Philippines
Tel. (632) 426-59-84 / Fax (632) 426-59-09
Email: unipress@admu.edu.ph
Website: www.ateneopress.org

Cover design by Rebecca V. Yu

The National Library of the Philippines CIP Data

Recommended entry:

Galam, Roderick G.
Women who stay : seafaring and subjectification in an Ilocos town / Roderick G. Galam. – Quezon City : Ateneo de Manila University Press, 2018, [c2018].
xii, 238 pages ; 22.86 cm

ISBN 978-971-550-848-3

1. Housewives – Ilocos (Philippines) – Social conditions. 2. Migrant laborers' spouses – Ilocos (Philippines) – Economic conditions. 3. Housewives – Ilocos (Philippines) – Economic conditions. 4. Emigration and immigration – Ilocos (Philippines) – Economic conditions. 5. Women employees – Ilocos (Philippines) 6. Subjectivity (Sociology/Anthropology) I. Title.

305.4364 HD8039.H84 2018 P720170286

For Marilyn,
Gabrielle, Daniel, and Jacob

CONTENTS

ACKNOWLEDGMENTS

Although "I'm much more aware of pain than I am receptive to joy," as the writer Akhil Sharma said, I write this acknowledgment with quiet joy, remembering the profound loss that drove me to finish *Women Who Stay*. Within a period of just over a year, my wife and I lost three loved ones: her brother, my father, and her cousin she considered a sister. I dealt with their deaths by burying myself in the work of writing this book. Even as grief gifted me with some lucidity, many people gave generously of their time for which I am very grateful.

I am, of course, most indebted to the women who participated in my research and their husbands who agreed to talk to me. Without them, there simply would be no *Women Who Stay*. I benefitted from the encouraging comments of Mick Bloor and I am grateful to him for his continued support of my work. I thank Teret de Villa, Lily Rose Tope, Leavides Domingo, Itaru Nagasaka, and Lilia Quindoza Santiago for their comments on chapters, which helped me strengthen my arguments.

My involvement in the work of the Apostleship of the Sea (AoS) Manila deepened my understanding of the lives and experiences of seafarers and their families. I thank its chaplain, Father Paulo Prigol, CS, for his friendship and enormous contribution to my work, as well as the staff of AoS-Manila, Stella Maris Ermita, and Scalabrini Center for People on the Move (SCPM): Franz Agravante, Roberto Canta, Ate Evelyn del Rosario, Sister Vilana Laluan, (the late) Kuya Greg Pedernal, Ate Malou Pedernal, Dorie Salomon, Marie San Andres, Sister Victoria Sanchez, Sister Cecilia Santiago, Leonardo Servidad, Sister Raycee Sumampong, Delia Umbao, and Isa Yniguez. Living with seafarers at the SCPM helped me see the dynamic of being home in the country but not home with the family and the financial strain caused by prolonged waiting for their next contract. What I saw and heard from them corroborates what the women of this book say about the hardship caused by their husband's contractual work. My research visits to the Philippines enabled me to renew friendships with Aurelio Agcaoili, Raquel Avante, Romel Bagares, Lorina Calingasan, Aida Cuanang, Jabeth Dacanay, Teret de Villa, Portia Dimabuyu, Jean Pia, Pia Ramirez, Wowie Salbibia, Marj Tangog, and Dedet Vargas. Their dedication to the work that they do inspires me.

My entire family is profoundly indebted to Teresita Rafanan for her important contribution to our lives. I thank our friends for their help and thoughtfulness: Jeannette Balangcod, Janet and Dom Barcega, Arthur and Rhoda Blanco, Moonyean and Buboy Cuanico, Norma and Ron Cuthbertson, Francis and Marilyn D'Acosta, Elsie and Danny Damo, Bernadette and Luther Diaz, Ate Agie and Kuya Jap Faytaren, Medalyn and Edsel Flores, Imee Caperocho Harris, Junar Ibasco, Janet Josue, Ada and Paul Maspinas, Sarah Mukombe, Frederick and Joy Pagaling, Hazel and Hassan Patel, Faye Paz, Fei and Sherhan Que, Alan and Darlene Ragpala, Leslie and Kurt Robles, Jun and Minnie Sayson, Graham and Hilda Stafford, Santa Steen, Marlon Valdez, Gigi Verano, and Ate Zenaida Yanga. I thank Maricel Agustin-Parrau for hosting me in her beautiful Brandenburg home for a few weeks, and Rami Kaplan and Jojo Nem Singh for various help and conversations. During a particularly difficult period, the support provided by Birgitt Roettger-Roessler immensely helped me and my family. I am grateful to Birgitt for her inestimable support. Thank you, too, to Gabriele Haensel for all her help.

That I have been away from my family for long periods of time for several years now has profoundly contributed to my understanding of the subject I deal with in this book. I thank Marilyn for her insights into the experience of being a stay-behind wife and for being the rock upon whom our family has stood. I have been sustained by her goodness, faith, hope, courage, resilience, and more. Gabrielle Himig, Daniel Kired, and Jacob Ilian carried and continue to carry me on their young shoulders. When they were much younger, they scribbled, wrote, and drew on my notes—superimposing their presence on what I was doing, and sat on my lap while I wrote, their profound way of reminding me of time I did not spend with them, of things that surely were equally, if not far more, important. Although over the years they have come to understand what a closed door meant when I was writing, I am thankful for the many times they disregarded it. My debts to my *dungngos* are many, my gratitude profound, my love beyond language. To them I would like to add Flordelis, Willie and Vangie, Edgar and Dang, Joey, Mel and Noel, Charles, Jr and Greeny, Cheryl and Ricky, Robert, Lawrence and Jenny, Gary, and Kristine.

I am most thankful to the Nippon Foundation and its chairman, Dr Yohei Sasakawa, for the Nippon Foundation Postgraduate Fellowship that funded my PhD on which *Women Who Stay* is based. I also thank the Dahlem Research Schools of the Free University of Berlin for a Postdoctoral International (POINT) fellowship, funded by the German Research Foundation (DFG) and the Marie Curie Foundation, which enabled me to conduct additional field-work. I thank Selie Tumacder, Gren Galam, and Gliceria Budol for fieldwork assistance. I am especially grateful to Ruby Calma for her research assistance.

Finally, I thank the Ateneo de Manila University Press for publishing this book, its director, Karina Bolasco, and staff for their contribution to its publication.

None of the people I mentioned is responsible for any of this book's weaknesses. I alone bear responsibility for its shortcomings.

I thank the publishers of the following journals for permission to include in this book material that first appeared in their publication.

Chapter 3 is a revised and longer version of "Through the Prism of Seamen's Left-behind Wives: Imagination and the Culture of Migration in Ilocos, Philippines," published in *Asian and Pacific Migration Journal* (vol. 24, no. 2) 137–59. Copyright© 2015 Scalabrini Migration Center. <DOI: 10.1177/0117196815579953> Reprinted by permission of Sage Publications.

Chapter 5 is a shorter and updated version of "Communication and Filipino Seamen's Wives: Imagined Communion and the Intimacy of Absence," published in *Philippine Studies: Historical and Ethnographic Viewpoints* (vol. 60, no. 2, June 2012, 223–60). Reprinted with permission by Ateneo de Manila University.

Chapter 6 was first published as "Women 'Like Parched Earth in Need of Rain' and Who Relax by Working: Gossip and the Surveillance of Filipino Seafarer Wives' Morality and Mobility" in *Mobilities* (31 May 2017) Copyright© Taylor & Francis, available online: http://www.tandfonline.com <DOI: 10.1080/17450101. 2017.133101> Reprinted by permission of Taylor & Francis Ltd.

Chapter 8 is an extended version of "Relational Autonomy: Kinship and Daughters-in-Law Negotiating Affinity with Their Mothers-in-Law," published in *Families, Relationships and Societies* (25 January 2016). Copyright© Policy Press 2016. <DOI: 10.1332/ 204674316X14534751747450> Reprinted by permission of Policy Press.

CHAPTER I

INTRODUCTION
Durable and Enduring Selves

"I've gone through a lot. I experienced bad treatment from his family. I bore them all. All because of the children. Even though all his family and relatives, God, even though they did not talk to me. I bore them all on my own. I faced a lot, really if you think about it, I went through all. I begged my husband to leave me so that his family and relatives would stop persecuting me. It started when I began receiving my allotment. I do not know if they were jealous. I experienced them all. My husband had affairs with other women when he was home. I went through all, financial problem, I experienced it all. I wanted to separate from him but he refused. We start anew, he said. We start all over again. No change. Even if I left him, he would come looking for me, he would search for me, he would not let it be. I wanted to show . . . it is easy to separate from your husband but what about the children? It is not that hard to break-up but I thought that there will come a time when he would calm down. By God's grace, he's settled down.

By God's grace, I am not saying that we no longer have to worry financially because we still do but money is no longer such a problem. And my husband has calmed, he does not go out any more. Before, God, buddies, if not women, buddies, he'd come home at dawn. By God's mercy, when I went abroad, that was also when my husband began to be more responsible. I was abroad, that's when he started building a house so his money would go to something tangible. That's when I think he stopped having affairs with other women. God, I came back the house looked like a skeleton. Then, with the little money I made, I had the ceiling done then when my husband was at sea, I would have things done little by little depending on my savings. Tiles, gradually, up to now, we are still doing things. Come to think of it, it is only now that we can do the polishing. See, what year is it . . . twelve years. Every time he comes back, he has some work done. When he is not here, I get done whatever it is I can get done. I hope that God will not give us any more trials because our life as a couple now is calm and light. We seem to be

> harmonious and at peace. My life is sailing smoothly now. My husband was tempestuous then. In the past, God, it was rough and stormy!"[1]
>
> —Nancy, 45 years old, mother to four children

Nancy's juxtaposition of images of movement characterized by, on one hand, calm and peace and roughness and upheaval and, on the other, movement through time and space, from a past to a present and to a future that is alluded, conjures up a woman who has not only endured but also prevailed. She likens her "old" husband to a tempestuous sea (*nadawel ni lakayko idi*) and her husband now as calm or peaceful (*natalna*) and portrays herself as a woman who has not only handled a difficult husband but also successfully navigated a rough and stormy life. Her life was burdened not only by her husband's womanizing and profligacy but also by her difficult relationship with her in-laws.

The women, whose lives form the basis of this book, referred to life as constituted by *padas* (experience) and *labas*—going through (*naglabasan* or *paglabasan*)—which evokes time, the past (*napalabas*) or that which one has gone through (*naglabasan*). In talking about their lives, they conjured up tropes of selfhood as journeys. As Nancy above said, "Adu't naglabasak" (I went through a lot) and "Napadasak amin" (I experienced them all). Another woman, Marissa, described her experiences, thus, "Adun a ti nagnaakon" (I have walked through many paths), thereby pointing to ideas about space and the repeated nature of the experience of difficulty. In other words, going through some trying times does not happen only once. It happens again and again, albeit the difficulties met are not the same. These images do not so much evoke nostalgia as convey a sense of the hardship endured, and, hence, a sense of accomplishment. Indeed, these tropes speak of enduring selves.

Filomeno Aguilar Jr. asserts that "[t]he very act of departing for work overseas is a complex assertion of subjectivity" (2014a, 128). Within Philippine migration scholarship, the figure of the migrant worker as a social and political subject has had far more recognition than those who stay behind. Research that has addressed identity, subjectivity, and agency in Philippine migration has almost exclusively focused on the experiences and subjectification of those who migrated.[2] Aguilar's essay on the subjectivity and agency of migrant Filipino workers, originally published in 1999, aimed to counter their one-sided representation "as victims of larger structures" (2014b, 12). It raises the question of the possibilities for subject formation among those who do not leave but enable and support the migration of others and who are just as "enmeshed in migratory processes as migrants themselves" (McDowell and de Haan 1997 quoted in Kothari 2003, 4).

Attention has been paid to what young children (Aguilar 2009a; Asis 2006a), teenagers and young adults (Parreñas 2005), and househusbands (Pingol 2001) undergo. In this book, I explicate the gendered subjectification of those who stay behind who enable or support the migration of others. I focus specifically on women married to Filipino seafarers working in the global maritime industry. I pay attention to wives of sea-based workers, marginal in migration scholarship that has focused primarily, if not exclusively, on land-based workers and their families in order to address, if not redress, the peripheral status of this specific group in migration scholarship. There has been increasing interest in Filipino seafarers, and research on international seafaring and seafarers has given ample critical attention to Filipino seafarers in part because of their numerical significance. However, little research has looked at their families.[3] Where migration research has examined the lives and experiences of those who stay behind, the focus has been on the families of land-based workers.

By examining the phenomenology of staying behind, I also address a lacuna in Asian migration research, an analysis of the experience itself of staying behind (Toyota et al. 2007). My empirical and conceptual elaboration of this experience through the prism of subjectivity provides the advantage of simultaneously situating the women in spousal, family, kin, and wider social relations thus demonstrating gender and subjectivity as "lived relations" (McNay 2004). I look not only into how the alternating absence and presence of the women's husbands shapes their everyday lives and family, kin, and social relationships but also how it engenders an environment of possibilities for subject formation. I look at experiences where women, consciously or compelled by their circumstance, engage in work that significantly defines and redefines their sense of who they are and what they can be and do. I analyze practices that bring about changes in their sense of self efficacy and independence, as well as strategies they devise that problematize gender relations and practices between them and their husbands, as well as hierarchies and structures of relations with family and kin.

I adopt a *relational* perspective, following Doreen Massey's insights on the "power-geometry" of mobility. Massey (1994) proposes two important characteristics of mobility. First, it is differential: groups and individuals have different access to, and possibilities for, mobility. Second, mobility is relational. Someone's mobility has direct negative consequences on somebody else's: "The time-space compression of some groups can undermine the power of others" (150). I do not examine here how Filipino seamen's mobility decreases or prevents the mobility of their wives. Rather, I look into how the women's staying put enables the sustainability and legitimacy of their husbands' mobility. I also pursue relationality here to examine gender practices because they are linked to the women's subjectification. The category of gender is important not only because those who leave are men and those who stay are women but also because the men's absence engenders the possibility for the perpetuation and/or interrogation of gender ideologies, relations, and practices. I examine the various mobilities that the women experience within their "staying put" (Reeves 2011), ones that I trace and map in transformations in their subjectivity. Furthermore, I examine the women's subjectivity within a perspective that considers both space and time as simultaneously involved in the production and representation of gendered subjectivity. There is a growing body of important work that links subjectivity and agency with both space and time in processes of migration (Aguilar 2002b, 2014a; Anderson 2007; Faier 2009; Parreñas 2011), particularly with respect to precarity (Ahmad 2008; Anderson 2009, 2010; Cwerner 2001; Jackson 2008; Rogaly 2009; Vigh 2009). Research into the simultaneity and mutual implication of time and space in subjectivity within migration, however, has predominantly focused on the migrants themselves.

If the times and spaces of migration direct the women, how might they in turn direct the times and spaces of migration? I draw attention to the women's spatiotemporal mobility in relation to their being wives who stay behind. In relation to this, I examine whether and how the subjective experiences of the women may be linked to wider social and political histories and narratives. I examine the implication of the women and their experiences in broader Philippine historical processes and economic conditions. I undertake this by reconceptualizing the role played in migration by women who stay through establishing a link between imagination and the concept of "culture of migration." I probe how the women's perceptions of migration draw on experiences and sociocultural categories that have been vitally shaped by the history of the Ilocos region where the fieldwork was done, in particular the migration of Ilokanos to work in Hawaiian sugar plantations and the continuing migration of Ilokanos to Hawaii.

Understanding the meanings the women attach to their experiences is an attempt to "retrieve the modalities of self-conceptualization" (Laliotou 2004, 199). Self-conceptualization joins together subjectivity and agency. Ortner (2006) argues that agency is based on subjectivity, "a necessary part of understanding how people (try to) act on the world even as they are acted upon" (116). The seafarer wives play a vitally important role in enabling and sustaining the labor migration of their husbands, and examining their subjectification within and through this process and experience of migration provides a critical standpoint from which to reveal how they have acted on, and been acted upon by, their world. Their subjectivity, as I will show, is deeply relational. Although I focus on their subjectivity, I make sense of their lives, experiences, and concerns in the context of their existence with others. In other words, I am also concerned with intersubjectivity. Furthermore, I look at subjectivity from a dialectical perspective, putting the personal and the social in dialogue with each other (see also Kleinman and Fritz-Henry 2007). As Biehl and Locke (2010, 320) have written, "[i]ndividual biography is replete with collective inflections and implications, just as collective categories and alternative solidarities can come through only in the understanding of individual lives and stories." I look at subjectivity from a generative paradigm, which "grasp[s] subjectivity as becoming—rather than structural dependence" (Biehl and Locke 2010, 337).

A GENERATIVE PARADIGM OF SUBJECTIVITY

In their introduction to *Subjectivity: Ethnographic Investigations*, Joao Biehl, Byron Good, and Arthur Kleinman define subjectivity as "the agonistic and practical activity of engaging identity and fate, patterned and felt in historically contingent settings and mediated by institutional processes and cultural forms" (2007, 5). This definition points to subjectivity as a process of becoming, that it forms through people's thinking and acting on their condition. Their modes of thought, reflection, feeling, sentiment, and action are constituted not only by the specificity of their temporal and spatial locations but also by social structures and cultural formations. It would appear that subjectivity is the space created by the juxtaposition of structure and agency, a space that encompasses feelings, desires, sentiments, and imagination (Laliotou 2004, 9; Holland and Leander 2004).

Subjectivity, for Ortner, refers both to the "inner states of acting subjects" and the cultural formations that shape them (2006, 107). Each is implicated in the other: subjectivity is "the ensemble of modes of perception, affect, thought, desire, and fear that animate acting subjects" as well as "the cultural and social formations that shape, organize, and provoke those modes of affect, thought, and so on." She considers subjectivity to be "a specifically cultural and historical consciousness" (110) that is simultaneously personal and social and collective (111). At the collective level, it refers to a sensibility shared by "socially interrelated actors" (111). At the individual level, it bestows upon actors the capacity to know and exercise a degree of reflexivity about how they have been shaped by their particular location in social and cultural structures and relations (111). Thus, a cultural consciousness is "multi-layered and reflexive" and it is this "complexity and reflexivity" that enable us to interrogate our world (127).

Ortner conceptualizes subjectivity as the means to understand our submission to authority, our formation in conditions of power domination, and our struggle against that authority (Luhrmann 2006, 356). She acknowledges that "there is no necessary link between questions of subjectivity and questions of power and subordination" but nevertheless aligns her work with those that "see a close linkage between subjectivity and power" (Ortner, 106). Indeed, there is a privileging of political subjectivity, that is, the subjectivity borne out of experiences of war, violence, political oppression, social suffering, etc., that become closely associated with and come to define *subjectivity* (see Luhrmann 2006; Simon 2014). Simon (2014) has argued that although anthropological accounts have "attended especially to experiential ruptures, instances in which individuals are unable to rely on set cultural solutions to make themselves or their worlds seem right and whole," critical attention should not neglect subjective formations that happen in "more settled forms of social and cultural order" (210). Subjectivity should not be associated only with extremely negative or difficult conditions of suffering. My work focuses on gendered subjectification in the context of male emigration. Although I do not deal with state and political oppression, war and violence, political struggle, and so on, I nevertheless examine the location and positioning of women in intimate structures and relations of power within spousal, family, and affine relationships, which are also characterized by authority, hierarchy, and conflict. My analysis of the women's gendered subjectivity depends on an examination of the women's negotiation and navigation of these spaces of power.

Lois McNay's generative theory of subjectivity has been conceptually useful in my critical analysis of the notion of "self" that emerged from the women's narratives of their lives and experiences. Her temporalized conceptualization of subjectivity argues that "the self has unity, but it is the dynamic unity of change through time" (2000, 74). This implies the coherence and durability of the self and means that "there are limits to the way in which subjectivity may be transformed."

> Gender identities are not free-floating: they involve deep-rooted investments on the part of individuals and historically sedimented practices which severely limit their transferability and transformability. Although subject

> formations receive their shape from prevailing social conditions, certain predispositions and tendencies may still continue to effect embodied practices long after their original conditions of emergence have been surpassed. This durability partly suggests that a coherent sense of self is not just an illusion. (18)

In order to allow for an active dimension of agency, subjectivity has to incorporate an account of how the coherence of the self is maintained (74). Such durability is vitally important in informing the way a subject understands and locates itself temporally (18).

The ontological claim of the durability and coherence of the self is central to the generative paradigm of subjectivity, which addresses the limitations of the negative conception of subject formation. In the negative paradigm, associated with Michel Foucault and Judith Butler (Allen 2008; Burkitt 2008; McNay 2000), although identity is taken to consist of multiple subject positions, the temporality of the subject or self is not adequately accounted for. The negative conception of subjectivity considers the coherence of the subject as "the externally imposed effect of power" (McNay 2000, 27). In other words, it is the negative moment and process of subjection that is privileged (McNay 2000, 2; McNay 2003a). It considers solely the idea of temporality as retention—"the sedimentation of disciplinary effects upon the body" (31). In this paradigm, the subject is essentially passive (McNay 2000, 161; McNay 2003b). Biehl and Locke (2010, 323), in their discussion of Gilles Deleuze's critique of Foucault, write that Foucault's "archaeology of the subject traces the ways in which he or she is constituted and confined by, for example, the categories of expert discourses in again what might crudely be sketched as a vertical or top-down movement." In Foucault, the subject is determined "by entangled regimes of power and knowledge" (Biehl and Locke 2010, 323). Moreover, the self in the Foucauldian-derived perspective "is constituted by a series of disjointed incommensurable subject positions that have no chronological relation" (Bryant and Schofield 2007, 336).

The coherence of the self relies upon the generation of "a singular, connected life trajectory" by "linking previous experiences to subsequent ones" (Bryant and Schofield 2007, 336). Here, anticipation and remembering as temporal aspects of the construction of the self become important, pointing to individual action as consisting of the dialectic of the retrospective and the prospective (Daly 1996). Daly argues that anticipation concerns the conception of the self in its lived and yet-to-be-lived parts and involves imagining events that, precisely because they are imagined, are not real but which, because they are perceived as possibilities, are invested with reality.

Remembering accompanies anticipation and confers upon individuals an awareness of their location in the past and present and their future trajectory. The construction of the self hence embodies a process of connecting the past, present, and future, and making sense of their connections and disconnections. This involves remembering and reconstructing the past and interweaving them with the present with which images of the future are shaped. These images or conceptions of the future refract on the present making individuals see it with new meaning (Daly 1996, 51).

McNay (2008) has argued that because we cannot predict what will occur next, action is not mere reproduction. Similarly, Bryant and Schofield (2007) argue that the development of a human subject does not occur through a "linear process of addition and accretion" (336); rather, it is attended by critical reflection on actions and experiences accumulated over time, a process that is "generative, involving actions that are predicated on their predecessors but never in an automatic and mechanical fashion that ensures their mimetic reproduction." The coherence of the self is thus something that develops over time through making sense of what it goes through. Vital to the formation of this coherence is the self's exercise of reflexivity, which informs later events and actions in life. As Desjarlais and Throop (2011, 88) have written, "[o]ur existence as humans is temporally structured in such a way that our past experience is always retained in a present moment that is feeding forward to anticipate future horizons of experience." The coherence of the self is constituted by and forged through, to borrow from Richard Sennett (1998, 98), the "sustained human relations and durable purposes" through which we orient our lives. Nancy's life story with which I began this introductory chapter demonstrates "these sustained human relations and durable purposes" that both formed part of the sources of her difficulties and the resources through which she endured and prevailed. Nancy's durability registers her negotiation of ideology and cultural formations, including the compromises and bargaining that she had to do. She stayed with a womanizing husband for the sake of her children yet also left them behind in the care of a woman she had only recently known to work overseas in order to extricate her family from debt as a result of the profligacy of her husband.

> "I was wallowing in debt. That's when I thought of working abroad. My youngest child was two years old at that time. My husband did not know; he was at sea and only learned about it when I was already there. He couldn't do anything anymore. He knew [it was because of him that I left]. He knew. He was a spendthrift. Spendthrift. Money had no value to him.

> Buddies, drinking. I was away for only two years. I looked after an infant. It is truly hard to go away. Sacrifice. Sacrifice but what I thought then was that if I did not go abroad, I would not be able to pay off my debts. At that time, I thought it was my only way of being freed of my debts."

Sennett's (1998) discussion of how coherence is achieved is useful in clarifying the dynamic that Nancy's case represents and which I wish to explicate. He turns to the concepts of "*maintien de soi*, maintenance of oneself, and *constance a soi*, fidelity to oneself: the first sustains an identity over the course of time, the second invokes such virtues as being honest with oneself about one's defects" (145). Sennett explains further that the "maintenance of oneself is a shifting activity, as one's circumstances change and one's experience accumulates; fidelity to oneself, as in being honest about one's faults, ought to be constant no matter where or what age one is." Nancy's fidelity to herself vitally included her sense of responsibility to her children, whose welfare she had considered in her decision to stay married to an unfaithful husband and consequently leave them behind to work abroad. For Sennett this sense of responsibility to other people points to the social dimension of fidelity to oneself. Nancy's durability of self, saw her achieve "calm and peace" in her life, one that coincided with the building of her family's own house.

The self is durable but at the same time amenable to and capable of change. The unity of the self is attained through and defined by change through time (McNay 2000). And as Biehl et al. (2007, 14) also say, subjectivity "provides the ground for subjects to think through their circumstances and to feel through their contradictions, and in so doing, to inwardly endure experiences that would otherwise be outwardly unbearable. [...] Subjectivity is the anticipation and articulation of self-criticism and renewal." The renewal that Biehl and his colleagues speak of must be understood alongside their characterization of subjectivity, quoted earlier in the chapter, as "historically contingent" and "mediated by institutional processes and cultural forms" (2007, 5). This change or renewal has its limits. Subjectivities "may be relational and performative but they are not free floating or indefinitely changeable" (McDowell 2012, 584) and are not "momentarily generated and then vanish as the next discursive construction occurs" (Bryant and Schofield 2007, 337).

A generative theory of subjectivity considers the temporal aspects of subject formation dialogically (McNay 2000, 4). In addition to retention, it incorporates protention—"the future-oriented dimension of praxis as the living through of the embodied potentialities, and as the anticipatory aspects inherent within subject formation" (McNay 2000, 4–5; 2003a). The subject is neither only the effect of power nor solely the product of human intentionality. Subjectivity "does not merely speak as resistance, nor is it simply spoken (or silenced) by power. It continually forms and returns in the complex play of bodily, linguistic, political, and psychological dimensions of human experience" (Biehl and Moran-Thomas 2009, 270). McNay's (2000, 2003a) development of a generative paradigm of subjectivity, however, has relied exclusively on a theorization of the temporality of subjectivity. It omits an explicit discussion of spatiality, which is vitally important to the subjectification of the Filipino seafarers' wives. To incorporate space into this generative paradigm, I turn to the work of Henrik Vigh on crisis. Rather than put crisis *in* context, he examines it *as* context, that is, "as a terrain of action and meaning" (2008, 5). Viewing crisis as a prolonged condition, that is, a state of affairs, rather than as a turning point or "a defined period of transition," he considers agency not simply as a matter of capacity but as a question of possibility (10). The issue is hence: "to what extent are we able to act within a given context" (11). He links this sense of agency to the concept of horizon, which has both temporal and spatial dimensions that need to be negotiated (16). Vigh argues that crisis situations compel agents to consider how they may move within a social environment but also how this social environment moves them as they seek to realize their goals (18). Crisis-as-context "clarifies the extent to which action must be seen as motion within motion, and the limitations of a faulty understanding of the relationship between act, environment and plot" (18).

Vigh (2006, 2009) has called "navigation" the way one moves within a social environment and how one is moved by that same environment. The central ideas of navigation—how a person moves within, and is moved by, social forces, and the concern for the horizon (understood as having temporal and spatial dimensions)—resonate with McNay's (2000, 2003a) dialogical conceptualization of the temporality of subjectification. It involves both retention (being determined by social relations) and protention (responding to constraining social relations). Vigh's (2006, 2009) concept of navigation involves negotiating the temporal and spatial dimensions of a social environment. To that extent, agency and subjectivity are both spatially and temporally implicated.

In the epigraph, Nancy's use of maritime images (rough, calm, tempestuous, stormy, sailing smoothly) evokes a particular strategy of survival: that of navigation. Younger women to whom I talked and who are still facing their own share of hardship, especially concerning their difficult relationship with their mothers-in-law (and family-in-law), also referred to spatiotemporal images of dealing with their situation. One wife referred to her strategy of relating to her in-laws as "lumuglugarak lattan." This means positioning herself accordingly, sometimes subsuming her interests to theirs, at other times asserting them. "Lumuglugarak," which comes from the word *lugar*, place, clearly indicates a consideration of space, of one's position within a constellation of relationships. But it also implies a temporal element because the act for the wife involved strategic waiting, and knowing that the time will come when she would not have to compete with her family-in-law in her husband's universe of affection and priorities. She just needed to bide her time.

The women therefore navigated. Their subjectivity is intimately braided with their life experiences and with the ways they positioned themselves within spousal, family, kin, and social relationships, which are shaped by cultural norms. It takes shape in "situated practices" (Pratt 2004). A sensitivity to the spatial and temporal contexts of the women's lives and experiences helps us see the ways by which their subjectivity forms, emerges, and develops from and through the times and spaces that their lives occupy. For these seafarers' wives, there are spatiotemporal dimensions embodied in the experience of waiting and preparing for the return and departure of their husbands; of their spouse's absence; of the tasks they become responsible for while their husbands are away; of becoming the recipient of their husband's remittances; of freedoms and constraints that accompany their being stay-behind wives. The absence of the women's husband had spatial consequences that are not only physical but also social and ideological.

Narrative and Subjectivity

My account of the women's navigation of migration, of their negotiation of its spatial and temporal dimensions that shape their subjectivity, draws on narratives the women shared. In reflecting on their lives and experiences, the women talked of having gone through a lot in terms of having walked through many roads or paths, hence drawing attention to how they have moved in the flow of time in space. They also talked about limits, boundaries, and crises that defined their experiences and tested their resolve, resilience, and capacity.

Narratives are crucial to how the women made sense of their experiences; it was through narratives that they expressed how they understood and saw themselves in relation to their "past, present and imagined future" (Henriques et al. 1998, xiii). As Somers and Gibson (1994, 58–59) have also written, "it is through narrativity that we come to know, understand, and make sense of the social world, and . . . that we constitute our social identities." In his work on the corrosive consequences on people's subjectivities of the insecurity of work in flexible capitalism, Sennett (1998) underscores the important role of narrative in interpreting, framing, and organizing experiences and in achieving coherence in time. His view resonates with Seyla Benhabib's (1999, 227) argument that the "continuity of self in time" is enabled by "one's ability to keep telling a story that makes sense to oneself and others about who one is." Human narratives then involve "the construction of a self" through reflecting upon and presenting experience (Maher 2005, 20). It is through experience that we directly understand the conditions of our existence, and developing an account of agency depends on analyzing experience, which is in turn linked to broader social structures (McNay 2008, 181). Lieba Faier, drawing on Mary Steedly, writes that narrative experience is useful "to evoke the ways that stories and experience are coproduced in everyday life" (2009, 82). She explains that for Steedly, "stories do not simply express life experience; they are themselves lived out, structuring imaginations and assuming flesh and quotidian form" and that narratives are "part of the ongoing, dialogic, and constrained ways that people selectively make and remake the past as they craft lives and selves in the present."

Yet, how the women experienced their present and saw themselves was profoundly informed by their consideration of their future. Their present was inextricably bound up with the horizon. Indeed, what shaped the resilience and tenacity of the women is their hopefulness, their sensing of the arrival from the future of something good—the fulfilment of a longed-for aspiration or the just reward for their sacrifices. As Nancy above said about her philandering and profligate husband, "I just knew that there will come a time that he will calm down." And as Nora, whose life was defined by debt, said, "something will come, life is not all hardship." One wife concluded her narration of what her life was like when her husband was away as "like bearing a cross," an allusion to Jesus Christ's bearing His own cross on the road to Calvary for his crucifixion. On the surface, she referenced the weight and suffering of her having to single-handedly manage all of her family's affairs, but the metaphor is also about renewal and redemption. The cross is both burden and source of strength. The imagery she used is suggestive of how the present is inextricably bound up with the future. The subjectivity of Filipino seafarers' wives is vitally informed by and forged in imagination and hope.

Such links created by the women not only between their present and their future but also among the past, present, and future shaped their perception of their emplacement in the world and how they experienced and interpreted their lives; which is to say, how they have endured difficulties and struggled and fought their battles. These links indicate not only how the women saw themselves moving in time and space but also how they were making sense of their selves. They were engaged in an active process of reconciling, and finding meaning in, what they were going through. In other words, they might be seen to be trying to find and give coherence to their lives, experiences, and selves. In his study of moral subjectivity in Minangkabau, Indonesia, Simon (2014, 214) notes the "enduring tensions of multi-dimensional selfhood as they emerge in social life, and by the self's need to navigate those tensions in a workable way" and that "reflection and subjective work remain an inherent part of the process of flourishing." In a similar way, my work is concerned with explicating how seafarers' wives navigated the tensions, constraints, and possibilities for subjectification that their husbands' absences engendered in order for them to foster growth, find themselves, and realize autonomy. Ultimately, I want to shine a light on how they assert their place in the world.

MIGRATION AND THE CHRONOTOPES OF SUBJECTIFICATION

Staying home engenders a multi-layered experience and process of subjectification. The home alone is already a place for the contestation and formation of identities and subjectivities. As Matthew Desmond writes of the relationship among life, personhood, and home, "The home is the center of life. [. . .] We say that at home, we can be 'ourselves.' [. . .] The home is the wellspring of personhood. It is where our identity takes root and blossoms. . . . The home remains the primary basis of life" (2016, 292). He adds, "[l]ife and home are so intertwined that it is almost impossible to think about one without the other" (300). Feminist reflections on the relationship between space and gendered subjectivities not only problematize the heteronormative conceptualization of space but also recuperate domestic spaces traditionally associated with women as productively subjectifying (Meah 2014; Meah and Jackson 2013; Young 1998). Iris Marion Young (1998) has drawn attention to how feminist thinkers such as Simone de Beauvoir and Luce Irigaray saw the home as depriving women their active subjectivity since their work consisted of "serving and supporting men in the home" (135). Young reclaims the home for feminist agency by highlighting the "creatively human aspects of women's traditional housework" (135) she calls "preservation." She asserts that the "preservation of the things among which one dwells gives people a context for their lives, individuates their histories, gives them items to use in making new projects" (153). Young thus alerts us to the life-giving, life-sustaining, and life-affirming activities that housework (and care work) also encompass and, hence, to the house-home as a space that enacts a different "mode of subjectivity and historicity" (149).

This book examines the constraints and possibilities for the women who stay behind or home. The home and, of course, the family, are vitally crucial to the Filipino seafarers' wives' lives and experiences, and, hence, to their subjectivity. The home does not only locate them in a physical space but also provides a very important site for the social, ideological, and gendered relations that shape their subjectivity. The seafarers' wives are deeply implicated in the changes in family and kin relationships and practices engendered by the migration of their husbands. Their repeated and chronic experience of the prolonged absence and distance of their husbands altered the composition of the family, which had consequences on the tasks and responsibilities that the women had to perform. This engendered situations and conditions that problematized, and held tremendous possibilities for, their gendered subjectification.

Within the "mutually constitutive relationship between migration and family formation," Yeoh et al. (2002, 8) raised the issue of the "extent to which gender roles and identities are reconfigured in the migratory process" and noted the absence of uniformity in the consequences that women who stay behind experience. On the one hand, some women "might find themselves taking on a wider range of roles and responsibilities and may become more autonomous and involved in decision-making within the family and community" (Yeoh et al. citing Hugo 2002); on the other hand, although stay-behind Filipino women may have "more authority over family governance," the experience is "also disempowering since it increases their domestic burdens and overall workloads, thus reinforcing traditional gender roles" (Yeoh et al. citing Espiritu 2002).

Rhacel Salazar Parreñas (2005, 2008a) has shown that a retraditionalization of gender roles and responsibilities occurs in and through migration specifically for women who leave for overseas work. She documents caring or mothering practices performed through communication technologies that intensify the link between female gender and care work. Distance and absence change the way mothering and caring are performed but not the gender ideology that underpins the social expectation for women to perform reproductive labor even when they already undertake productive labor through migrant work. In addition, the stay-behind men fail to adapt their masculine ideology and practices to the absence of their wives; they leave the work of caring for their children to relatives and others when it would have made more economic sense if they did this themselves.[4]

Alicia Pingol (2001) provides another perspective through which to look at the gendered subjectification of those who stay behind. Focusing on husbands-fathers whose wives are overseas contract workers, Pingol shows that men suffer a diminution in social status because they could not perform their role as family provider. Like women who stay behind who are saddled with responsibilities, these men also become burdened with domestic work and child-care responsibilities, while also trying to make some money in order to salvage whatever they can of their dignity. Men who perform what are considered by their community as women's work are ridiculed. Nevertheless, they counter social criticism, expressed through gossip primarily by their in-laws, by constructing a personal narrative built on endurance, that is, a masculinity defined by the capacity to overcome sexual deprivation and take care of and raise their children on their own. Pingol explicates the various ways these men reinterpret their experiences as househusbands and, consequently, redefine and reconstitute their gendered subjectivities as men doing what is traditionally a woman's job (see also Parreñas 2015, 159–82).[5]

The seafarer wives discussed in this book demonstrate the complexity of the experience of staying behind. As numerous research has shown, the consequences of male emigration on wives who stay are complex, uneven, and contradictory. They are nuanced, mediated, and conditioned by a variety of factors, such as existing gender ideologies (Chant 1992; Menjivar and Agadjanian 2007) and the rigidity or flexibility of prescribed gender roles (Chant 1992), household composition, and residential arrangement, specifically the presence of a mother-in-law (Desai and Bannerji 2008; Gulati 1993; Hadi 2001). Other researchers have noted that male emigration has the potential to strengthen stay-behind women's association with traditional gender ideologies and roles (Parreñas 2005) and their subordinate position in the family (Menjivar and Agadjanian 2007). Although migration helps introduce more secular values and attitudes to the community (Hadi 2001; Hugo 1992, 1995), in other instances, social remittances can lead to negative changes in gender roles (De Haas 2007a; De Haas and Van Rooij 2010).[6]

Other migration scholars have also pointed to the need to take into account how women who stay perceive these changes themselves. Bever (2002) notes in her Yucatan study that both men and women defended traditional gender ideology despite the changes brought about by the migration of husbands. The judgment that male migration engenders "positive" or "negative" changes to the women's position "always has a normative dimension" (De Haas and Van Rooij 2010, 46). Valuations depend on who is making the assessments and the particular set of values they espouse or represent. As Menjivar and Agadjanian (2007, 1260) have noted: "what to outside observers may appear to be increased control of the women's lives and decreased emancipation, to the women these outcomes may signal a partner's love and care for themselves and their children." De Haas and Van Rooij (2010) note in their Moroccan study that the women did not always appreciate, nor even aspire to, the increase in their responsibilities and tasks, which expanded their spheres. Their taking over of their husband's tasks was by default rather than sought by the women who were not prepared for or did not want the potential backlash from their society that was not ready for, and indeed may even be hostile toward their new status. De Haas (2007a, 20) argues that the increase in women's responsibilities "should not be equated with emancipation in the sense of making independent and conscious choices against prevailing norms of gender roles."

Male emigration's consequences on women who stay are part of broader social changes (Aysa and Massey 2004; De Haas 2007b; De Haas and van Rooij 2010). De Haas (2007a) says that it is difficult to disentangle the sociocultural and economic consequences of migration and remittances (including social ones) from broader processes of social change. This is because migration is a constituent part of these broader transformation processes that encompass social, cultural, and economic fields. Such transformations "integrate emigrant communities into global social, economic and migratory systems" while also being "an independent factor in perpetuating and intensifying, magnifying, and accelerating these processes at the local and regional levels" (19). This book examines the experiences of seafarers' wives within the transformations in seafaring labor brought about by the globalization and neoliberalization of the maritime industry. It also examines how the women draw, consciously or unconsciously, on ideas and sociocultural categories that owe their provenance to the historical experience of the Ilocos region, in particular its becoming a primary source of workers to Hawaiian sugar plantations. The region's becoming linked to US sugar capital under the auspices of American imperialism in the Philippines subsequently enabled family settlement migration to Hawaii and California, a settlement migration against which the seafarers' wives viewed and measured their husband's labor migration.

FIELDWORK SITE AND METHODOLOGY

I chose San Gabriel (pseudonym), a town in Ilocos Norte, as my research site for its location in a region with a long history of internal and international migration. To see how migration affects individuals, families, and societies, it was necessary to conduct the research in a place that has participated in, and been significantly affected by, migration.

The Ilocos Region, on the northwestern coast of Luzon, has had a long history of outmigration. The massive migrations of Ilokanos that began in the mid-1850s have been collectively referred to as the "Ilokano movement" (McLennan 1980, 105). The Ilocos Region, comprised of the provinces of Ilocos Norte, Ilocos Sur, La Union and Pangasinan, has been characterized as resource-poor, its small and rugged land mass inhospitable to large-scale cultivation of cash crops (Sharma 1987). Ilocos Norte has consistently been described as resource-poor (e.g. Arnold and Abad 1985) and where outmigration has consistently been a response to the province's economic difficulties. The high level of outmigration in Ilocos Norte and in the Ilocos Region more generally has a longer history, which has been dated to the middle of the nineteenth century (e.g. McLennan 1980). Jane Margold (1999, 67) has written that "[b]y the end of the nineteenth century, the region's soil had been depleted and its limited arable areas divided up into tiny, scattered smallholdings." The economic situation of the region, however, is not due only to poor soil and the environment's adversity but also to the region's greater vulnerability to natural hazards, such as typhoons (Bankoff (2007). The Ilocos Region also faced severe population pressures. Outmigration has been identified as one important response to relieve the mounting population pressure in the Ilocos Region.[7] This outmigration was linked to the economic policies pursued by the Spanish colonial government, most crucially the shift to tobacco production. As a consequence, by the end of the nineteenth century, the region had become a rice-deficit area (Trager 1988; also de Jesus 1980). There had also been the collapse of its traditional industries (such as indigo).

San Gabriel is an agricultural town and, based on income, is classified as a third-class municipality. The National Statistical Coordination Board (NSCB) of the Philippines defines a third-class municipality as one with an annual income in the last three calendar years of more than 35 million pesos but less than 45 million pesos. It consists of 43 barangays (roughly, villages) 18 of which comprise the *poblacion*, the town proper or urbanized area. According to latest available figures, its population in 2015 was 32,215. There are 11 grocery stores, 376 sari-sari (small variety/ convenience) stores, seven pharmacies, and 30 agribusiness establishments. The town's public transport system consists of 1,500 tricycles (motor bike with a sidecar) and more than 40 passenger jeepneys, all of which are privately owned. San Gabriel has a labor force of 19,766, almost 43 percent of whom were unemployed (Municipality of San Gabriel 2009a).

I used a purposeful sampling strategy in inviting participants and used the following parameters to select them: women who were in full-time employment; women who were not in employment; women with dependent children; women with adult children; women with no children; women who lived with their in-laws; women whose husbands have risen to top officer positions (chief engineer or captain); and women whose husbands have retired and stopped seafaring due to illness or other reasons. These parameters were based on different circumstances, residential arrangements, points in the lifecycle of the seamen-husband and wife, and points in the seafaring career of husbands. I identified informants in two ways. First, I asked family members, relatives, friends, neighbors, former schoolmates and teachers if they knew anyone I could interview. Second, I negotiated with the principal of San Gabriel High School if I could ask students whether they were related to, knew, or was a neighbor of a *married* seaman. In all I interviewed 60 women. I interviewed 40 during my fieldwork in 2010. From late December 2011 to mid-January 2012 I talked to ten wives whose husbands were no longer going to sea because of retirement, illness, or some other reason. Their inclusion was important to developing an understanding of how life was different without international contract labor as a source of income. I also did ten follow-up interviews during this time. More additional and follow-up interviews were made between 2013 and 2015. In 2010, I spoke to ten husbands who were home from sea during my interviews, and I have talked to more seafarers in San Gabriel in 2013 and 2014. In 2015, I conducted the last of my interviews and follow-up conversations with the women.

Figures from a village-by-village listing of migrants from San Gabriel conducted in 2009 by the municipality's Office of Planning and Development show that 4,090 residents were living or working abroad. This overseas population comprises 13 percent of the town's population (Municipality of San Gabriel, 2009a). Of this number, nearly 73 percent are in the USA: about 58 percent in Hawaii and around 15 percent on the US mainland, mostly California (Municipality of San Gabriel 2009b). Just over 800 are listed as living or working outside of the USA, with the following countries as top destinations: Italy (163); Hong Kong (130); Saudi Arabia (83); Singapore (74); Spain (58); Taiwan (48); United Arab Emirates (48); Canada (35); Norway (28); Greece (23); South Korea (20); Kuwait (15); Qatar (9); Malaysia (6); UK (6); and Japan (5). Of these countries, only Italy, Spain, Canada, Norway, and the UK offer the possibility of settlement migration. The other destination countries allow migrant workers to stay on a contract basis. Perhaps because they do not reside in a host country, only a few seafarers were included in the list.[8]

The youngest interviewee was 21 years old, the oldest, 58. The youngest husband was 30 years old, the oldest, 61. The longest-serving seaman has been working for 37 years while one husband was on his first ship. The average number of seafaring years was 17. The average length of contract is 10 months and stay at home between contracts, three months. In 2010, four of the women did not yet have a child yet. By 2014, only one of them was not a mother. The average number of children was three. Only nine of the women were in full-time paid employment, seven in the public sector (teacher, social worker). Of the 51 who were not in employment, four used to work as domestic helper/nanny in Hong Kong, Singapore, Taiwan: three of them stopped working overseas after marriage, and one left for work abroad while already with children. One used to be a top insurance agent until the collapse of the company she worked for in the mid-2000s. Twenty-nine were engaged in informal economic activity (farming; raising livestock; buying and selling of food items; selling cosmetics, lingerie and other clothing items; and owning a *tianggi* (small store). The rest neither worked nor engaged in any informal economic activity.

I conducted all the interviews, which were all in Ilokano except for two that were done in Filipino. A number of interviewees, however, mixed Ilokano, Filipino, and English. Most of the interviews were done in the residence of the research participants. Because of this, I saw husbands (hand)washing clothes with their wives, cooking lunch for the family, looking after babies, and doing house repairs or improvements. One interview was done while the husband was on Skype, talking to and watching the family: children going in and out of doors or playing. Two wives were interviewed at the waiting areas of their children's school, while four were interviewed in their place of work. These provided me with opportunities to observe women in the different locations of the performance of their various roles as wives and mothers as well as how the wives and their husbands helped each other do house work. I also encountered some of my interviewees in San Gabriel's hospital (one wife took her seaman-husband to the emergency room after he suffered from dizziness), while taking my own children to school and waiting for them to come out, on jeepneys on the way to the province's capital, Laoag City, and at different fast food stores which provided me with some opportunities to have conversations with them—informal and outside of the context of a research interview. More opportunistic observations included seeing interviewees walking with their husband to the village church or a number of them participating in "libot," a Roman Catholic rite of procession of saints. These observations enabled me to think more about what women did outside of their homes and in what context these activities were performed.

I attended church services upon the invitation of one interviewee whose faith and church activities were central to her life and family. I was also invited by a number of the women to gatherings that marked the arrival of their husbands. These were attended by a few seamen's wives related either to the seamen or the wives. In these gatherings, I heard the women exchange sexual banter. In the last one, the women, all related to each other, mercilessly teased one wife whose husband had left for his first contract only two weeks before. They repeatedly asked her when her husband was coming home (which they already knew) and said, "ah, you'd have to wait quite a long while" (*a ket mabayag pay ngarud ti panaguray mo a*) and broke into laughter. Her husband happened to join the same vessel of the host's husband's. In my interview, the latter shared her husband's description of the ship: it was old, they spent so much time just removing rust and repainting it, and it did not have adequate heating. The women proceeded to "scare" the young wife that her husband would have to deal with the same conditions that the host-wife's husband did. While the women laughed, the host-wife assured the young one, "But look, my husband made it home" (*Ngem kitaem ket nakaawid met*). I thought that the women's teasing was pedagogical. It was not so much to remind the woman of her "loneliness" or of the possibility of her becoming widowed as about telling her to just laugh about it. In this sense, they were showing her a strategy to survive the long wait. The young wife, who bravely smiled amidst the barrage of the older women's banter instead of breaking into tears, might be said to have understood at a deep level the lesson they were trying to teach her. It was also in such gatherings that I got to observe how these women shared stories, gossip, and resources. I listened to them ask if they had heard of what happened to so and so and update one another on other matters (such as when one was due to give birth, etc.) and when they will get their allotment (which meant the promised dates of paying back a loan had to be renegotiated). These invitations enabled me to see how the women drew sustenance from family and social relations, themes that this book examines.

ORGANIZATION OF THE BOOK

Chapter 2 provides a discussion within which to frame and better understand the experiences of seafarer wives who stay behind. It looks at Philippine seafaring labor in the context of the country's labor export policy. It examines how it has been shaped by the country's need for employment and remittances, a need that has vitally determined its fostering of an economic and business environment conducive to the interests of shipping capital.

Chapter 3 considers how the women's experiences are linked to a "migration imagination" that is historically constituted, and one which informs their "migration subjectivity." It examines the historical and cultural underpinnings of the women's "migration subjectivity" through the concept of *lung-aw,* which conjoins migration, better life, and navigation. Lung-aw embodies a specific mode or strategy of navigation and the very state of better life and social possibilities that the seafarers' wives desired. By looking at how the women position themselves in projects for lung-aw, I conceptualize the role they play in the migration process, linking their imaginative investments into their husband's migration to the development of a culture of migration in the Ilocos. I probe the constitution of the women's perception of the social possibilities enabled by migration more generally, and their husband's seafaring more specifically, in the Ilocos region's history of migration to Hawaii and California.

Chapter 4 examines the work that separation and return entail for the women. Here, I look at the shaping of the women's subjectivity in routine activities, especially of care work. I conceptualize routine to include situations that do not happen every day but which form part of the pattern of the women's lives. This conceptual move enables the analytical inclusion of moments when the women felt overburdened with responsibility (*bukodmo amin*) and how they use this state denoted by bukodmo amin to make their husbands understand what it is like to be on their own. Through practices of "surrendering tasks" and "sharing tasks," women initiate what I call "gender negotiation" when their husbands are home. My analysis of gender negotiation, which underpins practices of "undoing gender," reveals inherent differences and conflicts in the orientation and use of time by the wives and husbands. I therefore also examine the "politics of family time" and what this reveals for the women's subjectification.

Chapter 5 extends the work women do "at home" and examines the transnational reproduction of family life and intimacy. It analyzes the communicative practices engendered by absence and separation and the wives' activities that bring their husbands home and bring "home" to their husbands. It examines how new communication technologies, particularly the cell phone, have engendered new ways of becoming present and intimate. For seamen's families, cell phone-mediated intimacy creates a space of imagined communion, which becomes the locus of the reproduction of family and affective ties. I reflect on how cell phones enable the expression of longing and hence the mediation of sexual subjectivities.

Chapters 6 and 7 examine how the women justified through the Ilokano concept of *isu pay* the particular modes or practices of subjectification they engaged in, namely *dibersyon* and staying in paid work or engaging in business activities. Chapter 6 investigates gossip, which transnational migration intensifies, and how women who were not in paid work counteracted its surveillance of their morality and constriction of their mobility. As women whose husbands were away for long periods of time, they were seen as being "like parched earth in need of rain" and therefore susceptible to temptation and seduction. They engaged in *dibersyon,* activities that turned income-generating and money-saving work into recreation and which they rationalized through *isu pay.* The financial benefits of their activities, the *isu pay,* enabled the women to enjoy more mobility and sociality outside of the domestic space of the home without putting at risk their reputation.

Chapter 7 frames *isu pay* in the context of male emigration's consequences on the labor force participation and economic activities of the women who stay behind and puts it in dialogue with the concept of "gendered moral rationalities." *Isu pay* provided justification for the women's continued working or helping provide for the family as part of their gendered subjectivity. The women deployed *isu pay* in the context of their husbands' insecure employment and linked *isu pay* to a notion of "the good of the family" in order to go against their husband's wish that they give up what they were doing.

Chapter 8 examines the women's project toward autonomy, focusing particularly on their problematic relationship with their mothers-in-law. I examine this autonomy project within the quotidian, material, and affective practices of living together in order to explicate the dynamics of gender, generational hierarchy, family life, and kinship relations that inform the autonomy and agency that daughters-in-law achieve. I discuss three dimensions of their experiences: breaking their silence/talking back; becoming their husband's designated recipient of their remittances; and having their own house. Their autonomy, approached through the concept of "cultures of relatedness" that highlights the processuality of kinship, is relational, hence demonstrating how deeply embedded an individual is in intersubjective relations.

The concluding Chapter 9 synthesizes my discussion of the women's subjectivity. I call their subjectivity "hopeful and strategic" to capture how their lives have been vitally shaped by imagination and hope. Strategic and hopeful waiting underpins the women's navigation of their lives, a navigation that I try to map through "waiting game," another concept I elaborate on to capture the various ways the women navigated their lives and the futures they hoped to realize.

CONCLUSION

In this introductory chapter, I looked at the gendered subjectification of women who stay behind within the broad issues of gender and migration. I developed a theoretical discussion of subjectivity that looks at its social implication, enabling me to link the seafarers' wives—their lives and experiences—to broader Ilokano and Philippine historical, political, and economic contexts as well as to changes and developments within the shipping industry brought about by its globalization and deregulation. This might be said to link biography and history (Mills 1959). In examining subjectification—the conditions of its possibility, the processes and factors that engender and constitute it, as well as the relations and relationships that attend and structure it—I build on Ilokano history and concepts that the women's narratives themselves invoke or allude to in order to provide the women's experiences historical and cultural specificity while at the same time giving an analysis that links to and dialogues with broader social issues and discourses. In the next chapter, I examine developments in the global maritime industry that have vitally shaped Philippine seafaring labor and the lives and experiences of Filipino seafarer wives.

CHAPTER 2

SEAFARING LABOR AND SEAFARERS' WIVES

In 2015, more than 2.3 million Filipinos were deployed for overseas contract work. If this figure is multiplied by 4.4, the average Filipino household size for 2015, it could be argued that about 10.12 million Filipinos depended on overseas contract labor migration. Of this, more than 1.78 million relied on sea-based work. It is not just the number of people who depend on seafaring labor that is remarkable but also the scale of seafarers' contribution to the Philippine economy. In 2015, the 406,531 Filipino seafarers working on ocean-going vessels remitted US$5.8 billion to their families, about 2 percent of the country's GDP of around US$292 billion. Although they comprised just 4 percent of the 10.2 million Filipinos living and working overseas, their cash remittances constituted 22 percent of the total amount of money sent home by overseas Filipinos for that year. Moreover, the spectacular growth of Filipino seafaring labor has led to the expansion of the country's maritime labor infrastructure. The manning/ crewing industry is comprised of more than 400 agencies.[1] It has also led to the expansion of education, training, and banking/ financial services vital to the country's maritime infrastructure. These sectors themselves have generated employment and economic activities for others. In 2014, the education and training of seafarers contributed PhP11.9 billion pesos or US$242.89 million to the GDP through tuition and training course fees, while maritime review centers, which help seafarers prepare for licensure examinations, contributed more than PhP123 million or US$2.54 million (Richter 2016).[2] Equally remarkable is the number of Filipino seafarers onboard ships in the international fleet. In the late 1960s, only about 2,000 worked in international ships (S. McKay 2007). Now, they make up about 25 percent of the global labor force estimated at 1.65 million.

I examine in this chapter how Filipino seafarers came to dominate international crewing, highlighting the factors that enabled and shaped their participation in the global maritime labor force, as well as developments within the Philippines that have had significant consequences on the employment of Filipino seafarers, which in turn had consequences on their families. I aim to provide a discussion within which to frame the experiences of seafarer wives who stay behind, which the succeeding chapters will develop. I begin by situating seafarers within Philippine overseas labor migration.

FILIPINO INTERNATIONAL CONTRACT LABOR MIGRATION

The Philippines' labor export policy began in 1974 to help address the economic and unemployment problems that the country was facing.[3] Through international contract labor migration (ICLM), defined as the "temporary, contracted, and highly controlled international circulation of Third World workers exported from labor surplus to capital-rich nations" (Ball 1997, 1603), the Philippines exported its unemployment problem (Tyner 2009). Estimates indicate that "unemployment levels would be 40 percent higher without labor migration" (Castles 2000, 108).[4] Equally important, the export of labor was undertaken as a development strategy to provide the country with a vital source of national income (Gonzalez 1998; Kelly 2000) and foreign exchange for the country's international transactions, as well as to address balance-of-payments deficits and pay its external debt (Ball 1997; Battistella 1999), which had grown from US$355 million in 1962 to US$2.7 billion in 1972, US$24.3 billion in 1983, and US$28.3 billion in 1986 (Boyce 1990; Krinks 2002; Montes 1992).

Under the Marcos regime, foreign borrowing was a major component of the country's development strategy (Boyce 1990; Broad 1988). Economic growth in the early years of martial law was in fact spurred and sustained by international loans (Hutchison 1997; Hutchcroft 1998; Krinks 2002). The Philippine economy's dependence on the continued flow of loans from international institutions, namely the World Bank and the International Monetary Fund, meant that the country became much more vulnerable to IMF-WB economic policy prescriptions, particularly from the end of the 1970s when these lenders made further loans conditional to macroeconomic structural adjustments (Bello et al. 1982, 1994; Boyce 1990; Broad 1988).[5]

How are foreign-debt servicing and ICLM linked beyond the obvious answer provided by foreign exchange earnings/remittances? Ball (1997, 1608) traces the relationship to "changes in the composition of loans to the Third World and a centralization of loans in the hands of multilateral agencies."

Ball explains that in 1981 commercial banks accounted for 42 percent of net loans, whereas multilateral financial institutions accounted for 37 percent. By 1988, however, commercial banks only accounted for 6 percent and multilateral agencies, 88 percent of net loans (1608). The consequence of this is that in order to establish their credit worthiness, states "have followed the dictates of structural adjustment and export-oriented policies of the IMF and the World Bank, and redefined the development process as participation in the world market" (1609). These policies prioritize debt servicing and foreign-exchange earnings through export intensification (McMichael 1996). In order to comply and keep their "good debtor status" and so have continued access to foreign loans, borrower-countries cut spending on social services, on the one hand, and accelerate "the path of export-oriented development through industrialisation, largely unmitigated resource exploitation, and labor export, on the other" (Ball 1997, 1609).

The labor export policy was thus meant as a stop-gap measure to address the Philippines' unemployment problems, trade deficits, and ballooning external debt, but it has become a structural feature of the Philippine political economy (Rodriguez 2010; Tyner 2004). More than 40 years after it was begun, there are no signs of it being phased down. On the contrary, since 2001, the Philippine state has pursued an even more aggressive program of deploying at least a million Filipino workers annually. How the Philippines became a major source of seafaring labor for international shipping is examined next.

THE GLOBAL MARITIME INDUSTRY AND FILIPINO SEAFARERS

As recounted by Steven McKay (2007), Filipino seafarers caught the attention of the world shipping powers quite by happenstance. In 1966, a Greek vessel docked in Manila and requested a Philippine company, El Greco Shipping Enterprises, owned by Peter Toundjis, to provide it with Filipino seafarers to replace some of its crew. The Greek vessel offered employment on a trial basis. Although El Greco was principally "an owner's protecting agent," which provided "foreign vessels in port with food, water, bunkers, lubricants and spare parts as well as arranging for repairs and other requirements," it acceded to the request (Toundjis 1975, 7). Toundjis believed that this Greek experiment proved providential as it marked the beginning of Filipinos working on Greek ships. As he recounted:

> The word quickly circulated in Piraeus, London, New York and other international maritime centers that Filipino sailors are good and dependable.

> El Greco thereupon launched an information campaign to sell the Filipino seaman, undertaken through brochures distributed to more than 2,000 shipowning companies all over the world. The brochures generated inquiries from all directions and helped put the Philippine crewing industry firmly on its feet. (7–8)

Filipino seafarers' coming to the attention of international shipping might have been an unintended consequence. The Philippines' status as a major source of workers, nevertheless, could be accounted for by two factors: the deregulation of the shipping industry and the labor-brokering of the Philippine state and the manning industry.

The Deregulation of the Shipping Industry

The deregulation of the shipping industry began in the 1970s (Alderton et al. 2004; Alderton and Winchester 2002), during which the global shipping industry faced the economic repercussions of the oil crises of 1973 and 1979. The industry suffered from heavy losses due to a slump in the world trade, an overcapacity of shipping, and depressed freight market conditions. To reduce its losses, the shipping industry looked to cut its operating and labor costs. Shipowners registered their vessels with flags of convenience (FOC) (Stopford 2008).[6] Up until the 1970s, ships and their crew were considered "extensions of their nation states" (Ruggunan 2009, 182). This direct link was severed by "flagging out." Whereas only 5.5 percent and 21.6 percent of the world fleet was registered under FOCs in 1950 and 1960, respectively (Ruggunan 2009), by 2005 89 percent were registered with flags of convenience (Stopford 2008). Flagging out enabled shipowners to circumvent the regulatory frameworks as well as labor and maritime laws of embedded maritime nations (Ruggunan 2011; Stopford 2008). The liberties include the hiring of an international crew who can be paid much lower wages and who can be made to work in inferior conditions (see Couper et al. 1999). As Alderton and Winchester (2002, 37) explain:

> In the "traditional" maritime states there have historically been some restrictions on labor, both in terms of their nationality and pay and conditions. FOCs, by contrast, have few such restrictions and the crews aboard vessels flagged to these states are often labelled "crew of convenience." This is for a number of reasons. Firstly, such seafarers tend to be from the less developed countries of the world. Secondly, and partly as a result of the former point, they tend to be less well paid than their counterparts from the more developed nations of the world.

Swift (2007, 5) writes that shipowners "who did not take advantage of FOCs were quickly disadvantaged—especially if their governments failed to make alleviating tax concessions—and many were forced to follow suit to [*sic*] FOCs or at least to newly created secondary registers of 'embedded' flag states that retained some regulatory machinery while loosening restrictions about crew nationality." This shift in employment strategy prompted by FOC shipping created massive opportunities for Filipino seafarers as shown by Table I below.

Table 1. Number of Deployed Filipino Seafarers 1960s–2015

Late 1960s	2,000
1975	23,534
1980	57,196
1985	52,290
1990	111,212
1995	165,401
2000	198,324
2005	247,983
2010	347,150
2015	406,531

Sources: Amante 2005; McKay 2007;
POEA Overseas Employment Statistics

Labor Brokering: Filipino Seafarers as Cheap Workers

The state's aggressive labor export policy helped make the Philippines become a major supplier of seafarers. A look at the state's program regarding the deployment of Filipinos especially as enunciated in the *2002 POEA Rules and Regulations Governing the Recruitment and Employment of Seafarers* demonstrates this drive to seek out new markets to send seafarers to. Under "Licensing and Regulation," which directly concerns the participation of the private sector in the maritime employment program, an applicant for a license to operate a manning agency must, among others, show proof of marketing ability, which very importantly includes crew orders of not less than 50 seafarers from its new market. The applicant must also provide a verified undertaking stating that the applicant shall "deploy at least fifty (50) seafarers to its new market within one-year from issuance of its license which shall also be a condition to the accreditation of old principals." There is not only pressure on manning or crewing agencies to deploy a minimum number of seafarers but also a not-so subtle push to look for more shipowners to partner with.

The drive to deploy Filipino seafarers might be said to have been complemented by two strategies. First, the country might be argued to have engaged in the past in a strategy of "niching" to keep its dominance of the ratings position (S. McKay 2007) and maintain its position as, up until recently, the number one supplier of seafarers to the global market. Shipping has a practice of filling in positions according to nationality, as Olivia Swift (2010, 218 n136) notes: "it is common for ratings to be of one nationality—often from the global South—and officers from another—often from the global North such that Imperial histories resonate in the division of labor." The segmented character of the seafaring labor force, McKay (2007) has argued, played into how the Philippine state positioned its seafarers. For example, Japanese and Greek ship owners hire Filipinos to fill in the majority of lower-level ratings positions, and Filipinos fill in only 40 percent and 14 percent, respectively, of senior officer positions in Japanese and Greek ships (69). The Philippines then created a niche for Filipino seafarers in the ratings position, for many years happy to maintain dominance of this lower market segment. But as will be discussed below, Filipino seafarers now have more opportunities to become officers opened up by the global shortage of qualified seafarers for such positions.

The second strategy is keeping the cost of hiring Filipino seafarers cheap. For example, the POEA, which is responsible for implementing the Standard Employment Contract (SEC) for seafarers, delayed implementing for several years the wage recommendations for seafarers set by the ILO (S. McKay 2007, 71).[7] Also, Captain Gregorio Oca, then president of the ITF-affiliated Associated Marine Officers and Seamen's Union of the Philippines (AMOSUP), the biggest union of Filipino seafarers, exerted influence to freeze a scheduled increase of US$50 in the salary of able seamen (AB). POEA's standard contract in 2003 pegged the basic minimum wage for AB at US$385 a month, which was $50 less than ILO's recommendation of US$435. Oca argued that increasing the wages of Filipino seafarers would make Filipino labor more expensive and therefore less competitive. The US$50 increase, Oca said, would put Filipino seafarers at a disadvantage, as they would be priced out of the labor market. He thus claimed to be concerned more with securing the long-term employability of Filipino seafarers than with the increase (Amante 2004, 87). Oca's intervention reckoned with the power of manning agencies as AMOSUP depended on them for the employment of its members.[8] There is a systematic effort, of which manning agencies are at the forefront, to keep the cost of seafaring labor low. This effort is rationalized as a way to keep Filipino seafarers competitive and therefore protect their employment opportunities, which in turn protects the interests of the nation-state as it helps sustain the flow of cash remittances from overseas Filipino workers.

Table 2. Monthly On-Board Salary of Ratings
According to Nationality and Type of Vessel (in US $)

Nationality	Dry Cargo	Tanker
United Kingdom	3300 – 3960	4620 – 4950
South Africa	1430 – 1650	1650 – 1950
Russia	1330 – 1485	1430 – 1485
Croatia	1430 – 1485	1430 – 1485
Montenegro	1420 – 1485	1485 – 1595
India	1280 – 1485	1335 – 1485
Poland	1210 – 1485	1540 – 1650
Romania	1210 – 1485	1430 – 1650
Philippines	1155 – 1485	1210 – 1485
China	900 – 1100	1060 – 1320
Ukraine	935 – 1045	1045 – 1155

Source: International Shipping Federation, cited in Ruggunan 2011, 87

KEEPING FILIPINO SEAFARERS COMPETITIVE

Maintaining the global maritime labor market competitiveness of Filipino seafarers has meant making seafaring labor cost as low as possible, thus making it as amenable to capital and profit as possible. The manning industry has played an important role in subordinating seafarers to the interests of the shipowners, whom the manning industry represents.

The manning industry links seafarers to shipowners. Filipino seafarers get work on-board ocean-going vessels through manning or crewing agencies that recruit for and supply seafarers to foreign shipowners and operators around the world. These agencies are employed or contracted by shipowners for this purpose. Nevertheless, they also assume bigger responsibilities. For example, the *2002 POEA Rules and Regulations Governing the Recruitment and Employment of Seafarers* directs manning agencies to "assume joint and solidary liability with the employer for all claims and liabilities which may arise in connection with the implementation of the employment contract, including but not limited to wages, death and disability compensation and their repatriation." It also instructs them to "guarantee compliance with the applicable labor, social and maritime legislations of the Philippines, and applicable regulations of the flag state and international maritime bodies such as the International Maritime Organization (IMO) and the International Labor Organization (ILO)." These legal obligations open them up to potential cases or actions that might have heavy financial implications. This helps to explain why the manning industry, which has become a powerful player in the seafaring labor sector of the Philippine labor export program, has sought to influence judicial decisions, legislation, as well as state policy concerning important seafaring labor matters. Its success has led to the diminishment of the rights and welfare of Filipino seafarers. I turn to this in the next section.

Seafarers as Contractual Employees

In July 2002, the Supreme Court ruled that Filipino seafarers were contractual employees, overturning its own decision in March 2000 in which it ruled that they were regular employees.[7] In its earlier ruling, the SC ordered the reinstatement of two seafarers who had worked for twenty years on successive one-year contracts. The high court's reversal of its own decision came as a result of the motion in intervention filed by the Filipino Association of Mariners Employment (FAME), an organization composed of manning agencies, which saw the decision as having significant negative consequences on the Philippine manning industry. Because they are workers to whom "regular employment" does not apply, seafarers do not enjoy security of tenure, minimum social security benefits, and other rights as provided for in the Philippine Labor Code (Dacanay ongoing).

Narrowing the Legal Space for Crew Claims

Shipping companies and manning agencies look at crew claims for work-related personal injury or death as detrimental to the long-term sustainability of Filipino seafaring labor. The manning industry (and the shipowners its represents) depicts the issue as a reason that could potentially drive business away. The report "The Impact of the Maritime Industry on the Philippine Economy," published by the German-Philippine Chamber of Commerce and Industry, makes very clear these repercussions.

> One challenge in the future of the crewing and manning sector is the issue of crew claims. This legal issue poses a threat for a continuing prosperous growth of the Philippine maritime industry as a whole. With inconsistent

> and seemingly unjust verdicts being a regular occurrence, foreign ship owners might no longer re-employ Filipino maritime professionals. This possible decline in employment opportunities can lead to the decrease of the annual billion dollar remittances they bring into the country. (Richter 2016, 4–5)

The same report strongly asserts that "unjust claims must be avoided through fair arbitration" for Filipino seafarers "to remain competitive in the long-term" (4). It calls for the qualifications of volunteer arbitrators and the reasons for their disqualification to be reviewed. Finally, it recommends that "incorrect and unfair decisions should entail more grave consequences. Furthermore, the labor laws may require to be reviewed if they balance the interest of employees and employer in a fair way" (4–5). It calls, no less, for labor laws to be changed, in what could only be logically thought of as making seafaring labor subservient to shipping capital.

The legal recourse for Filipino seafarers to pursue claims has been considerably limited by the Revised POEA-SEC (Seafarers Employment Contract), first adopted in 2000 and finally adopted in full on 5 June 2002. The SEC lists the rules and regulations that govern the relationship between seafarers and shipowners to which both parties must adhere during the term of employment. It defines the seafarer's duties; specifies working hours and overtime; lays down the procedures for termination of employment, filing of grievances, and repatriation; and provides a schedule of benefits for injuries or illnesses suffered during employment. The schedule of benefits establishes a definable amount to compensate seafarers in the event of accidents that result in a disability (Terry 2009, 472). Broadly, therefore, the SEC aims to provide protection for Filipino seafarers by providing a framework guaranteeing that a certain set of minimum standards of employment are met (Terry 2009). These minimum standards, however, create "limitations for workers that make them more attractive to foreign shipowners" (472).

Terry identifies two changes in the SEC that have significant consequences on the legal recourse of seafarers for compensation. The first is the introduction of the term "work-related" to the type of injuries or illnesses deemed compensable. Before this amendment was made, all that was necessary to trigger compensation was for an illness or injury to occur during the seafarer's employment (Terry 2009). This amendment not only delimits the scope of liability of employers to work-related injury, illness or death (Dacanay ongoing) but also shifts the burden of proof from the shipowners to the seafarers and their families (Terry 2009). This has also made the process of determining benefits more litigious (Pabico 2003 cited in Terry 2009). The second change to the SEC "involves an added clause that removes the liability from shipowners once a seafarer or his or her family has filed a claim for death or disability" (Terry 2009, 473). Once a seafarer claims disability according to the injury schedule stipulated in the SEC, he or she can no longer file torts cases or damages "based on negligence against a foreign ship" (Terry 2009, 473 citing Binghay 2005). This amendment "indemnifies shipowners from any future claims, thus limiting the damages for which they may otherwise be held accountable" (473).

Furthermore, in the past, Filipino seafarers could file claims in foreign courts where there was potential for more generous compensation. Due to the lobbying of the manning industry, the POEA-SEC was revised to specify the Philippines as the single entity that has jurisdiction over Filipino seafarers' and their family's claims for compensation for injury, disability and death (Dacanay ongoing). This change "represents an erosion of the historical protection of seafarers within the global economy" as it has "directly led to legal decisions that have significantly infringed upon Filipino seafarers' rights to find legal remedy in U.S. courts" (Terry 2009, 473). The changes to the SEC have significantly reduced, arguably, to the minimum the scope of Filipino seafarers' claims for compensation and clearly demonstrate the SEC's protection of the interests of foreign shipowners and their manning agencies (Dacanay ongoing).

In November 2015, the Philippine Congress passed RA 10706 or the Seafarer Protection Act,[8] a piece of legislation that further addresses the issue of crew claims by limiting acts of so-called ambulance chasing by what are considered predatory law firms or lawyers intent on profiting from the compensation claims of seafarers or their families.[9] Before the law took effect in May 2016, it was said to be standard practice for such lawyers to charge claimants exorbitant fees, including legal fees amounting to between 30 and 60 percent of any compensation awarded to seafarers or their heirs. The new law makes it much less lucrative for them to represent seafarers, as it limits what lawyers can claim or charge to a maximum 10 percent of the total compensation or benefit awarded to the seafarers or their heirs. It also criminalizes the act of ambulance chasing, imposing monetary penalty or a prison sentence on those found guilty.

The manning industry vigorously lobbied for the passing of the Seafarer Protection Act. Shipowner clubs and P & I (Protection and Indemnity) clubs applauded its passage into law. There is now a stronger clamor from sections of the maritime sector, specifically shipowners and P & I clubs for the Escrow proposal to be adopted and enacted into law by the Philippine government to deal more fairly with crew claims. Tony Nicholson, Senior Claims Director at UK P&I Club, in a published reaction[10] to the passage of the Seafarers' Protection Act, stated that employers are unfairly and unnecessarily losing money due to some flaws in the Philippine legal system. He noted the frustration of employers, exacerbated by perceptions of a lack of impartiality on the part of arbitration bodies, specially the National Conciliation and Mediation Board (NCMB). In the Philippines, he said, payment is made in full to a claimant even if the decision is later appealed by employers so that even if the appeal is successful, it is impossible to recover the money.[11] The Escrow proposal is presented as an alternative to the current system of enforced payment of arbitration awards:

> When an employer wishes to dispute an arbitration decision, the judgement amount would be deposited in an Escrow account pending the decision of a higher court. This would also leave the door open to an amicable settlement being agreed at any time during the pendency of the case before the higher court. Legal title to the money in the Escrow account would rest with the employer but the claimant would hold beneficial title.

Filipino legislators, leaders of the manning industry, shipowners, and various P & I clubs claim that the Seafarer Protection Act was introduced to protect seafarers and their families. Others, however, assert that it protects and serves the interests of shipowners. Walker (2016), for example, sees the Escrow system as a means for P & I clubs (whose members are rich shipowners) to make it even more difficult for Filipino seafarers "to receive reasonable compensation for career-ending injuries and illnesses." Withholding payment of awards pending an appeal "will encourage the wealthy employers … to place financial pressure on the injured seafarers and force them to accept cheap settlements." Together, the Seafarer Protection Act and the Escrow proposal heavily disadvantage Filipino seafarers. As Walker puts it quite strongly: "Imprisoning lawyers who advocate greater rights for seafarers, and permitting maritime employers to withhold the payments of arbitration awards, make a further mockery of a system, which works to protect the rich while screwing the injured and impoverished seafarer."

These developments in Philippine seafaring labor show how the interests of shipowners are not only taking precedence over those of seafarers. More importantly, they show how these interests influence both the thinking and practice concerning Filipino seafaring labor in the Philippines. By flexing their financial muscles, shipowners, through the manning industry which represents them, are able to have their interests translated and codified as law or state policy in a country desperate for employment opportunities for its citizens and the resulting billions in remittances. The country adapts to the demands of shipping capital, with little real capacity to set its own agenda other than to deploy as many of its seafarers as possible. On this, the country's maritime organizational infrastructure aligns its efforts with what the global industry demands.

THE GLOBAL DEMAND FOR FILIPINO SEAFARERS

The world merchant fleet (of 68,723 ships) continues to face a shortage of 16,500 qualified and competent officers, and a surplus of 119,000 ratings (BIMCO/ICS 2016). This shortage for officers, which stood at 27,000 in 2010, brought about by the significant decrease in the number of seafarers from embedded maritime nations and the increase in the number of ships needed for the global trade in goods and merchandise, has provided a lot more opportunities for Filipino seafarers to occupy senior officer positions, contingent on their successful completion of required trainings and passing of licensure examinations.

Table 3. Seafarer Positions According to Level and Department

LEVEL	Deck Department	Engine Department
Management (Officers)	Captain Chief Officer/Mate	Chief Engineer First Engineer
Operational (Officers)	2nd Officer 3rd Officer	2nd Engineer 3rd Engineer (Electrical Engineer, Electrician)
Support (Ratings)	Bosun Able Seaman (AB) Ordinary Seaman (OS) Deck Boy Chief Steward Chief Cook 2nd Cook Messroom Steward Catering Boy	Fitter/Repairer Pumpman Oiler/Greaser Wiper Motorman

The need for officers, however, as clarified by Pia (2017), is most acute at the management level positions, which include the captain and chief officer or chief mate for the deck department and chief engineer and first engineer for the engine department. Two factors have been identified to account for why Filipino seafarer officers are concentrated in the junior or operational level positions (second officer, third officer, second engineer, etc.). First is their uncertainty over whether they are ready for the responsibility that such positions, especially the captainship, entail. Second, promotion to these positions means a considerable financial outlay as seafarers would need to undergo training and pass the relevant licensure examinations (Pia 2017). Prior to taking the licensure exam, they go through a review program with review centers for which they are charged steeply. Many seafarers postpone doing the courses and trainings for these more senior positions until after the financial needs of their families are more settled. Many others already have the requisite experience and license but have yet to be given the promotion. For example, someone who has obtained a license for a captain is still going to sea as a chief mate.

Shipowners and their manning agencies want to ensure that their fleet of ships is assured of the necessary complement of qualified and competent workers. To address the shortage of officer seafarers and have a stable of officers who will take care of their expensive ships and ensure their business, many have implemented a career development program in which they provide in-house courses and trainings to their seafarers for free. By investing in their seafarers, shipowners and manning agencies not only cultivate these seafarers' loyalty to them, particularly those in very high demand, the approach also ensures the survival of the manning agencies while, very crucially, protecting the shipowners from losses (Pia 2017). These in-house trainings cater to the particular requirements of each company. Seafarers get training on "maintenance systems, company safety management system, commercial operations, and the business side before they are sent on-board" (129). Additionally, for a chartering company, "the senior officers are considered the representative of the owners, or substantially the managers on-board." They undertake a course "on how to run a ship business, how to deal with charterers and sub-charterers. In this way, they will be able to know and appreciate the perspective of the shipowner and care for the ship more" (128). These trainings therefore include making the seafarers the caretakers of the properties and interests of the shipowners and manning agencies.

As part of the effort of shipowners and their manning agencies to ensure access to a stable supply of the full complement of seafarers they need, many of them have established various programs in cooperation with maritime schools to: a) sponsor the maritime education of high school students who qualify through their selection process; b) offer a cadetship program to the most qualified of those who have finished either the first two or three years of their maritime education and need a ship to undertake their shipboard training; and c) for those who didn't qualify for either of the first two schemes, provide a walk-in cadetship qualifying exam that can be taken at the manning agency. In return, recipients of any of these schemes will work on the shipowners' vessels for a certain number of years. For many, this is a win-win situation for both parties. Shipowners/manning agencies gain access to seafarers whom they can nurture to stay with them beyond the five years, while new seafarers are assured of work for the foreseeable future and, if they show potential, could even be put by the manning agency on a career track.

While officers have plenty of opportunities provided by their employers to advance in their careers, ratings face stiff competition from other seafarer-ratings. As the latest BIMCO/ICS Report showed, there is a global surplus of 119,000. This is further complicated by the persistent concern over the competitiveness of Filipino seafarers. The view goes that if the cost of Filipino seafaring labor continues to rise, shipowners and principals will cast their nets farther afield to hire cheaper workers from Asia (such as China, Indonesia, Burma, and Vietnam) and Eastern Europe, which are developing their seafaring labor to compete better for a share of the global labor force. Filipino seafarers already face a lot of challenges getting work, competing against fellow countrymen and women. Were a significant slice of the labor market to move elsewhere, Filipinos' employment prospects would obviously become even worse.

FILIPINO SEAFARERS AND THEIR WIVES WHO STAY BEHIND

Building on the discussion above, I wish to foreshadow here in this short section some of the themes I will develop in the succeeding chapters. Despite industry pressure to bring down labor costs, seafaring still offers some of the highest-paying jobs overseas Filipino workers can have. Filipino seafarers who are officers, especially those in management level positions, can specially enjoy a truly financially comfortable life because of the demand, the higher salaries, and the special enticements that employers/manning agencies give to keep them. It is increasingly becoming an industry practice for shipowners/principals to offer officer seafarers additional benefits if only to retain them: payment of salaries while on vacation, completion-of-contract bonus, re-joining bonus, and stand-by pay; as well as medical benefits (which also cover their dependents); and housing or car loans (Pia 2017, 128–29).

The vast majority of Filipino seafarers, however, are in the ratings position. As such, there are so many of them competing for a job. This adds to

Table 4. Salary of Seamen According to Position, 2014 (in US $)

	Differential	Basic Salary (40 hrs)	Guaranteed Overtime (103 hrs)	Overtime rate	Leave pay (7 days)	Leave Subsistence	Total
Master	3.369	2864	2127	20.65	668	126	5786
Chief Engineer	3.062	2603	1933	18.77	607	126	5270
Chief Officer	2.175	1849	1373	13.33	431	126	3780
1st Engineer	2.175	1849	1373	13.33	431	126	3780
2nd Officer	1.742	1481	1100	10.68	346	126	3053
2nd Engineer	1.742	1481	1100	10.68	346	126	3053
RO	1.742	1481	1100	10.68	346	126	3053
Elect Engineer	1.742	1481	1100	10.68	346	126	3053
Chief Steward	1.742	1481	1100	10.68	346	126	3053
3rd Officer	1.679	1427	1060	10.29	333	126	2946
3rd Engineer	1.679	1427	1060	10.29	333	126	2946
Electrician	1.498	1273	946	9.18	297	126	2642
Bosun	1.117	949	705	6.84	221	126	2001
Carpenter	1.117	949	705	6.84	221	126	2001
Fitter/ Repairer	1.117	949	705	6.84	221	126	2001
Chief Cook	1.117	949	705	6.84	221	126	2001
Donkeyman	1.117	949	705	6.84	221	126	2001
Pumpman	1.117	949	705	6.84	221	126	2001
AB	1	850	631	6.13	198	126	1806
Fireman/ motorman	1	850	631	6.13	198	126	1806
Oiler/Greaser	1	850	631	6.13	198	126	1806
Steward	1	850	631	6.13	198	126	1806
2nd Cook	0.852	724	538	5.22	169	126	1557
Messroom Steward	0.852	724	538	5.22	169	126	1557
OS	0.744	632	469	4.56	147	126	1375
Wiper	0.744	632	469	4.56	147	126	1375
Deck Boy	0.599	509	378	3.67	119	126	1132
Catering Boy	0.599	509	378	3.67	119	126	1132

Source: ITF Uniform "Total Crew Cost" (TCC) Collective Agreement for Crews on Flag of Convenience Ships, 1 January 2015–2017
These are salary rates set by the International Transport Workers Federation (ITF). The Philippine Overseas Employment Agency (POEA) has its own rates, but salaries are determined by the companies or employers.

the insecurity of their employment, which, by its contractual nature, is already precarious. Older seafarers (those in their 40s and 50s) who are still ratings become easily replaceable by much younger ones. The sheer number of available workers makes them dispensable. The length of time a seafarer takes to get his next contract has consequences not only on the financial well-being of their families but also on the emotional and mental well-being of wives who have to rely on quickly disappearing savings or on debt to manage and look after a family while their husbands are in Manila chasing after an elusive contract.

The insecurity of seafaring employment impacts on the capacity of families to plan for the future, which wives feel particularly acutely because it is they who have to manage while their husbands are away aboard a ship or in Manila looking for their next contract. Low-ranking seafarers have trips that last for as long as 12 months, and requirements to get training and certification considerably reduce their leave time with their families. A lower position also means lower pay, and this has implications not only on the needs of the families but also on their capacity to achieve personal and family milestones, such as owning a house, which have vital consequences on the well-being and autonomy of stay-behind wives.

While it could be assumed that Filipino seafarers' wives share these conditions that impact on their husband's work, certain experiences can be uniquely shaped by other factors. Swift's (2010) study, centered on the Seamen's Village in Cavite, highlighted specific issues vitally linked to its being a union village of the Association of Marine Officers and Seaman's Union of the Philippines (AMOSUP), the country's biggest seafarers' union. Among those she highlights, the issue of house ownership is most pertinent to this book. Swift attends to problems that some residents have encountered, specifically evictions as a result of their failure to keep up with mortgage payments. She notes that those who have had problems with payments were seafarers who were ratings. Most of the recently approved house purchase applications, she adds, show a preference for officer seafarers and their families whose incomes were far more stable.

I highlight here the issue of housing not only because it demonstrates the gap in the financial strength between ratings and officers and thus its importance to the lives and experiences of seafarers' wives. I do so also because it brings into relief how the experiences of seamen's wives can differ depending on their location in structures and relations of power. The presence of couples or families in the Seamen's Village is, in the first instance, dependent on their capacity to purchase a house from a union that is both landlord and patron (Swift 2010). They live in a village where all other residents are also seafarer families who might have originally come from other parts of the country. As such, their relationships are not fundamentally based on blood but are instead built on fictive kinship, common interests, friendship, and other forms of solidarity. Their behavior was governed or influenced to a significant extent by village rules set by the union.

How the women of San Gabriel, Ilocos Norte framed their husband's seafaring or contract labor migration and their implication in it was vitally and fundamentally informed by the province or Ilocos region's specific social and cultural histories of migration. Furthermore, how they experienced the absence of their husbands and dealt with its consequences and social expectations was shaped by the the level of economic development in the place (that certainly determined the availability of employment opportunities), the state of the infrastructure of communication technology, and the availability and spatiality of services in the town (such as banking, transportation, education, and health/medical) that helped to determine their mobility. They lived with or near their own or their husband's family and relatives who, because of blood or affinal kinship, felt they had particular responsibilities and obligations to or entitlements over the wives. These and other factors nuance the experiences of the women so that even though there are conditions and experiences that are broadly shared by Filipino women married to seafarers, the research participants' geographical and cultural specificity ultimately add dimensions to their experiences that differentiate them from others.

CONCLUSION

I have developed in this chapter a discussion of seafaring labor in the Philippines, focusing on developments that have led to the country's becoming a major source of seafarers. This includes making the country conducive to shipping capital through judicial and legislative acts that have helped to bring the cost of their employment down and minimize the financial risk that shipowners face in engaging their labor. The aim has been to contextualize, albeit at a general level, the experiences of the seafarer-wives who stay behind. I framed this discussion within international contract labor migration. Various Philippine communities have their own specific histories of migration and these also shape the women's conceptualization and interpretation of their experiences vis-à-vis the seafaring of their husbands. In the next chapter, I examine how the women have been shaped by the Ilocos region's particular culture of migration as well as how they conceive of the role they play in the labor migration of their husband.

CHAPTER 3

LUNG-AW AND MIGRATION SUBJECTIVITY

"Agsakripisyo tapno makalung-aw met iti panagbiag."

[I have to sacrifice so that we can have a better life.]
—Nora, 51 years old, mother to five children

Nora, whose husband has been seafaring for 26 years (as a second engineer for the last two), makes an explicit link between her role as a wife and the project of obtaining a better life through international contract labor. She uses the word *lung-aw,* which refers to keeping one's head above water so that one can breathe and not drown. *Lung-aw* not only describes what a person does to remain alive but also alludes to reaching refuge. Nora's choice of word is instructive in that *lung-aw* conjoins better life and migration while simultaneously conjuring migration as a particular way of navigating social and economic difficulties.

That wives who stay sustain male emigration through the responsibilities and tasks they do in the absence of their husband is by now an established fact in migration scholarship (Brettell 1986; Kanaiaupuni 2000). As Kanaiaupuni (2000, 2) says of Mexican migration to the USA:

> . . . women and their labors in origin villages are crucial to the migration process—*they make men's migration possible and ensure its continuity across space and time.* As such, they form the invisible backbone of this transnational migration process that has endured for over a century. [Emphasis in original]

I examine in this chapter the role that the Filipino seafarers' wives play in migration by looking at the "imaginative" component of their participation in migration projects. I show how wives who stay behind may be linked more explicitly with the concept of "culture of migration." Examining the women's persistent references to settlement migration to Hawaii within which they frame their husband's contract labor migration as seafarers, I probe the historical constitution of the women's desires and aspirations for a better life in the context of a culture of migration in the Ilocos that has been vitally shaped by Ilokano migration to Hawaii beginning in the early twentieth century. Examining this closely is necessary because "[b]ringing subjectivity to the foreground of the study of migration entails a reconsideration of the complex interaction between the psychic and the social dynamics of historical process" (Laliotou 2004, 3). In undertaking this, I am situating the women's "migration subjectivity" in its historical specificity through the cultural prism provided by *lung-aw,* a concept a number of the women used to configure their lives and experiences particularly in the context of migration. I use "migration subjectivity" to refer to the women's sense of self and agency that develops and emerges from their participation in migration projects even though they are not the migrants themselves. The term includes acts and practices of the imagination that are expressive of their desires and aspirations (the focus of this chapter) as well as the physical, emotional, and mental work entailed by the absence of their husbands in order to make migration sustainable and viable.

Discussions of a culture of migration in the Philippines have looked at the confluence of factors that have contributed to its development, resulting in an analysis that is pitched at the national level and in an understanding of the concept as mainly meaning "a predisposition to migrate," hence putting the focus on the migrants. I aim to cut a conceptual space in which to examine the relationship between women who stay and a culture of migration. Clarifying the link between the two helps delineate how the women participate and are implicated in migration. Equally important, incorporating the women's historically shaped conceptions and perceptions of the link between a better life and migration is vitally important in conceptualizing their "migration subjectivity" and an Ilokano culture of migration.

WIVES WHO STAY BEHIND AND "CULTURE OF MIGRATION"

Scholars of Philippine migration have pointed to a by-now pervasive Filipino culture of migration (Asis 1995, 2006b, 2008; Baggio 2008; Sills and Chowthi 2008). Asis (2006b) traces its emergence to the confluence of historical, political, social, and economic factors at various scales—national, regional, and global. She argues that the development of a Philippine culture of migration has been greatly facilitated by the Philippine state's institutionalization of migration. Its reliance on the remittances of overseas Filipino workers to help keep the Philippine economy afloat has provided the impetus for the state to become actively involved in promoting, facilitating, organizing, and managing the continued deployment of Filipinos for work abroad. Similarly, Sills and Chowthi (2008) attribute the development of "a culture of labor migration in the Philippines" to the country's history of emigration, the state's promotion of overseas labor, and its reliance on remittances to prop up the economy (see also Sills 2007). Asis (2008, 79) observes that "over the years, the idea of working abroad spread from a few pockets of the country in the 1970s to the whole archipelago." So pervasive has migration become in the Philippines that commentators now speak of it as "a social fact" (Aguilar 2009a), "a fact of life" (Asis 2008), "a way of life" (Sills and Chowthi 2008), "routine and taken-for-granted" (Asis 1995), and "prosaic" (Aguilar 2014a). Aside from those already mentioned, the banality, that is, routineness, of migration in the Philippines may also be attributed to how recruitment agencies and educational institutions have both capitalized on, and reinforced, the migration aspirations of Filipinos (Asis 2006b, 2008).

At its core, "culture of migration" refers to the "establishment of norms within a community" that sustains migration (Massey et al. 1998, 192; see also Alarcon 1987). It is considered a process belonging to the cumulative causation theory of migration, which "refers to the tendency for international migration to perpetuate itself over time, regardless of the conditions that originally caused it" (Massey et al. 1998, 192). In their most explicit effort to explain the development of "culture of migration," Massey et al., drawing mainly on Mexican-Hispanic literature, write of its distinct features. First, successful migrants provide a powerful demonstration effect of the financial and material benefits of international migration. Others in the community admire and are drawn to emulate their new lifestyle and aspire to gain access to the same ability to consume goods and acquire property. Second, while the attractiveness of migration is partly and initially due to financial and material gains, migration becomes a social norm in which overseas work becomes integrated into the community's structure of values and expectations. Third, as migration becomes more widespread and important in the community, it comes to acquire the status of a rite of passage by which men prove themselves and against which others are measured. Finally, with their participation in migration, women become more powerful and influential in their family through their financial contribution. Their stay abroad exposes them to more egalitarian gender relations, and they push for greater equality as well as working toward settling abroad (105).

Kandell and Massey (2002), in their essay that provides the first quantitative evidence for the concept of culture of migration, describe the social mechanisms involved in the transmission of a culture of migration within a community:

> The more a community's families become involved in migration, the higher the likelihood that children will aspire to work in the US, which causes them to look northward rather than locally for opportunities and social mobility. As a consequence, they reduce their investment in the acquisition of resources (education), and increase their investment in the prospect of migration, substantially raising the odds that they actually will migrate as they get older and, through their involvement in international migration, ultimately pass pro-migration values on to their own children. (1002)

As in the Mexican case described by Kandell and Massey, in the Philippines, the social institutionalization of migration is also seen to occur through the family, except that Filipino families invest in education to improve members' chances of migration. Asis (2000) writes that where there is continued reliance on migration to provide for the needs of families, "migration values develop and are nurtured in families" (264). International labor migration becomes one of the major components, if not the major component, of a family's livelihood strategy (Asis 2008). Although she points to the centrality of the family, Asis seems to have the migrating member/s at the fore of her argument when she writes, "Once a family member starts to migrate, other members tend to tread the same pattern" (2008, 86). What remains to be explicated is the link between those who stay and the culture of migration. How might their part in the perpetuation and legitimization of a culture of migration be accounted for within how the concept "culture of migration" has been defined?

In order to answer this question, we need to disaggregate "culture of migration." Three useful categories for understanding the concept are offered in the literature. One, it "refers to the way that migration becomes a cultural fact in the communities of origin" (Horvath 2008, 773). Two, it "relates to the system of norms and ideologies that create a framework of interpretation and evaluation for the stability or mobility in a given society" (774). Three, it "refers to adjustments in the behavior and changes in the relationships between all local residents in the absence of the people with certain functions on different levels of the community" (Elrick 2008, 1505).

It is vitally important to pose the question regarding the role of the wives who stay in the development and spread of a culture of migration because, in its most empirically grounded conceptualization, the "culture of migration" offered by Massey et al. does not explicitly address the place of non-migrants, let alone women (1998). Nevertheless, the same study explains that over time and with the extensive back and forth movement of migrants, a "culture of migration" develops that is distinct from the culture of both the sending and receiving societies, changing the context within which migration decisions are made (105). It thus represents a "third culture" (Elrick 2008). We might thus look at "culture of migration" in terms of category 1 above, that is, a culture of migration grows out of, and develops from, the fusion of the foreign and local cultures (Elrick 2008). This "third culture," i.e., culture of migration, embodies the mixing of newly adapted values and existing local ones (Elrick 2008). It "concerns the emergence of new artifacts, habits, perspectives, ideas and values that become a part of the sending society's culture" (Horvath 2008, 773). Category 2 refers to migration acquiring a socially normative status, that is, how it comes to be seen as akin to a rite of passage (Massey et al. 1998) bestowing upon those who undertake the journey a status that is socially valued and against which other members are measured. Category 3 refers to the social and cultural adaptations that societies make in the departure and absence of members (Aguilar 2009a; Horvath 2008; White 2010).

Looking at culture of migration not only in the sense of a "predilection to migrate" but also in terms of a dynamic that gives rise to a culture characterized by experiences of migration (category 1) opens up a conceptual space for the incorporation of wives who stay behind and their contribution to the perpetuation of this "third culture." Equally important, by looking at culture of migration as encompassing the ways the migrant source societies adapt in order to continue existing, thereby demonstrating resilience and flexibility (category 3), we are able to more clearly locate the contribution of women who stay behind in the maintenance of these societies. Not only do these wives help prevent migrant source communities from disintegrating; they also make migration economically viable and provide it with social legitimacy (Oishi 2005).

The link between wives who stay and culture of migration (understood in terms of category 1 above) might be established in the way they share in the imagination of migration as social navigation. They become agents in the diffusion of a culture of migration through their integration into their own mentality and horizon of the economic and social possibilities offered by migration. The following section explores how seamen's wives share in the social and collective cognition of migration as the key to a better life, a sharing that is tightly woven with what their lives used to be and the changes that labor migration has brought about.

MIGRATION, IMAGINATION, SOCIAL NAVIGATION

The desire to improve one's socio-economic situation remains the most significant reason for overseas Filipino labor migration (Asis and Battistella 2013). Rita, 35 years old, mother of two children and whose husband has been seafaring for 10 years as an oiler puts it simply but powerfully: "so we would have food that has a bit more flavor." She does not reduce migration to the provision of a family's most basic needs, albeit this is an important component of it. Rather, her answer to my question on why she is willing to endure the long absences of her husband evokes the desire for a more comfortable life, one that goes beyond the alimentary. She also points to her place in this migration. She endures the difficulties and challenges brought about by her husband's absence so that she and her family would not have to endure the difficulties and challenges of a hard life. That is, subsisting on the paltry income from a local job (if there is one), income that will not enable them to afford "food that has more flavor," let alone secure their future. This future, characterized by improved socioeconomic possibilities, is what Nora, quoted in the epigraph to this chapter, referred to as *lung-aw*—meaning a better life but also connoting a survival strategy of keeping one's head above water so that one can breathe and not drown. This reveals how she sees migration as swimming for survival. She imagines migration as a way of navigating the uncertain waters of life in the Philippines, as a way of responding to the risks or threats of social and economic crisis and death. Such a conception might be argued to rely upon the work of imagination.

Migration as Social Navigation

Extending Nora's insight, we might look at migration as social navigation (Vigh 2006, 2009). In the context of youth soldiering and migration within which he writes, Vigh defines navigation as "simultaneously keep[ing] oneself free of immediate social dangers and direct[ing] one's life through an uncertain social environment, towards better possible futures and improved life chances" (2009, 97). It is geared towards overcoming the present: a condition that is characterized by social and economic limitations. It is aimed at realizing a better future.

Migration, following Vigh, might be seen as "a technology of the imagination . . . an act through which people come to imagine better lives in other times or places" (94). For seamen's wives, it is a way of bridging the gap between what is socially desired and what in the Philippines is economically possible, which the wives have pronounced limited, if not unavailable, in the context of improving their social possibilities. In order to live, and to live a better life, one must leave. Futures are imagined at home (a "home" or locality that has, however, been linked to an outside economy) but are realized, or at least actively worked for, elsewhere (see Vigh 2009, 103). To the extent that migration is seen as a way of negotiating social, economic and temporal (future) uncertainties, and of obtaining a better life, imagination is a crucial component that underpins not only migration but also the development of a culture of migration.

Seamen's Wives and the Wages of Migration

Seamen's wives consider their husband's undertaking of contract labor migration as a lifeline. The reality or threat of nothingness, of life becoming impossible or not viable, looms large for them. They say that if their husbands did not leave, their families "would not have a life" (*awan met biagmi, ana ngarud biagmi no di mapan*), would face a "life of pure hardship" (*puro rigat met ti biag, rigat met latta ti adda*), or have a "life that revolves around debt" (*utang met laeng ti pagpuligosan*). Wives themselves see migration as offering the possibility of escaping this condition. It makes it possible for them to think of a future. The women's desire for a better life entails sacrifice. They exchange one form of hardship with another, but one which offers a promise of a better life. Irene, 33 years old, mother of two children, and whose husband has been seafaring for 10 years, describes the affinity between their life and hardship as *rigat met laeng ti adda* ("there is nothing but hardship/hardship is all that there is"). Emilia, 45 years old, married to a bosun seafaring for 15 years, and mother of four children, describes her life as akin to bearing a cross (*kasla agibaklay ti krus*). As suggested by Emilia, wives who stay behind might be seen as undertaking a journey, during which they carry a burden, but also one that will hopefully bring about economic and social upliftment, if not redemption.

In order for the whole family to have a life and a future, it has to be broken, torn apart, albeit temporarily. As Rosa, 21 years old, mother of two children (a two-year-old and a two-month-old) and whose husband has been seafaring for 10 years, said, "awan mabalin a ta no agtiptipkel kami, awan met biagmi" (we have no choice because if we stayed together, we would have no life). This breaking apart might be seen as an effort to link together space and time, that is, the seeking of life in another place is an attempt to secure and guarantee the present and future life of a family. The domestic territory of the Philippine nation-state is crossed for the sake of another domestic institution, the family. What wives do to sustain their families in the absence of their husbands must be seen as a contribution to the securing and guaranteeing of the family's present and future. In addition, it may be argued that the Philippines is also a domestic entity, the survival of which (and future, too) is partly the labor of Filipino seamen's wives. This is precisely because the remittances are sent back home, crucially through the banking system. It is a move by the Marcos government to ensure that remittances pass through the state (Rodriguez 2010), thus temporarily guaranteeing the Philippines' present. Seafarers have had no choice since their salaries are paid by manning agencies located right in the Philippines. It is in the shipping industry, as Aguilar (2003) has noted, that the Philippine state has exercised most its extractive reach.

In San Gabriel, local government personnel certainly do not earn much.[1] A seafarer's income easily dwarfs what local workers make. According to the salary rates set by the International Transport Workers' Federation (ITF) for 2012–2014 (ITF 2014), the lowest-paid ship crew, deck boy and catering boy, would earn a monthly salary of US$1,132, or about PhP51,000, which significantly exceeds that of the mayor, the highest-paid employee of San Gabriel.[2] As a result, many of the wives mention visible signs of improvement, such as being able to buy more electrical appliances; afford private schooling for their children; and even pay for piano, ballet, or voice lessons. Many have been able to purchase status-symbol objects, such as cars and sports utility vehicles (SUVs), sometimes owning two or three. But without a doubt the most important of all, they have been able to build a house. Indeed, in a number of instances, when people gave me directions to find the house of seamen's wives I was going to interview, I was simply told to look for the big house, which, I was assured, I would not miss. This was especially the case for interviews in villages outside of the *poblacion,* the town's urban area. Such visual descriptions index the economic and social status these seamen and their families have achieved.

Many of those who have enjoyed the most significant material improvement are those married to senior officers, clearly because they are paid a lot more. Amelia, 55 years old, mother of three children, and married to a captain (of five years but who has been seafaring for 25) owns four cars (one each for her and her three adult children). Nevertheless, there were some women whose husbands' rank could not fully account for the situation of their families. The husband of Aida (41 years old, mother of two children) is an oiler, while the husband of Josefa (51 years old and mother of one child) was a fourth engineer. Their family's economic standing was due, in large measure, to the two women's success with their business ventures. Josefa's natal family also owned tracts of land, on which they farmed rice and other crops, saving them considerable amounts of money that would have otherwise gone to buying the staple.

Several other families who were doing well already had some migration-enabled resources to begin with: many of them had parents who were themselves migrants, particularly to the United States of America (USA). Two other officers' wives were professionals (accountant and head teacher). In contrast, Lourdes' family owned three sports utility vehicles (SUVs) even if Lourdes was never in paid employment and her husband has only been seafaring since 2002. Their house was also under construction. Lourdes' parents and all of her siblings were in Hawaii and three of Lourdes' sons, all in their twenties, were themselves seafarers. The combination of these circumstances has led to Lourdes' family's ability to enjoy a very comfortable life.

Wives, including those whose husbands have only been on a few voyages, note the life-changing benefits of separation due to migration. In the words of one interviewee, *nakakaluwag*: with more money, they feel less constrained and better able to breathe. This description is apropos because the financial and material gains of separation-through-migration provide families with more spending power and the social space in which their family is positioned expands. With many constraints removed by this improvement (no longer will they have to worry about the next meal or each family members' medical needs), wives also feel some physical, embodied effect—they can breathe more easily. Life begins to become easier, more comfortable.

Women, whose husbands have decided to retire due to age or for health reasons note a big difference in their life now compared to when they could still rely on the salary of their seafaring husbands. But all of them expressed thankfulness for what seafaring has given them. They have built their houses, sent their children to college or university, and enjoyed years of what the women modestly described as enjoying some degree of comfort in life. Although their lives are obviously no longer as comfortable—and they note this financial diminishment—they also expressed a sense of accomplishment (their house, the education of their children, the much better life they were able to provide for their children), an accomplishment that clearly gives them a sense of satisfaction, fulfilment, and pride.

A number of the women have children who have gone on to become overseas contract workers themselves. They could therefore rely on financial assistance from them. Amanda, 48 years old, with four children, and whose husband, a wiper for 10 years but who could no longer get a job as a seafarer due to illness and had since worked as a tricycle driver, could rely on financial support from her son, himself now a seafarer. Genoveva, 58 years old, with three children, and whose husband now farms, earns some money by selling cosmetic products and by serving as a barangay *kagawad* (village council member), for which she gets an annual honorarium of 12,000 pesos, paid quarterly. Her eldest son, an engineer in Abu Dhabi, also sends her money monthly.

Other seafarer families invest in the labor migration of family members in order to obtain some economic and financial security. For example, Grace—35 years old, with two children, and whose husband has been seafaring since 2006 but whose career is increasingly at risk of prematurely ending due to illness—had an agreement with her husband that when he stopped working, it will be her turn to work overseas. Her husband has a number of siblings working in Italy and whose move there was financed by her husband. Dolores, 52 years old, and her husband who has been seafaring for 19 years (as bosun for the last eight), fully supported the migration aspirations of their daughter (one in a brood of three) and financed her training and application for a caregiver job in Canada, for which Dolores said they had spent half a million pesos. This money, according to Dolores, had been earmarked for retirement, but they were prepared to gamble it for their daughter's migration to a country that, if she was lucky enough, would let her bring them, her parents, there in due time. In my follow-up interview with Dolores in March 2014, she shared that her daughter ultimately withdrew her application to Canada as it had seemed hopeless, a wise but costly decision as she was unable to recover all the money she had paid to the recruitment agency. She instead went to Hong Kong where, while employed as a domestic helper, she pursued her goal of going to Canada. She eventually moved there in 2013, after two years in Hong Kong. On why her daughter specifically targeted Canada, Dolores said, "it's where she can go, we can't go to Hawaii." She not only referred to the job opportunities available to her daughter in Canada but also to how migration projects are haunted by Hawaii. The following section explores why Hawaii looms large in the migration imagination and discourse in San Gabriel and in the Ilocos region.

HAWAII IN THE IMAGINATION OF SEAMEN'S WIVES

Of the 2.8 million Filipino immigrants and their children (first and second generations) living in the USA, around 814,000 reside in California and about 110,000 in Hawaii (MPI 2014). The significance of migration from San Gabriel to Hawaii and mainland US (specifically California) is not only numerical (73 percent of its migrant population); this trend has also transformed the appearance of the town by way of big houses, the construction of which began in the 1970s. People from other towns, particularly those that are not sources of emigration to Hawaii, would frequently remark, in quick succession, that San Gabriel's residents are *babaknang*, or rich, that it hosts many big and beautiful houses, and there reside many Hawaiianos. That wealth, a big house, and Hawaii are closely linked in San Gabriel is not lost on seamen's wives.

In my interview with Dolores in 2010, she explains her husband's decision to go to sea:

> "We do not have family members and relatives in Hawaii. We have no one to rely on except him [husband]. If we had Hawaiianos, oh how much better it would be! We would be in a good position. That [seafaring] is our only source of life so what can we do?"

For Dolores, becoming a Hawaiiano is better than being a seafarer. Seafaring is contractual and temporary, contingent on the health and employability of the seafarer. As discussed in the Introduction, the financial and economic benefits that families could glean from it depends on the seaman's position (whether officer or rating), which determined not only the length of their contracts but also their salary.[3] That Dolores looks at her husband's seafaring as a notch below migration to Hawaii, and that she looks at it in the context of migration to Hawaii, reveal how Hawaii looms large in the imagination and historical experience of San Gabriel. She not only refers to family members or relatives who would be able to financially help them but also, more crucially, alludes to the possibility of also moving to Hawaii. This is demonstrated further by the case of Leonora, 26 years old and mother of one, who spurned what her parents saw as their golden opportunity to improve their material, economic, and social position by refusing to marry a "Hawaiiano" and marrying a seaman instead. According to her, her parents were disappointed that she threw away the chance at a more secure and better life for herself and her entire family. She herself would have been an immigrant with a real chance at permanent settlement in the USA, starting a chain migration for the rest of her natal family. She could have sponsored her parents' immigration to Hawaii, who in turn would be able to sponsor their other children's immigration, who will then sponsor their spouses' and children's immigration. (These spouses would also then be able to sponsor the immigration of their own parents, hence repeating and widening the cycle of immigration.) Leonora's case reveals the hierarchy of migration reckoned through the social possibilities that it enables and the extent to which migration has become an escape route, a strategy for improving one's life chances. People recognize the different (and differentiated) possibilities afforded by settlement migration and temporary labor migration.

Dolores and Leonora were not the only wives who referred to Hawaii. Although my interview questions on the challenges that came with the absence of their husbands were never intended to bring up Hawaii, many of the interviewees framed their situation within the better possibilities offered by migration to Hawaii. Anita, 45 years old, mother of three children, and whose husband has been seafaring for 20 years (third engineer), summed this up:

> "It would be better if it's Hawaii, we could stay together, we could all work, we could all help each other make a living. True, we are better off now but there are times when we do not have any since he has no pay when he is at home. And you could sponsor others to follow."

That Hawaii is quickly and readily drawn on in my conversations with the seamen's wives regarding migration clearly indicates how Hawaii has come to inform and shape their migration imagination and discourse. In his work on the development of a culture of waged labor in American-occupied Philippines, Bankoff (2005) has argued that this development expanded the life expectations of Filipinos beyond their attachment to their barrio (village) and ethnolinguistic group.[4] This, he suggests, was most clearly instantiated by migration to Hawaii:

> Just how deep the notion of a further mental horizon had sunk into the psyche of ordinary people, especially the young, comes through in four complaints filed at the Bureau of Labor in 1910 by parents requesting to have their underage sons, who were working in Hawaii without their consent, returned home. (85)

To give a sense of how powerful a shaping force migration to Hawaii (and California) is to the consciousness of people in San Gabriel in more contemporary times, it might be useful at this point for me to look at it from personal experience. As a child, I first encountered the word "citizen" in the context of the migration of the people around me (family, relatives, and neighbors who were also my relatives) to the US. I did not understand the word as indicative of an individual's relationship to a particular nation-state (I was too young for this anyway) but rather as something that happened in Hawaii (or California) and which served as a precondition for the immigration of those in San Gabriel. I heard "*agcitisen-en*" (will soon become a citizen) or "*nagcitisen-en*" (has recently become a citizen) used not only to indicate the migration status of my relatives in the USA but also to temporally mark my own family and relatives' location of their own migration to Hawaii or California. Becoming naturalized American citizens allowed my relatives in the USA to formally petition for their family members in Ilocos. It meant a quickening of the migration process. In contrast, those who have only recently moved to Hawaii (or California) and therefore are a long way away from becoming a "citizen" evoked descriptions of waiting for those in Ilocos as "*pagurayan patay*" (waiting for death to come). A relative acquiring American citizenship brought in its wake discussions in my family in San Gabriel of the words and phrases: "petition," "passport," "medical exam," "interview" [with an embassy consul], "visa," and "flight," all of which I understood in the context of migration to the USA. I therefore grasped (at) the abstract concept of "citizenship" as something that one obtained in the USA, and which was very important because it had consequences on the lives of one's other family members. This "instrumentalist" understanding of citizenship has uniquely been informed—indeed defined—by a historical consciousness and experience indelibly shaped by my family and relatives' immigration to Hawaii and California. Disregarding for the moment the irony and paradox this evokes, my story conveys a sense of how lives in Ilocos had been so linked to and oriented toward Hawaii and California that "citizen" came to connote the impending migration of those waiting in the Ilocos. Conversations with a number of my contemporaries in San Gabriel certainly suggest that the notion of "citizen" as understood and imbued with an idiosyncratic nuance through the prism of immigration to Hawaii might be more widely shared.

Aguilar (2014d) has noted that the USA has ceased to be the dominant nation against which Filipinos imagined their emplacement in the world; Filipinos have managed to undertake a reserialization of nations, which has enabled them to look at other countries as places of immigration. But while indeed many in San Gabriel have rerouted their (im)migration dreams to the United Kingdom, Norway, Italy, and Spain, the USA, especially Hawaii, remains a point of reference for the women I interviewed. Hawaii is often a shorthand for settlement migration, but the USA in general, too, as the country allows those already there to sponsor the immigration of parents and even unmarried adult children, something that is not possible in other countries such as the UK and Norway. How did Hawaii come to index better socio-economic opportunities and possibilities through migration? How did it acquire the status of a cultural signifier, a trope that represented the promise of migration—the possibilities for upward social and economic mobility? The following section explores these questions.

Ilokano Migration to Hawaii and its Impacts on Ilocos Communities

Ilokano emigration to Hawaii and California in the 1900s is an important part of the history of Filipino migration (España-Maram 2006; Griffiths 1988; Lasker 1931; Sharma 1987; Teodoro 1981). The strong presence of people from San Gabriel in Hawaii and California follows the pattern established by Ilokano migration to Hawaii and California during the early years of the 1900s. The liberalization of US immigration laws in 1965 enabled the immigration of large numbers of Filipinos to the United States. Those who moved to Hawaii and California immediately after this liberalization were able to do so because of family members who were already there—mostly those who went there to work as agricultural laborers.

American capitalist interests and those of Filipino elites determined the flow of Ilokanos to Hawaii to work on the island's sugar plantations (Sharma 1987). Officials of the Hawaiian Sugar Planters' Association (HSPA) conducted aggressive recruitment missions beginning in 1906 in the Philippines, at that time an American territory. This meant that although Filipinos were citizens of the Philippines, they were also US nationals (Aguilar 2010) and were therefore not covered by immigration restrictions. In 1908, the Gentleman's Agreement was signed, restricting Japanese immigration to the United States. Japanese workers had hitherto comprised the majority of Hawaii's sugar plantation labor force. With the immigration restriction and with Japanese workers increasingly becoming militant, plantation owners looked for alternative sources of workers (Ngai 2004). Even so, the early missions of HSPA officials to the Philippines were not successful primarily because there was resistance from the local sugar industry, which feared that the exodus of workers would adversely affect their interests.[5] To be sure, when HSPA officials came to the Philippines, they saw the potential in the local sugar industry and invested heavily in it. So as not to jeopardize their own interests, they recruited from the Ilocos Region, which traditionally had been a source of (the cheapest) workers for the sugar plantations in Central Luzon (specifically Pampanga). Not tied to the competing interests of Philippine sugar that had been infused with Hawaiian/American capital and considered "superfluous for the development of the Ilocos" (Sharma 1987, 28), Ilokanos became the ideal workers.[6]

From 1915 to 1946, the Ilocos provinces would become the major source of workers for Hawaii recruited by HSPA. Of the 100,137 emigrants from the entire Philippines from 1916 to 1931, 67,279 came from the Ilocos region (Abra, Ilocos Norte, Ilocos Sur, La Union, and Pangasinan). Ilocos Norte alone contributed 30,641. Their presence changed the ethnic composition of the plantation labor force. Whereas in 1915, Filipinos comprised only 19 percent of the workers and Japanese 54 percent, by 1930, Filipinos comprised 70 percent and Japanese, 19 percent (14). In 1923, the first large group of Filipino workers, numbering more than 2,000, the majority of whom were Ilokanos, were recruited to work in California. The predominance of Ilokano workers among this group might be explained by the fact that 84 percent of them came from Hawaii (España-Maram 2006). Between 1924 and 1930, with the establishment by steamship lines of better direct routes from Manila to Pacific Coast ports (such as, Los Angeles, San Francisco, and Seattle), more Filipino workers arrived in California directly from the Philippines. By 1928, 57 percent of arrivals were from Manila, although the number of those who embarked from Hawaii remained significant at 35 percent (España-Maram 2006, 19).

This labor migration would pave the way for Filipino, but especially Ilokano, family-selective migration to Hawaii and California beginning in the mid-1960s. The Immigration and Nationality Act of 1965 liberalized US immigration policy, and its family reunification provision had accounted for the increase in Filipino immigration to the USA since. In particular, immediate family members of US citizens or permanent residents—parents, spouses, and unmarried sons or daughters—contributed significantly to the continuing immigration of Filipinos to the USA. From 1981 to 2013, an annual average of 38,835 immigrated to the USA (CFO, 2013). Ilokanos have become the dominant Philippine ethnolinguistic group in Hawaii, comprising almost 80 percent of the Filipino population (Aquino 2000).

Studies that have looked at Ilokano migration to Hawaii have identified two significant social consequences on source communities: social inversion and the accentuation of economic differences (Griffiths 1988; Lewis 1971; Pertierra 1992). Social inversion was put in motion by emigration between the landless but "moneyed" Hawaiianos and the Ilocos elites who were increasingly experiencing difficulties as a result of the deteriorating economic condition in the region. Henry Lewis (1971, 18), in his study of rice farmers in two barrios in a municipality of Ilocos Norte, noted that "a paradoxical situation developed where upper class landlords often mortgaged lands to their own tenants, at least those with savings income from relatives overseas" (see also Lasker 1931, 252–53). In other cases, Griffiths (1988) explains that landlords in the Ilocos region sold their land to take advantage of two new opportunities—entry to the professions and politics—made available by American rule. These landlords used the proceeds to finance their children's education or their political ambitions. Unsurprisingly, it was village peasants with families and relatives in Hawaii who had the financial resources to buy these holdings (see also Young 1982). In Ilocos, where farmland is especially scarce due to the region's physical characteristics and population density, land is a highly prized possession and ownership of it is a key indicator of one's (new) wealth and status. It is the "most valued and prestigious sign of economic well-being" (Griffiths 1988, 55).

Emigration to Hawaii not only provided the resources by which the families of Hawaii emigrants acquired land. Griffiths (1988) points to how these resources led to an increase in and consolidation of material and economic resources among those already in possession of some measure of it. They had access to money to invest in agricultural and other business activities. This created a new form of social distinction as emigration to Hawaii created changes in people's "horizons of expectations" (Pertierra 1992, 2) even as it also exacerbated inequality. In San Gabriel today, many of the biggest and grandest houses, a number of which are uninhabited, are owned by those who immigrated to Hawaii and the US mainland by way of family connections established by the migration to Hawaii and California of Ilokanos as farm workers. To be sure, many other grand residences, by San Gabriel standards, have been built by those who went to the US as skilled migrants, by those who migrated to other countries, and by those working as seafarers. Yet it is telling that when people initially comment on such houses, they say that a Hawaiiano perhaps owns it, especially when the identity of the owners and where they are working are not known. In this sense, "Hawaiiano" has come to stand in for those working overseas and who have made some financial and economic success to show for it.

In informal conversations with neighbors, former schoolmates, friends, and family members, when we touched on the topic of what we could do to improve our lives, one of the stock responses was "marry a Hawaiiano/Hawaiiana." Although frequently made in a jocular manner, such statements nevertheless express a social fact or truth. Marrying a Hawaiiano or Hawaiiana clearly refers to a strategy of using settlement migration to improve personal and family social possibilities. Indeed, in interviews I conducted in 2014, two women described their not having been married to their seafarer-partners as a strategic decision made according to family policy (*palisi*) or rule/regulation (*patakaran*). According to both women, it was the policy of their partners' parents not to allow their sons to marry just yet so as not to jeopardize their son's migration to Hawaii. These women, who now have children, have agreed to enter into a live-in partnership because, according to them, they themselves saw the wisdom and advantage of such a decision. A seafarer I interviewed in 2014 who had stopped going to sea after surviving captivity in the hands of Somali pirates and who has been "petitioned" by his parents to immigrate to Hawaii explained his being in a common-law partnership as "isu met ti aramid ti tao ditoy San Gabriel" (it's what people here in San Gabriel do), clearly pointing to how the practice or strategy of not formally and legally changing civil status to protect or preserve one's chances of immigrating to Hawaii has become common. This has been thematized in Ilokano literature and Ronelyn Ramones (2013), an award-winning writer from Bacarra, Ilocos Norte, touches on this in her short story "Ina" (Mother):

> "Namnamaek idi nga agtungpal iti simbaan ti relasionmi ta isu ti maysa a planomi idi ken papam aglalo ket imetkan, ngem naklaatak iti desision dagiti dadakkelna—katulagan ti panagkasarminto laeng ti intedda a pagsammakedak, gapu kano iti panangorderda ken ni papam idiay Hawaii. Narigrigat kano ngamin a makapan no naasawaanen."
>
> [I was expecting we would have a church wedding because getting married was part of my and your father's plan especially since I was already pregnant with you, but this was thwarted by his parents' decision. Our marriage was only going to be an agreement—and this was the only assurance I was given to seal the relationship—because of their petition for your father to immigrate to Hawaii. It would be more difficult for him to go if he was married.]

Although San Gabriel is predominantly Roman Catholic, cohabitation is widely practiced, and there is very little moral condemnation or even criticism for those who choose to enter into common law relationships and partnerships. Ilokanos have been seen to have a pragmatic and flexible attitude toward moral and sexual issues (Pertierra 1992; Pingol 2001) but especially with cohabitation linked to migration to Hawaii (Pe-Pua 1991; cf. Williams et al. 2007). This approach has certainly served the purposes of migration to Hawaii and the USA, an area where such a flexible attitude toward cohabitation shows its instrumental deployment. When the two women finally marry their partners, they will be getting married to Hawaiianos because, by then, their seafarer-partners will have moved to Hawaii and come back to marry them, thus initiating the women's own move to Hawaii. That such a strategy is now understood and talked about as "policy," "decree" or "regulation" suggests a "codification" of a social and cultural practice that has sustained Ilokano migration to Hawaii and the mainland US. It speaks of how these women and their family's lives in San Gabriel are oriented toward migration, specifically a future life in Hawaii.

LUNG-AW/BETTER LIFE, NAVIGATION/MIGRATION

Lung-aw not only describes what a person does to remain alive but also alludes to reaching safety. Putting these two ideas together means two things. One, migration is a form of social navigation (Vigh 2006, 2009), with consequences on women who stay behind that themselves have to be navigated. Two, these women do not only deal with the consequences of their husband's absence due to contract labor and hence sustain migration; equally importantly, they contribute to the development of cultures of migration.

I have shown here the "social, emotional and existential stakes" (Lucht 2012, 185) of the wives not only on the labor migration of their husbands as seafarers but on migration in general, revealing a culturally-shaped preference for chain migration. Such chain migration harks back to the family-selective stream of migration (Liu. et al. 1991) put in motion by the migration of Ilokano workers to Hawaii and California in the early 1900s. I have tracked the social and economic referents of the seafarers' wives' statements on migration to Hawaii through examining its impact on the economic, social, and cultural life of Ilokano communities. In doing so, the history of Ilokano migration to Hawaii is used to illuminate the migration imagination and discourse of a particular Ilocos town and shows how it has shaped the "migration subjectivity" of the women whose husbands are seafarers. Through the prism of the experiences and insights of seamen's wives in San Gabriel, this chapter has not only provided a discussion of what could be an Ilocano culture of migration but also linked women who stay behind to the development of this culture of migration.

The movement of Ilokanos to Hawaii, which began in the early twentieth century and which continues to this day, and the socio-economic improvement that this movement has brought into the lives of those who moved there or those closely related to them, have profoundly shaped the migration imagination of Ilokanos and the wives themselves. This chapter shows that among Ilokanos, particularly in Ilocos Norte, the culture of migration is heavily informed by Ilokano migration to Hawaii and what Hawaii has come to stand for in the historical experience of migration in Ilocos. There is a preference for migration that enables the migrant to petition for the immigration not only of spouses and minor children but also of parents (and in cases where the parents are the immigrants, their adult, single children). This preference for Hawaii/the US mainland (mainly California) might be linked to the considerably better economic opportunities that could be shared or distributed. In other words, because migration represents for many families their only real means of obtaining a better life and future, migration to Hawaii/the US mainland itself becomes a resource that becomes distributed and sustained.[7]

The statements of the seamen's wives that indicate their preference for migration to Hawaii clue us in to the socio-cultural and historical context that shaped this preference. This preference is part of a culture of migration that puts a premium on enabling the migration of others. This is to say, the cultural value placed on migration is fundamentally linked to a consideration of the family. This is what one wife referred to as *makaala ka pay* (one can get [petition] others to immigrate). This extension of the possibility to migrate is related to a term frequently used to refer to migration to Hawaii (and California)—*makatawing*—which comes from the Ilokano word *tawing*, the act of drawing water from a well. The preference for migration to Hawaii therefore points not only to a concern for getting or bringing in others but also for lifting up others or lifting them out of their present condition. Thus, the act of *tawing* both refers to the process of chain migration and, metaphorically, to migration as the water being drawn, a basic resource of life.

The socio-cultural theme of sharing or extending better social possibilities by enabling migration encoded by *makaala* and *makatawing* are inextricably bound up with the affordances gained from and witnessed through Ilokano migration to Hawaii and California. A flexible attitude toward cohabitation (or more commonly, living in) is a social and cultural strategy that has been adapted in order to sustain, or keep open, the possibility of, migration. This points to the development of a culture of waiting, of leading a life inextricably linked to the lives of their sponsors in Hawaii. People wait until their sponsors become permanent US residents or citizens, when they become eligible to petition them. Meanwhile, life goes on, children are born and grow up. A wedding that would otherwise have occurred before children are born now occurs as a rite that prefigures migration, done to initiate the spouse's and children's move to Hawaii.

CONCLUSION

I conceptualized the participation of the seafarers' wives in migration by establishing a link between imagination and the development of a culture of migration. Through the concept of *lung-aw*, I showed how notions of "better life" and "migration as navigation" are conjoined in the women's imagination. The women's migration imagination is historically constituted, shaped by the social and economic possibilities enjoyed by families of Ilokanos who migrated to Hawaii as sugar plantation workers, a migration that occurred under the auspices of American colonization. The women set their husband's contract labor migration against the background of settlement migration to the USA, revealing how their perceptions and experience of migration as a process are haunted by Hawaii and what it represents. The meanings the seamen's wives invest in their husband's migration and the social possibilities they believe migration helps them realize justify and rationalize separation from their husbands. The images conjured by their explanations of why their husbands have to go away—images that simultaneously evoke both the hopes and aspirations pinned on migration and these women's participation in migration—show how migration depends on, because it is facilitated by, imagination. They also show how migration becomes a form of social navigation.

The aspiration for a better life is encoded by such responses as *tapno makalung-aw* (to keep one's head above water so as not to drown, that is, to have a better life), *tapno adda met raman ti kanen* (to have tasty or flavorful food), *tapno adda met bassit nam-ay* (to have a little bit of comfort). Migration is therefore that which offers the promise of social and economic well-being and security so that one can eventually leave a life that revolves around debt (*utang met la ti pagpuligosan*). The women's sharing in the cognition of migration as social navigation helps to account for how they nurture and foster a culture of migration. Examining their role in it through their "imaginative" investments provides the space in which to situate their "migration subjectivity." Furthermore, these imaginative investments—what they hope to glean and realize from migration—enable the wives to endure the absence of their husbands as well as deal with the consequences on their lives of their husband's absence, consequently shaping their subjectivity and agency as women who stay behind. Migration is vitally linked to the women's and their husbands' desire and aspiration for a better life and because of it they are willing to endure, indeed will themselves to endure. They see it as part of their life because if their husbands did not leave, they "would not have a life." All of the women describe their lives of being on their own as hard, and which entails longsuffering and sacrifice and demands fortitude and steeling one's body and inner self.

CHAPTER 4

BUKODMO AMIN

Routine, Responsibility, and Subjectification

> "When he is not here, it is hard becoming a solo parent. Everything becomes your responsibility. Your children are your responsibility, you alone, especially when someone falls ill, it is all yours, ay, it is all yours. You are on your own. All problems are for you to deal with on your own. The maintenance of your house, the maintenance of your children, everything, which is what makes it difficult. You are also worried about your husband whether he is safe because he is at sea. Your worries pile up. You worry about those who are here with you and you worry about your husband. That is what makes it hard. That is what makes it really hard. I think it is what has caused my illness. That's because you have to deal with everything on your own. Stress. Everything falls on you."
>
> —Lilia, 44, mother to two children aged 17 and 11

Lilia's repeated reference to everything becoming her problem all her own (*bukodmo amin*) points to the heavy burden of responsibility she bears while her husband is away. Her husband's absence doubles (*doble-doble*) her work and adds a variety of layers to it. Not only is she concerned with the very vital work of caring for and looking after her children, which is intensified by illness and hospitalization, she also has to see to house maintenance and repairs. Moreover, her concerns extend beyond the home and include thinking and worrying about her husband. I examine in this chapter the mothering work that the women performed, focusing on two major aspects. First, I look at how the women's everyday practices of housework and care work are linked to their subjectivity. Second, I look at care work and other activities that women perform not on a daily basis but which are part of their life's rhythm. I focus here on situations when they were, as Lilia said above, in a state of "bukodmo amin," when they particularly acutely felt overburdened with responsibility.

I conceptualize routine, which is conventionally seen through its repetitiveness and therefore as being oriented in the here and now, as not just habitual and mindless. Focusing on routines of care work, especially of women with children, I show that the performance of these repetitive, mundane, and quotidian activities is invested with thought and intentionality oriented toward the well-being and growth of those the women have responsibility for. As Feldmand and Pentland (2003, 95) have written, routine activities "can also involve . . . reflecting on the meaning of actions for future realities." I look at the women's routine of care work in the context of the chronicity of their seamen-husbands' repeated and alternating absence from, and presence in, the lives of their families. This alternation of their husbands' absence-presence and departure-return happens repeatedly and regularly in the course of the seamen's career and comes to shape the structure, cycle, and rhythmicity of the lives of their wives and families.[1] Indeed, the women's domestic or family temporality is bracketed by this broader life schedule. Consequently, not only does this chronicity shape the women's routine of care work, it also becomes part of the routine or pattern of their lives. I therefore frame my examination of the women's routines, and hence of the temporal organization of family life, in the context of when the husbands are away and when they are home. These "timeframes" (Adam 1995; Nowotny 1994) shape their family temporal order, one that "regulates the structure and dynamics" of family life.[2] Between these two timeframes exists a transition period, one that is most linked to the departure once again of the husband.

ROUTINE AND SUBJECTIFICATION

Routine, in western Marxism, "indexes the systemic reification or colonization of everyday life, and always constitutes a diminution of agency or increase of alienation" (Slater 2006, 218). In this sense, routine embodies the non-exercise of consciousness or reflection as activities are done mechanically, without much thought or creativity. Routine, particularly in the context of the home, has been most associated with women. In the home, mothers play a pivotal role in the construction and structuring of the family schedule and therefore of family activities (Larson and Zenke 2003, 86). Because they take charge of the family, the women's awareness of time is tightly oriented and attuned to the needs and concerns of the family (Daly 1996). Care work has also been historically associated with women. Tronto (2003, 122) asserts that "[e]ven if we do not assume that care is essentially linked to women, historically women have borne disproportionately the burdens of care."

Here, I shine a light on routine's subjectifying potential through seeing it as activities that support life and the flourishing of individuals. I investigate the mutual constitution of the women's gendered subjectivity and their routine activities *for* others, especially young and even adult children whose well-being and future they have responsibility for. In other words, routine can be a path toward the affirmation of vitality and of life itself. Ehn and Loefgren (2006, 100) point out that routine is the diminutive form of route, "the making of small paths in everyday lives." I trace how routine, particularly of care work, are seen by the women as paths toward maturity, growth, and independence for their children. I define care work as "the daily physical and emotional labor of feeding and nurturing" children and others, such as elderly parents, parents-in-law, and other relatives who depend on the women (Herd and Harrington Meyer 2002, 666). As there is a *for whom* or a *with whom* to their care work, the women's routines are thus also pathways toward relationality and intersubjectivity. Routine becomes "part of how we take a strategic position on self and other" (Slater 2009, 217).

The incorporation of women into paid work has not been accompanied by changes in traditional gender ideology that assigns to women the "second shift" (Hochschild 1989), the housework and care work that need to be done to reproduce family life (Brown 1982). Although changes in the division of work have been documented (e.g., Pesquera 1997), women continue to do more or most of the housework and care work (Craig 2006; Fagan 2001; Hochschild 1997; Maher 2009; Starrels 1994). Moreover, these tensions have been examined in the context of couple relationships, predominantly heterosexual, in which both husband and wife go home to a house with some sort of regularity—daily if not frequent—and where there is a gendered division of domestic labor. Where both husband and wife work, housework and care work remain predominantly done by women (e.g., Hochschild 1989).

Seafarer families represent a different arrangement in that husbands-fathers are away for long periods of time inevitably leaving the care work and housework to the women who stay behind. Scholars have noted that temporalities and rhythms of homework are linked to broader socio-economic developments and processes (Brown 1982; Hochschild 1989, 1997; Silva 2002; Smith 1987; Sullivan 2004). These include "consumer culture, the restructuring of labor markets, [and] technological innovations" that are seen "to re-order the temporalities of daily life" (Southerton 2009, 49). As mentioned in the Introduction, seafaring is implicated in contract labor migration facilitated by the deregulation of the global maritime industry that enabled it to source its workers from the developing world. The routine of seafarer wives, the rhythmicity of their life is a means of dealing with their husband's work, which helps to move and sustain the flow of global trade. It is also work upon which their lives depend. Their adjusting to the retemporalization and respatialization of their lives and responsibilities brought about by their husband's work has meant establishing order within their families, an order that relies on and embeds "gendered ideologies and strategies" (Hochschild 1989) as well as practices and kin-social relationships. What is notable about the domestic order put in place over time by the wives (and their husbands, too) is its ability to accommodate the "disruptions" caused by the husband. Indeed, it may even be said that, because this order was put in place precisely to deal with the cyclicality of their husband's absence-presence, it is built on both order and disruption. Disruption and a corresponding adjustment punctuate and rhythm their domestic temporality. This order is thus time-bound, that is, it works through this absence-presence timeframe. Yet, as I will show, there is also a limit to the "disruption" that wives can accommodate, a limitation determined both by economic and emotional considerations.

This order is achieved and works through the routines of the wives. How the wives organize their everyday lives depends on routine (cf. Silva 2002; van den Broek, Breedveld and Knulst 2002). Their routine helps them get a handle on their responsibilities just as these responsibilities help structure their routine. Thus, wives organize their lives but at the same time are organized by (the realities of) their lives, too. "The rhythm of families' daily lives," observe Roy, Tubbs, and Burton (2004, 172) is "shaped by the timing of obligations throughout the course of a typical day." Stage in the life course is an important factor. For example, wives with school-going children have a set of responsibilities and do a set of corresponding life-sustaining socio-material practices that organize and structure their lives, and which distinguish theirs, for example, from that of wives with adult children. These activities are done at particular times. There is thus temporality in action, that is, action implying a time element (Adam 1988, 1995; Pertierra 1997). And these actions are done in specific places. Time, then, has a topological dimension and "times and spaces are mutually produced through socio-material practices" (Nansen et al. 2009, 184).[3]

I look at the women's practices in "contexts" of temporality. The institutional and cultural structures of social time that Lewis and Weigart (1990, 83) identify are useful for this purpose. They identify the school as an example of a social institution that helps to structure time, while attending mass on Sundays is an example of the cultural structuring of time. We will see later how the routines of the wives are determined by or follow these institutional and cultural contexts. I would like, however, to add a domestic context to the constitution of time, a context from which the institutional and cultural cannot be separated. Both are bound up with the domestic and may even be seen as extensions of the domestic. Lewis and Weigart (1990, 84) have written that three cycles "organise social time into smaller and larger temporally embedded structures": daily, weekly, and yearly (see also Zerubavel 1979). These cycles provide people with meaningful ways of making sense of, marking off, and reckoning (the passage of) time. Routines of work and activities associated with school and church are ways by which the seamen's families experience, inhabit, and live time. "School" is Monday to Friday and thus has a daily regularity. "Church" is Sunday (at least for Roman Catholics and other Christian groups) and hence marks time weekly.[4] The wives' routines may therefore be seen within social time cycles (daily, weekly) and within temporality contexts (domestic, institutional, cultural). The routines of wives (and in many ways, of the family), which are structured by temporality contexts, are important not only because they are the means by which wives structure time. Routines also embed the wives in spaces or domains of responsibilities as well as in kin and other social relationships especially during their husband's absence. These routines enable us to locate these wives in spacetime since they show wives organizing and acting within the sociotemporal order (for example, the time structure imposed by schools and churches) even as this order organizes their domestic life.

WOMEN'S ROUTINES WHEN HUSBANDS ARE AWAY

In this section I look at routines of women who are in paid employment and those who are not and of women with help and those without in order to provide an empirical description of their various routine activities and how they combined various and often competing temporalities of paid work, housework, and care work. The use of these three categories of routines (see Silva 2002) is heuristic and is not meant to suggest that there are clear-cut delineations between them or that they can be compartmentalized as such. As I will show specifically in the case of mothers who had young children, these routines were intermingled, and how and when they were done can be characterized by the notion of "meanwhile," that is, the mothers doing tasks simultaneously.

Routines of Mothers in Paid Work

The nine mothers in paid employment I interviewed depended on others to do the housework or care work for them. Two relied on paid helpers and the rest on their mothers and other family members. In other words, for most of these women, kin relations made it possible for them to become both mothers and workers at the same time. Such reliance on them deepened and strengthened ties of dependence, indebtedness, and reciprocity. However, the mothers still helped particularly with looking after their children before and after work. Six of the mothers had school-going children and were involved in getting them ready in the morning. They did not, however, prepare their children's breakfast. For most of these working mothers, their paid-work day began at 8:00 a.m. For the teachers, however, theirs began at 7:15 a.m., their "time-in" at school. Classes began at 7:45 a.m. Four of the mothers went home for lunch from 12 n.n. to1 p.m., which gave them a little bit of time with their children who also went home for lunch. In the case of the mother whose son was only two years old, her lunch break also became an opportunity to check on him. For reasons mainly of distance and/or money, the other three mothers had lunch where they worked.

Because they relied on others to do the housework and much of the day-to-day activities that sustained the family, the work of mothers, particularly those who employed helpers, consisted of supervision, which is to say that their work consisted of making sure that chores and other tasks were done properly. For those who relied on mothers and other members of their own family, there was more trust and confidence (*kumpiansa*) that their children would be properly looked after and, hence, lessened this task. Both sets of mothers were involved in childcare and some form of housework (like helping prepare the evening meal) only after 5:00 p.m. when they finished work. Helping with housework, however, was the wives' prerogative. The mother whose son was not yet in school took over looking after him once she got home and left the housework to her helper. The others said that because they recognized how difficult it was to both look after children and do housework at the same time, they did whatever they could or what else needed to be done. One task that mothers did not pass on to their helpers was taking their children to a doctor when they were ill. Also, most of the mothers felt that helping their children with school work was their job. This activity would take place after the evening meal and prior to watching television, which mostly comprised the family's time together during the weekdays. When their children had gone to sleep, the mothers either read, watched more television, and, for the three public school teachers, corrected the work of their pupils or prepared for their lessons the following day.

It is clear that most of these mothers did not face any conflict between being able to pursue paid work and raising a family at the same time precisely because they had other people to take over housework and care work. For many of them, they did not have to face the dilemmas of "care deficit" that many working mothers encountered, who consequently had to employ "speed up" and "cut backs" strategies (see, for example, Hochschild 1989). However, the pursuit of other work- or career-related activities, such as graduate study as in the case of two mothers (see below), undoubtedly diminished the attention they could give their children.

Routines of Unemployed Mothers with Young Children

Unlike mothers in paid work, those who were not employed could devote their time and attention to housework and care work. Nevertheless, many of them still depended on the help of their families with whom they lived (and who also depended on them financially) or on paid help. This was especially the case for mothers who had both very young children and school-going ones. There were a number of wives, however, who neither had family nor paid help but still managed to do these responsibilities. In this section, therefore, I look at the routines of mothers who had family and/or paid help and those who had neither.

Unemployed Mothers with Family and/or Paid Help

For unemployed mothers with family or paid help to rely on, their day either began with preparing breakfast for their children or, for those with school-going children, getting them ready, which always included a morning shower. For the latter, it was either the mother or the paid help who prepared breakfast. Because school started at 7:45 a.m. (the flag raising ceremony began 15 minutes earlier at 7: 30 a.m.), the mothers said they got up from bed no later than 6 a.m. This gave them enough time to take their children to school depending on how far and accessible the school was.

Mothers who had young children other than their school-going ones left their younger children to either their mothers or the paid help while they accompanied the rest to school. For one wife who had paid help, it was her father-in-law (who lived in another village some distance away) who took her son to school. She would then look after her other child while her helper did most of the housework. Most of the mothers who took their children to school went home immediately to do a combination of care work and housework. To be sure, some of the housework would be done by their family members or paid help. Alternatively, they did the work themselves while their other child or children were looked after. Work included doing the laundry, cleaning the house, and preparing lunch. One wife took their goats to graze. Mothers who relied on paid help had much less housework to do than those who lived with their mothers. Housework was fitted around their school-going children's schedule. Lunch should be ready or be almost ready by the time the mothers picked up their children for lunch break at around 11:30 a.m. Children are taken back to school for the 1:00 p.m. resumption and fetched again by 4:00 p.m. In between, wives did whatever was there to do: looked after their other children, watched television, ironed clothes, had siesta or rested, or chat with neighbors or relatives.

Mothers who had no children to look after other than the one going to school waited for their child in school. For them, this time spent waiting for their children to finish was time to socialize with other mothers. Many of the wives considered this time important not only because they could at least be out of their house but also because they were able to meet other people and even become good friends with some of them. This time was considered "relaxing" as wives not only shared gossip and jokes but also got to talk about their problems in a way that was light and with other women they considered sympathetic to them. Some mothers, however, had a more complicated situation as the case of Jennifer illustrates.

Jennifer

Jennifer had two children who attended two different schools. Her older son went to a school in the capital city while her daughter attended a preparatory school in the village where she lived near her in-laws. Her son's school started at 7 a.m. and finished at 3:30 p.m., while her daughter's started at 1 p.m. and finished at 3:00 p.m. Her mother-in-law would go to her house by six a.m. while she (Jennifer) took her son to school. Her mother-in-law would then pick up her daughter and looked after her at her (mother-in-law) house. Jennifer would then go back for her daughter. Her brother-in-law, when available, would pick up her son from school. If not, she had somebody else pick up and look after her daughter while she picked up her son. She would then drop by her in-law's house to get her daughter and head home with both children. Now that both attend the same school in the capital city, things have become more manageable for her.

Without any paid helper, Jennifer began her day at 4:00 a.m. She prepared her children's breakfast (which they will eat in school upon arriving) and lunch, washed clothes, and cleaned the house. All of these she'd do before she woke up her children at 5:30 a.m. She gave them a shower, dressed them, and took them to school. A tricycle picked them up at 6:00 a.m., an arrangement she had made in advance, for the ten or so kilometer trip to school. They are there before 7 a.m.

Unemployed Mothers Who Were on Their Own

Unemployed mothers who did not have a paid helper or their own family to rely on for help were the busiest of all mothers in terms of the housework and care work they did. The way they did homework and care work involved time elasticity and time deepening (Roberts 2002). Most of them described doing several things at the same time (time deepening) and did these tasks in a more quickened manner (time elasticity). They also got work done while their children were asleep, work that they would not have time to do with the children up. When their children did wake up, it meant another set of routine or tasks. A mother who had to take children to school but who also had a younger one to look after managed to do both by bringing the whole brood with her. She eventually transferred her children to a nearer school to make her school trips easier. She also learned to drive a tricycle.

Maria

Maria, 51 years old, with four children, whose elderly parents-in-law lived with her, and who farmed and raised pigs, organized her day according to her children's school schedule and to the intensity of the sun's heat. This means she did her farming activities when the heat was at its most tolerable and prepared packed lunch for her children because, as she explained, picking her children up from school for lunch wasted a lot of time. Otherwise, she would have to stop doing her other tasks at around 10:00 a.m. to prepare lunch, pick up her children at around 11:30 a.m., then take them back to school before 1:00 p.m. For her, this got in the way of her farm work since the best time to do it was in the morning. This also meant getting up early to prepare breakfast, wash clothes, and feed her pigs so that by the time she came back home from taking her children to school, she would have done some of the work that comprised her daily routine. She could then go to the fields before it became too hot.

Maximization of time and opportunities could characterize the activities of the women. This could be seen in how all of the mothers talked about doing at least two things at the same time and trying to do things while their children were asleep. The cases of Jennifer and Maria, presented above, demonstrate the women's organization of their quotidian lives, based on their caring responsibilities for their children structured by wider social temporalities (such as temporalities of schooling) and the work they do (such as Maria's farming that is undertaken according to natural or seasonal rhythms of time (e.g. in the morning when the intensity of the sun's heat is much more tolerable). This temporal organization might be called "coordination," which rests on the interweaving of timespaces (Schatzki 2009). This coordination rested on the spatial distribution of physical distance (how far the women's homes are from their children's school) and resources of care help women had access to (relatives and in-laws).

For many of these mothers, training their children to be able to do things on their own was an important component of their strategy to make their work more manageable. Lessening the work required for one child enabled them to devote more time, for instance, to a younger one who needed more constant care. Some mothers who had teenage children, especially daughters, were able to rely on them to help in housework or care work, such as looking after their younger siblings. This was particularly the case in the afternoons when the children would have come home from school and the mothers would be busy again preparing supper and on weekends when they, for example, (hand)washed clothes or ironed school uniforms and other clothes. The presence of the older children would offer the younger ones company so that the mothers could at least just have one work to focus on and not multi-task.

After-School Routine

After school, most of the mothers allowed their children to watch television to rest. Some of them watched with their children. Others allowed their children to play outside the house. Thereafter, they or their helper prepared the evening meal, had supper, helped their children with their lessons or school work, and got them to bed. Some watched more television before retiring. For most of the mothers, the children saw minimal television during school days. The children, however, were allowed to watch more television during weekends, which the mothers considered family time. Watching television, specifically when mothers used it to occupy their children, was put to other strategic uses. The television performed a function of time deepening. In the case of one wife, for example, letting her children watch television after picking them up from school constituted rest time and entertainment for the children even as it simultaneously gave her time to prepare the evening meal. She would also spend time watching with them and so turned watching into family time. The television was also therefore something used to get other things done. Multitasking was aided by this appliance. It was something done to relax and something through which other tasks were done. Watching television composed a significant amount of family time, but this "family time" was not exclusively leisure time since mothers were also simultaneously doing housework and care work, demonstrating how these tasks were interwoven by the wives. There was, in other words, a "temporal integration of the multiplicity of tasks" (Glucksmann 2000, 114).

Weekend Routine

Weekends for most of the mothers represented a different tempo and pace of life. It was experienced generally as a time when both mothers and children relaxed. They did not have to wake up before six in the morning. They did not have to eat early. They did not have to take a shower in the morning. Weekends were not "school time." Most of their day consisted of family time by which they meant they ate together, watched television after lunch, had siesta, watched more television, and then had dinner. Weekends were also a time when working mothers contributed to housework. It consisted predominantly, however, of going to the town's *tiendaan* (market) for food.

For two mothers, however, Saturday was devoted to another aspect of their working lives: the pursuit of a master's degree. Although they were both part-time students with their classes only on Saturdays, this meant that their weekdays also included researching, reading, writing, and occasionally preparing for presentations. Both admitted that their studies took away practically the whole Saturday away from their children, something that their children noticed and often commented on. While they felt guilty, they justified it as the only way for them to rise through the ranks and therefore receive a higher salary. They explained that given how teachers receive appallingly low wages, such an increase would be most welcome. The consequence, however, was that they had not been able to attend to the educational needs of their own children. One mother felt ashamed that her son lagged behind in class, contrary to the social expectation on the son of a teacher. The other hired a private tutor to help her children with school work. During the summer break, she left her children with some work to do which she then checked when she got back from school (as head of a subject department, she was required to report for work even during the summer vacation). She also left for her sons written instructions tacked on walls on how long they can play on the computer.

Sunday was a day reserved for Mass (for Roman Catholics) or fellowship (for Baptists and other Christian groups) and was a time when the whole family went out together. For these mothers, going to church was important because it was time the family used to thank God for His blessings and time to pray for their husbands. Sunday was also a time mothers used to instruct children to remember their own father in prayer. These activities were a marker of the weekly reckoning of social time, and although wives allocated Sunday as primarily a day for the Lord, the "day" was only as long as the Mass lasted. The observance of a specifically delimited "sacred time" (Zerubavel 1985a; see also Zerubavel 1985b) represented by the practice of mass or fellowship exists alongside or is followed immediately by practices of profane time. What wives marked, then, is a time especially devoted to God whose goodness and protection they acknowledged and sought. That they prioritized church service registers this importance and only when this had been observed could the families proceed to their "worldly" concerns. Right after attending mass the family then made use of the rest of the day to do groceries, eat a meal together at a fast food establishment, and, for at least for one wife, whenever possible, communicate via electronic video with her husband, an internet-enabled facility she did not have in her own house. Sunday, therefore, did not signify a strictly "sacred time" but rather constituted the "devotional rhythm" (Sillars 2010) of the family.

BUKODMO AMIN AND WOMEN BURDENED WITH RESPONSIBILITY

As Lilia said in the epigraph, *bukodmo amin* encompasses her becoming a single or solo parent, which, by necessity, leads to her having to deal with situations and problems all on her own. This overburdening of responsibility has also been noted as definitive of the lives of Filipino women married to Filipino stewards in the US Navy (Espiritu 2002) and other women with migrant husbands (de Haas and van Rooij 2010; Wu and Ye 2016). Despite being surrounded by their or their husband's family who could provide them with assistance in times of difficulties, many of the mothers said that there were aspects in which others simply could not substitute for their husband.

I conceptualize *bukodmo amin* as encompassing not only the physical work wives had to do but also the cognitive and emotional work that went with holding the family together in the absence of their husbands. I focus on moments or episodes that, when they happened, revealed the complexities and tensions that characterized the life of a *nabati* (stay behind) and a *nabatian* (left-behind with something). These might be called the times of *when*, when these wives' alone-ness became most felt: when disciplining children became difficult, when children fell ill, when decisions had to be made, and when they had to deal with emergencies and life tragedies without the comforting presence of their husbands. It is, in short, in those times when wives felt a strong sense of having to think, act, and do on their own, when they felt overburdened with responsibility and obligation. These events do not happen daily, weekly, or even monthly, but they form part of the pattern of the women's lives.

Bukodmo Amin as Physical, Cognitive, and Emotion Work

Women being on their own overburdened with the responsibility of being in charge of all household affairs was described by one wife as *sika amin ti agpanunot* (it is you who have to think of everything). Another referred to being on her own as a time of *sika amin ti makaammo* (literally, "when you had to know about everything"), that is, when she was "on her own to deal with everything." *Agpanunot* (think) and *makaammo* (know) both refer to a mental or cognitive act that is the first stage in a series of actions that results in accomplishing something. It is not limited to acts of thinking, although it is an important aspect of it. It combines emotion, thought, and action. *Bukodmo amin* denotes a state, a time when the women had to think and know everything. I therefore conceptualize *bukodmo amin* as encompassing the physical, emotional, and cognitive work involved in looking after and raising a family. I develop *bukodmo amin,* however, as also vitally constituted by the strategic acts the women do when their husbands are home. They surrendered tasks or passed on to their husbands some of the most vital work involved in looking after their family in order to make them understand, and consequently develop a fuller appreciation of, their difficult situation when the husbands are away. This surrendering and sharing of tasks became the basis of the spousal negotiation of gender practices around housework and care work.

We might look at being "on your own" and "becoming a solo parent" as involving a time and process when the responsibility and obligation to sustain the families of migrant men become even more associated with women. This constitutes a "feminization of responsibility and obligation" (Chant 2006). This is also a time and process in which their primary responsibility of mothering becomes intensified (as it now has to encompass fathering), as indicated by their becoming "solo parents" but having to do double the work. I use the phrase here to describe both the process in which one, the responsibility and task of raising and looking after a family becomes clearly and more intensely associated with women, and two, as a result of the first, some changes in gender practices occur and women see how their sense of self-efficacy or agency has been positively affected. The experience, in other words, is subjectifying. The women whose husbands have been going to sea for quite a long time have developed the confidence and self-efficacy to deal with difficulties. As Luisa said: "Because of his absence, because he is not here for me to lean on especially when I need to deal with something that both of us should be dealing with, I have become capable of carrying them without him. You become stronger and that is because you learn to stand on your own feet."

This suggests that the women's gendered subjectivity is vitally shaped by mothering practices necessitated by the alternating absence and presence of their husbands. Wives learned to do things that were not conventionally part of domestic work, which, as Gutmann (1996, 149) has pointed out, is "generally considered to encompass cooking, washing, cleaning, and child care." Many of the wives persevered to learn to drive (a car, a small motorbike, a tricycle) for very practical reasons. They would not have to rely on or trouble others to drive them to work, take their children to school, or bring someone to the hospital (especially in unholy hours). It was especially useful for some as they lived in barangays that were not well-served by public transportation. Also, because their husbands were not always accessible due to the nature of their jobs, the women had to make decisions which their husband should have made or at least consulted. We turn to this in the next section.

Decision Making

A number of the wives said that their husbands would leave them with the assurance that if anything needed to be done or a decision taken, the wives would make the best choice (see also Espiritu 2002). Wives particularly felt burdened if decisions involved significant amounts of money, which, if they made the "wrong" decision, would have significant financial implications for the family. Thus, sometimes, making decisions was not always seen as potentially empowering but instead in terms of the possible consequences of making a "wrong" one that would affect the whole family. To be sure, however, husbands would accept the decision as done and irreversible. I present two cases to illustrate the nuances of decision-making processes and to underscore the contexts within which the women's decision making might be better appreciated.

Grace referred to a perimeter fence that she had had constructed for their eatery-variety store-billiard hall because of break-in attempts. She was concerned about her husband's reaction. She had discussed the need for it with him on the phone but at that time was not yet clear on what it was going to be like exactly. Her concern, therefore, was not the existence of the perimeter fence but whether it was the kind that the husband himself would have had built. In the end, however, her husband's opinion did not matter as the fence had already been built by the time he came home. In her case, the husband recognized that decisions have to be made, and whether or not it was the decision he would have made no longer mattered (as much). The wife said that her husband would just keep quiet or say it was fine. Both she and her husband have learned that their situation demanded understanding the dynamic of their lives of separation, which affected decision-making. As the wife said, "I can't always talk to him because signal is not always available. And it is different when he is here because you can really talk things over." Finally, the husbands, informed of decisions after the fact, viewed them with a bit more detachment and hindsight; they were not within the "crises" that the decisions were meant to address. Husbands were not in the eye of the storm, as it were, unlike their wives who were there and for whom the very making of these decisions in itself caused them worry.

Because her husband was the eldest in his family and whose parents were both dead, Alicia became involved in making a decision about her husband's younger brother. This was a particularly vexed situation for her because she was an in-law and was surrounded by her husband's relatives. Careful not to step on anyone's toes, she first consulted her husband's aunties, uncles, the *barangay kapitan* (village captain) who also happened to be a relative of her husband's. Only after the decision had been made and the deed done was she able to discuss it with her husband. Thrust in that unenviable position simply because her husband was the eldest sibling of his family, she went about her "responsibility" in a manner that protected her husband's position and that did not open her up to criticism.

Making decisions over matters that wives felt should have been first discussed with their husbands gave the wives no small measure of unease, relieved only when they had informed their husbands of their decisions. It is a complex dynamic that cannot be reduced to wives seeking the approval of their husbands or of wives clearly having less power to make decisions. These decisions were not merely personal; they also revealed their embeddedness in layers of social relationships and obligations. The wives' attitude toward making decisions in the absence of their husbands does not so much reveal indecisiveness as provide clues to the considerations they bear in mind and so shape the dynamic of their "(in)decisiveness." The sometimes unreachability of their husbands already shaped this dynamic. The consequences they tried to avoid cue us in on their social, kin, and economic obligations and standing. These wives' experiences show how circumscribed their decision-making was and provide us with a better understanding of how and why they cannot take decision-making lightly. Even if decisions were often initially accompanied by doubt, prevarication, and tentativeness, the fact remained that the decisions were made, and made with the best of intentions. To be sure, there was sometimes a refusal to take full responsibility for them, as with Alicia who consulted her husband's elders. This turned out to be a wise decision, for not only did it show her sensitivity to social norms but also became a mechanism for unburdening herself of the full responsibility of decision-making. These two wives demonstrate a competence for balancing the social implications of making decisions. They reveal that in these situations, decision-making was not just about being decisive.

Facing Tragedies and Emergencies

A number of wives have had to deal with emergencies and tragedies. Three had to evacuate their houses due to flooding and, after which, had to make their house liveable again. One's house was gutted by fire and had to find a place to stay only to move again. She referred to the difficulty of having a sense of stability and security (*narigat ti agsimpa*) as a result. One's child died eight hours after being born. Another faced eclampsia during her pregnancy, a life-threatening complication that can lead to seizures or coma. All throughout these trying times, their husbands were away, and although the wives could rely upon family, relatives, and friends, the task of lifting themselves and their families up to move on was principally theirs. As they assured themselves and their children that they would somehow pull through, they had to assuage their husbands' worry even as they (the wives) were desperate for their presence. Indeed, the wives comforted their husbands even though they were the ones most in need of help and care. As the wife who lost her child recounted, she told her husband: "Let us accept it. Let us accept it is really her fate (*gasat*). It is what was meant to be." "Yes, we should," the husband reportedly said.

One could surmise that the wife was saying this to herself even as she shared her grief and pain with her husband. At the time of my interview with her, it had been more than six months since the loss of her child, and her husband had not come back yet from sea. He still had ten months left on what the wife said was a 24-month contract (12 months then extended for another 12 months). As tragic as it may seem, they have had to deal with their loss separated physically, only comforting each other through mobile technology. At least for Alicia, 43 years old, her husband, who has been seafaring for 16 years, was home when she had an operation for breast cancer. Her husband also stayed home for more than seven months to be with her during her chemotherapy but finally had to go because they had used up their money for her medical bills.

Taking Care of Sick Children

A child falling ill brought immediacy and acuteness to the wives' being on their own. All the mothers mentioned this; asked what was most difficult with their husband's absence, a child getting sick was the first to come up for many wives. It could be as simple as a small baby catching a cold, but which was enough to leave the women sleepless and worried. It could also be a more serious condition such, as the fatal dengue (haemorrhagic fever), which often requires immediate hospitalization. A sick child did not only mean more physical work for the mothers, it also left them emotionally and mentally drained.

Taking a child to the hospital had, of course, financial implications, similar to every visit to a doctor. The women were careful to point out that, regardless of whether they had money or not, they would have taken a child to hospital because the only thing that mattered was the life of the child. They could worry about the money later on. It was nonetheless an important consideration, especially when the illness did not quickly manifest any serious consequences, particularly among those who were less financially established. The wives pointed out that just because they were at the hospital did not mean that they did not have a household to take charge of. Indeed, this was what made things very difficult for the women: they had to divide themselves between two places that required their attention simultaneously. Unquestionably, help was always available: a mother or aunt or a sibling would help look after the other children (if there were any), wash clothes or prepare meals, and surely even alternate with them at the hospital. It was impossible, however, for them to disengage completely from one space or set of responsibilities.

Although it was relatively easier for mothers who looked after sick children at home than those whose children were in hospital, the physical, emotional and mental demands of attending to what were virtually two sets of responsibilities also took a toll on them. Although they did not have to divide themselves between the hospital and their home, the attention demanded by a sick child competed with their other responsibility of running the household and of looking after the other children. A wife with four boys recalled her sheer exhaustion when her children fell ill one after the other, if not at the same time. Mothers whose children required hospitalization faced even more challenging prospects. A wife recounted the two times her children were hospitalized. With both her parents already old and her siblings with young children of their own, she had no one to alternate with her in the hospital.[5]

Although many of the mothers could rely on their parents, siblings, and other relatives and even friends for help, they said that it was in times like this that they sought their husband's presence. Indeed, it was times like this when they needed the assistance of their family yet also made acute their need to show they were capable of having their own family. There was the tension generated by the fact that this should be her and her husband's concern. I should make clear that this tension did not get in the way of what actually happened, which is that the wife would eventually rely on her family, relatives, and friends. They make clear, however, that the person they would most want to rely on was their husband. Even so, the wives would quickly say that if their husbands were not away, they would not be able to afford to pay for hospitalization in the first place.

A number of the mothers also worried that their husbands would think they had been negligent. As one wife said:

> "You know, when they [her children] were sick, even if I had to stay up all night. Because of course your husband is away he might then say you neglected your children if something happened. That's how, maybe that's why I seem to have aged too quickly because when the children were sick, I focused on them."

This concern for being faulted or even blamed put psychological pressure on the mothers to put in even more effort in looking after their children, especially when they were ill. Wives felt accountable to their husbands for what happened at home. Those who were in paid employment and who employed helpers said that one responsibility they did not delegate to them was taking their children to a doctor. As Rosario explained, there was a limit to what can be passed on to others. Their feeling of being on their own (*bukbukodam* or *bukodmo amin*) was compounded by this sense of accountability, of "owning" and "owning up" to everything, of having to make all the decisions that exhausted women.

Nabatian: Wives Giving Birth Without Their Husband Around

The long absences of their husbands have placed almost all of the mothers in situations where they gave birth without them. Some women with three children never had their husbands around for most of their pregnancy and delivery. Their husbands would be back home only when their children were already five or six months old. In other cases, the children had had their first birthdays when they returned. In most instances, the husbands left shortly after the women got pregnant or a couple of months after giving birth. The decision to leave shortly after the birth of a child was justified as being for the entire family's welfare and future. It is clear that the departure and return of the women's husbands, and, consequently, of the broad rhythms of their lives are dictated by economic imperatives. The welfare of the family was cited as the primary reason husbands did not want to stay home long. This, in turn, was linked to the availability of contracts which husbands feared they would lose if they did not yet leave. The now shorter contracts of seafarers (which many seafarers I have spoken to found "disadvantageous" to them) and the precariousness of job availability have therefore come to determine how much time their husbands can spend with their family without income. Husbands have to go, leaving behind wives to sort out on their own their deliveries and to deal with the additional work the birth of a(nother) child brings. In this sense, the women referred to themselves as *nabatian,* meaning, literally, "left behind with something."[6]

Wives were often left on their own to worry about their delivery. Money was an important concern. Leonora, 26 years old, recounted how stressed she was worrying about the sufficiency of the money she had at hand. Her last ultrasound had indicated that she might require a caesarean delivery. She explained that sometimes her allotment was delayed by two or three months, and so she borrowed from other people. Judith, 32 years old with two children aged 12 and 9, had gone to hospital for a check-up during her eighth month as she had wondered why she seemed to be passing water always. Once there, she was told she had to have a caesarean delivery as her water had ruptured, and there was very little amniotic fluid left (*awan danum a paglanglanguyan diay ubing;* literally, the child no longer had any liquid to swim in). She recounted that at that time, her only concern was the life of her child and it was only after the delivery that she got to think about how much she had to pay. Like the first wife, she had to source this money from other people.

After delivery, those who lived surrounded by their natal family and relatives were assured of abundant assistance, and this eased the absence of the husband. Those who already had other children but who had no relatives of their own to rely on, paid for help for at most three months after delivery just so they could focus on their new baby. The absence of their husbands became more acute, particularly because this absence had made it difficult for them to rely on their in-laws' help. Grace, 38 years old with a six-year old daughter, whose in-laws did not volunteer their assistance, later on welcomed their unwillingness to help. Had they done so, she explained, she would have been in their debt. The experience of Gina, 37 years old, with two children aged 11 and 4, who had no relatives in San Gabriel, and whose husband left only a week after giving birth gives us an idea of the practical difficulties arising from the absence of a husband:

> "It's hard, to give birth without any of your family and husband around. It's hard. You want to do something, you want to eat something in particular.

> You can't tell them because you do not feel comfortable doing so. Your mother-in-law, ask her to do something for you, you can't do that. It is really different with your own family or husband."

Wives did not only face practical concerns. Others had to deal with situations that involved more emotional and mental distress. Lilia, who gave birth to her two children both prematurely, said the delicate condition of her infants added to the issues she had to deal with. Although these wives lived with their natal family around them, it was only human for them to desire the presence of their husbands. They longed for their comfort, like the wives who looked after unwell or seriously ill children.

Disciplining Children

A responsibility that wives-mothers found difficult and which always reminded them of the impossibility of becoming both mother and father, no matter their attempts to doing everything, is disciplining the children, especially adolescents and older/adult ones, whom mothers described as "having or starting to have horns." *Bukbukodam* is how they said it: to be burdened with and perform a responsibility that was supposed to be a shared one. It is also a responsibility that the women thought their husbands were more effective at. As Dolores said: "The difference with a father around is they have someone to fear. Looking after the children especially when they are growing up, that is really hard. It is really hard when a man is not around. [. . .] The children don't listen to you."

The mothers considered discipline a critical part of raising good and responsible children. This became even more critical then with the absence of their husbands, who they acknowledged was the authority figure the children really recognized. This made visible tensions in their attempts to both mother and father. Linda conceded it as impossible to do: "You who are here, you fill in his absence. It is like you turn yourself into two [*dobliem koma ta bagim*] but of course you can't really do it because being a father and a mother are two different things. Being a father is simply different."

Another issue related to discipline that the wives alluded to concerns the connection made by the parents among raising children, discipline, and instruction. Disciplining was also seen as teaching or training children to be good, behaved, and responsible. Inasmuch as it is seen as instruction or moral pedagogy, wives felt burdened not only by the absence of their husbands (whose job it was to discipline children) but also because moral instruction was one of the wives' responsibilities. There are practical reasons why mothers wanted their children to be easier to handle (children can help with household work, help look after their siblings, or generally make situations easier for mothers), but these practical considerations were wedded to moral and social expectations. As such, it is burdensome. They said it was difficult because so much was at stake.

This matter concerned most especially mothers who had children approaching adolescence or older ones. They described it as particularly difficult since these ages brought with them specific issues such as rebelliousness and this was a period, according to them, when their children started to stay out more and later. With their other children and the business of running the entire family, they could not possibly keep an eye on them, or what they were up to. They were concerned that they would fall off the narrow and straight path, pick up vices, not do well in school, and the like. As one wife put it succinctly, "di ko matengngel isudan." (I can no longer handle them). What made the situation worse was that the wives felt that because they were with their children, their husbands expected them to be able to see to this part of raising the children. There was, therefore, an added psychic burden on the wives. As Maria said: "Sisiennaka ta asawam a no haanmo maisuro ta annakmo." (Your husband will blame you if you fail to teach and rein in your children.) Irene said that despite giving everything she had, she still got faulted by her husband. Still another, Nancy, whose teenage daughter got pregnant, felt very relieved that when the pregnancy was discovered, her husband was home. She said that aside from the fact that she would not have known how to break it to him had he been at sea, she was also worried that he might put the blame on her for failing to keep an eye on her daughter: "If he told me, 'you failed to keep an eye on your daughter,' what could I say to him in response? Even if I am strict, I can't keep an eye on them 24 hours."

What was clear from the wives was the importance of the presence of the father in the upbringing of the children, a presence that was, however, severely limited by the nature of their jobs. If one of the reasons for their seafaring was to provide for their future, this future was also potentially compromised by their absence since the raising of children implied ensuring they had the values that would maximize the fruits of this very labor. If the children grew up not valuing, for example, education or training that would help them secure a better future and life, then part of what is claimed as one of the reasons for the father's going to sea is not realized. Although the wives did their best to raise and discipline their children well, they knew that they could do this better with their husbands around. For this reason, all of the wives with children who were going to school (even the ones in kindergarten) encouraged them to study hard so as not to waste their father's hard work and sacrifices. They encouraged them to do so because studying hard meant that, particularly for those who were entering adolescence and adulthood, they stayed away from bad influences. A part, therefore, of the wives' strategy for motivating their children to be good and responsible was inculcating an appreciation for what their father was doing. Wives frequently reminded their children of their relatively better material comfort and the better opportunities for education they now had access to, opportunities that would only be wasted if they did not learn to listen to and heed them. A number of mothers shared the disappointments of fathers when their children abandoned their studies because they had gotten into serious responsibilities (i.e. got, or got someone, pregnant).

Becoming in charge was not a moment of empowerment in the first instance but rather a time when and through which the women became stronger because they learned to stand on their own feet. *Bukodmo amin* denotes the condition of the lives of the women when their husbands were away as a time when they were overburdened with responsibility. Becoming a solo parent not only "impose[d] heavy burdens and feelings of obligation and inadequacy" (Lewin 1997, 206) but also entailed a lot of physical and emotional work. This is why the women unburdened themselves and gave themselves a short break from carrying and shouldering responsibilities and obligations that should be shared. The women said that they, too, needed to be cared for, or even just comforted. Although they had their families to help them, as Julie pointed out, the assuring presence of the husband was different and irreplaceable: "Sabali latta tay adda tay asawam a kaduam. Adda inta sibaymo a pagibagaam. Adda katulongam." (It is something else when your husband is here. You have a companion. He is beside you, you can tell him. You have somebody to share the burden with.) Another wife described it as "awan mangtarabay kenka," that is, she had no one beside her to encourage and give her comfort. I think that this was what all of the women were trying to convey when they said they were responsible for everything despite the fact that they were surrounded by their own people who they knew they could always ask help from.

WOMEN'S ROUTINES WHEN HUSBANDS ARE HOME: LIBERATING SURRENDER (OF TASKS)

The women engaged in ways to impress upon their husbands when they were home the enormity of the task they had to shoulder on their own when their husbands were away. Wives "surrendered" or passed on responsibilities and tasks to their husbands when the latter returned. There is a strategic reason why wives "surrendered" tasks and unburdened themselves of some of their work, why, for example, they left their husbands to look after and discipline the children; do the budgeting, purchase of food and other provisions; and often do the cooking. The women wanted their husbands to "live" or see for themselves what being with children demanded and entailed. They wanted them to know how prices of commodities have gone up, to help dispel suspicions that they were not budgeting their money well and at the same time convince them to increase their wives' monthly allotment. The wives explained that it was so that their husbands would come to appreciate how difficult it was and is to be left behind with so much responsibility. They wanted their husbands to know what it was like to be made to think (*agpanunot*) and to know (*makaammo*) about practically everything. This is one way by which women initiated and negotiated changes in gender practices with their husbands.

While it is important to consider how wives involved their husbands in family life and in the tasks of maintaining family, it is also important to look at how husbands saw and felt about being home. I would like then to expand this idea of "surrendered tasks" as also a way of sharing the burden, task, and time of looking after the family. This surrender could also be seen as a form of sharing work and time. It is time for the father or husband to do his share for the family. When they were away, their absence was in the performance of their breadwinning role. During this time, wives often felt a profound sense of "being on their own." In contrast, wives saw the presence of their husbands as a time when they had their *kadua* (literally, companion) to do part, if not half (*kagudua*), of the work. Women referred to this time as having their *kabadang*, a person who shares and helps in carrying the load. For this reason, wives expected their husbands to help. I was fortunate to see husbands cooking for their families, handwashing clothes with their wives, cradling babies, and coming home from the market with food supplies. My conversations with husbands before or after the interview with their wives and interviews with seafarers from San Gabriel indicate that they were willing to do housework, look after children, and go to the market. Of course, this depended on what the husbands were good at. Some bought food from the market but did not cook. It is important to point out that the husbands who did not cook, for example, did not find it a disagreeable task for a man to do but were simply not good at it. Some husbands did not volunteer to wash clothes because their washing had been criticized by their wives in previous attempts. They would help in rinsing and hanging the washing to dry but wives would also find fault in how they hang clothes. One wife admitted that the house was tidier when her husband was around because he was very good at it, while another said that her husband was better than her at cleaning.

Most wives reported that they experienced a lightening or easing of their work load (*nakanamnam-ayak* or *malag-anannak*) as husbands took over some of the work they did (school run, budgeting, buying of provisions) and helped in housework and childcare. The men's contribution to the household maintenance involved a blurring of heteronormative gender boundaries. As one wife said, "obra ti babai, obraenna met" (a woman's job, he also does). Another wife said, "obra ti balay, obraenna" (housework, he does). This resonates with Virginia Miralao's (1984) observation in the context of the effect of women's employment on the gender division of labor in the household. Miralao concluded that although the employment of women did not appear to lead to "dramatic redefinitions of wives' and husbands' roles in household management," it nevertheless brought about "a greater amount of gender-crossing in the activities of the household" (Miralao 1984, 386 quoted in Chant and McIlwaine 1995, 300). What is notable here in the case of seamen's wives is that the women described a willingness among their men to do housework (see also Dalisay et al. 1996; Espiritu 2002; Eviota 1982; Pingol 2001; cf. van den Broek, Breedveld and Knulst 2002). The men who cooked, cleaned, washed clothes, and who did the groceries and marketing did not engage in masculinizing what they did in order to make it "accountable as men's work" (Coltrane 1998, 552). Men did not feel a diminution in their status or masculinity when they did housework and care work.

When husbands were home, the sharing of responsibilities demonstrated what I would call "gender negotiation," a process that made possible the crossing of gender boundaries when it came to the performance of housework and childcare. Whereas the husband's absence engendered a condition of *bukodmo amin,* the husband's presence instantiated moments when husbands shared in the work of caring for the family through what I called practices of "surrendered tasks" and "shared tasks." I would like to consider them here under the overarching idea of "gender negotiation."

Arlie Hochschild (1989) makes a distinction between gender ideologies and gender strategies in order to underscore the contradiction and tension between the two. Gender ideology denotes ideal types of masculinity and femininity and a person's identification with them. As such, it defines their expectations of themselves and others in terms of roles and responsibilities. Gender strategies are specific ways people resort to in order to reconcile the gap between reality and their ideal(ized) conceptions (George 2005). My understanding of Hochschild's concept of gender strategy is that it is something that an individual can do in order to cope with the messy reality of family life, and negotiating it with a partner is not always necessary. For example, a wife can it take upon herself to adopt certain gender strategies to adjust to her husband's recalcitrant demands for or expectations of who should do the housework and what kind. Although there is the element in gender strategies of both wife and husband agreeing to a certain way of sharing the work, a wife who gives up demanding her husband to share equally in housework and care work can, all by herself, adjust to her husband in order, for example, to keep the marriage intact.

My notion of "gender negotiation" as specifically practiced by wives in "surrendered tasks" and "shared tasks" attempts to capture the negotiated aspect of doing housework and care work. Its purpose, as explained by the wives, is to make the husband appreciate the work that the wives do, for them to see how difficult it is to be overburdened with responsibility. In a sense, it might be considered a form of gender strategy but one that specifically addresses the negotiated dynamic that underpins the husband's performance of their wives' many tasks. To be sure, this negotiation does not only originate in the wives' experiences of "being on their own" and "becoming a single parent" but also in the desire of the husbands to make up for those times they were away.

FAMILY TIME AND TIME OUT

Here I examine what the women did to shape family relationships and activities from the perspective of time when their husbands were home. I focus on practices of "time out" (Davies 2001), which I consider within "family time." Family time, according to Daly (2001, 284) "is not only a descriptive term that offers a perspective on some aspect of family togetherness, it is a prescriptive term that directs families to act in certain ways."

Time Out: Making Room for Father and Children

Mothers engaged in "emotional choreography" (Sillars 2010). Emotional choreography describes the way people hold and behold each other. I use it here to capture the work done by the wife to choreograph how her husband and children felt, behaved, and moved in each other's presence at least in the first few days of her husband's arrival.

Mothers, particularly of young children, gave their husband and children a time together all their own. As one wife said, no matter how much she sometimes wanted to join in what her husband and children were doing, she restrained herself, reminding herself that for almost a year she had the children all to herself. She thus enabled her husband to have his own time with the children within this family time, a time when the family was whole. Distancing, however it is done, becomes paradoxically a way of fostering ties.

This contrasts with the effort they made to make their children speak to their fathers when they are on board ships (discussed in the next chapter). They made sure that the father and their children talked or that the father talked to their babies. When the husbands were away then, the wives mediated relationships and made sure that a semblance of father-children ties were maintained. When the husbands were home, however, they limited their mediation. One wife explained that she could not force her children to warm up to their father. With her husband home, she let her husband find his own way of winning his children's affection.

Time out therefore has both external and internal dimensions to it, as well as spatial-temporal ones. Both are meant to foster ties, to deepen relations. One, mediation, is done to bridge a gap caused by absence and distance, while the other, distancing, becomes a form of emotional management. Paradoxically though, the internal aspect of time out does not make the wife any less important. Instead, the situation makes her even more central to the life of the whole family even as she momentarily and fleetingly takes a peripheral role during the time the father and children re-established broken bonds. Moving in and out of the timespace of emotion and relationships forms a vital part of the rhythmicity of a seafarer wife. She thus cuts out a space for her husband even as her husband, on his own initiative and desire, makes room for himself precisely by integrating himself into the family routine. This way he achieves temporal symmetry with the family from which he was distanced, a rhythmic harmony or symmetry he himself helps to conduct and orchestrate.

Time Out: From Maternal Care to Marital Care

Although most wives talked about taking care of their husbands, only two wives said that they looked after their husbands more than they did their children when their husbands were home. Only one of them, however, explicitly talked about a shift in the focus of her attention and care. I call this shift in care focus as time out from maternal care to spousal care:

> "I attend to him. It's his turn. When he's not here, all my time is focused on my children. But when he is here, I turn over my children to my mother, and I attend to him."

Because her husband was a (new) chief engineer whose work pattern consisted of three months of work followed by one month of paid shore leave, the alternation of the focus of her attention was not, according to her, a source of conflict since her two older children were already grown up (14 and 7 years old). However, when I interviewed her, she had just given birth to their third child ten days before and so had not lavished her husband with the usual attention. Her routine, she said, involved managing the children's behavior when he was home. She acted as the link between them. She would tell her husband how to handle the children. Hence, although she shifted her attention to him, this did not mean she completely abandoned her children for her time with him included fostering father-and-children relationship.

More Time (To Be) Out

When women went out during the time their husbands were away, most of it was in the performance of their responsibilities: taking the children to and from school, purchasing food, or going to mass on Sundays. All these were still part of their domestic responsibilities. Even the employed wives' movements outside of the house were due mainly to their work. A few of the older wives said they went to the provincial capital only when necessary (to withdraw some money, for example). Wives very rarely went out on their own for leisure. Indeed, some of these women pointed out when I asked them how they relaxed that they were not like other seamen's wives who have gone astray, implicitly asserting that staying close to the house/home was a sign of their virtuousness. The wives' associating of going out with impropriety is a response to the fear of being the subject of gossip about for sexual impropriety, which I discuss in another chapter.

When the husbands were home, the women had more time to go out, that is, to spend some family time outside of their house. Thus, they could more freely go out; the husband's presence "relaxes" them since going out with him would not put her under a cloud of suspicion. The women mentioned that this "time out" was not only pleasurable because they were such a welcome change to the space within which they moved most of the time and to the routine that structured their lives; women who lived with their in-laws said they felt rejuvenated not only by time spent relaxing and having fun with the whole family but also by the feeling of "being away," of "going away" even only for a brief period of time. Women, particularly those who lived with or near in-laws, felt happier.

However, one wife's time out of the house became time in the house. When her husband was away, the time waiting for her son at school was essentially her time to be out of the house in order to be with friends. She therefore found it such a pleasurable time, a time she considered her leisure time. With her husband around, she lost this time with friends. She and her husband would take their son to school together, go home together, and then pick him up. The time during which the son was in school was time the husband wanted to spend together. It made perfect sense for her to shift how, where, and with whom that period of time was spent. For her, going out took other forms as the whole family would drive to the beach, eat out, and attend Sunday mass together. When he goes back to work, she goes back to how, where, and with whom this time was spent. Again, we see in this particular case how a wife's routine and rhythmicity are structured by the husband's cycle of departure and return.

Contested Time

Some women found dealing with their husband's social drinking to be a vexed issue. While they understood their husbands' desire and even need to spend time with friends for drinks and other leisure activities, they wanted their husbands to strike a balance between their family obligations and their social needs. Because their husbands were away for a long time, they needed social relaxation. But for precisely the same reason did the wives want their husband's time for, and with, them. Because the husbands are home for only a few months, the wives wanted them to make the family the primary recipient and object of their time. Wives tried to negotiate the tension between the pull of family obligations and their husband's social integration, which had consequences on family time, the family's financial condition, the worrying imposed on the wives concerning their husband's safety while they were out, and the marital relationship in which husbands used their time to have liaisons.

The men's own "time out" from the family hence has the potential to strain domestic harmony, which, as shown in the previous section, husbands and wives achieve and establish through cooperative working in practices of "surrendered tasks" and "shared tasks." To be sure, a good number of wives reported that their husbands were good at exercising responsibility and good sense. One wife with two young children, for example, expressed gratitude for her husband's being considerably reasonable. The last time her husband was home, she did not allow him to go out at night since they did not have a helper at that time and she did not like the idea of being on her own with her husband at home. In the few times he had gone out when they had a helper, the wife expected him to be home by 10:00 p.m. as she did not want to worry about his safety. Such a "curfew," she added, was not too much to ask as he was no longer a bachelor who did not have any responsibilities to others.

Others, however, had to deal with husbands who did not seem to know their limit. Three wives were so displeased by their husbands' unbridled behavior (drinking, gambling, womanizing) that they sometimes wished their husbands went back to sea. To them, their husbands were "kunsumisyon," someone who gave them worry, or more precisely, a headache:

> "When he's home he's like a wild animal set free. But it is okay for him to go [drinking], what I do not like is that he comes home at dawn. Of course, what wife likes her husband to come back at such a time, right? He goes out early in the afternoon, and then comes back only at dawn. Who would like that?"

The husband's "time out" to socialize had consequences on the wives' routine as well. For example, when their husbands entertained their "barkada" (their group of close male friends), some wives were expected by their husbands to wait for them to have dinner together. Drinking also added to the wives' tasks, which they hated doing. One wife mentioned her husband, who in his drunken state, urinated in the corner of their bedroom thinking it was the toilet. Another recounted, in horror, cleaning away her husband's vomit. Husbands being out having drinks with friends, which could go until late evening or early morning, made wives worry about their safety, which deprived them of a good sleep. Wives also thought about the money involved in drinking since it would be their husbands who almost always certainly paid for these drinking sessions. Wives were rightly concerned about budgeting wisely for during this time they lived on saved money.

Also, the wives were concerned about the health and safety of their husbands, a concern that is tied to their ability to get a new contract and hence to the well-being and life of the whole family. Wives preferred their husbands to stay as healthy as they possibly could. The risk of a career cut short or permanently ended was a thought that had real consequences even on the wives' "routine," that is, on the demands and expectations they had on how husbands spent their time home. When husbands persisted in drinking, gambling, and womanizing (which involved spending money, danger, or disease), they became a burden to their wives, which the latter said they rather did not have. It was in these times they wanted their husbands back to sea.

Daly (2001, 284) observes that family time "does not typically include portrayals of . . . the negative aspects of family activities or the different meanings and entitlements associated with family time for each family member." Here, the wives' conception of "family time" clashed with their husbands' "taking their own time," that is, time spent away from the family that the wives felt constituted "wasting time" (that also involved wasting money and wasting or risking their "health capital"). The wives were concerned with "making up for lost family time" as well as "saving time" in the sense of accumulating times of family togetherness that would sustain the whole family when the husbands were away again. The husbands' "own time" also differed from the wives' practices of "making room," which they occasionally did to exclude themselves from what their husbands and children were doing in order to facilitate and foster warmer father-children relationships. Such conflicting conceptions, practices, and use of time reveal, as Daly (1996, 211) has noted, that "decisions about time are decisions about values. When people experience time conflicts, not only are there competing demands placed on that time, but divergent underlying values shape how the time is spent."

Bittman and Wacjman (2000, 167) explain that "[f]ree time is a residual category. It is the time that remains after maintaining one's body in a healthy and socially acceptable state, contracting time to the market, and meeting domestic and family responsibilities. Free time encompasses both time devoted to activities undertaken explicitly for leisure and time used to engage in discretionary pursuits such as religious and civic activities." My discussion of contested time shows that husbands are able to have time that remains only for themselves (whether this time be spent with friends); in other words, they can have time away from their family. Seafarer-husbands who are home can have a leisurely "me-time" that is not linked to or associated with others or care work. More importantly, their "free time" for leisure is uncontaminated by "family time." Some husbands went out on their own and returned home as and when they pleased. In contrast, the women did not. Their time for themselves, especially those spent when their husbands were home, was the time they spent with the "whole family." The husband's "time out" also shows that some of these women did not really have a time out of their own, that is, a time they could devote to themselves and not have fun *with* the family. When their husbands were away, the women had home-bound leisure dominated by watching television. When their husbands were home, they were able to have leisure outside of the home but in the context of having "family time." Theirs is a "linked" leisure time, one defined by it being spent with others. This demonstrates a gendered use of leisure time. Their experience of leisure is bound up with time spent on leisure with their family.

ROUTINES OF "GETTING USED TO" HUSBANDS' DEPARTURE

I have thus far discussed the temporal organization of the lives of seafarer families through the timeframes marked by the seaman's absence and being home. In this section, I examine how these two timeframes (and the temporality of life they engender) are mediated by the work women do to prepare themselves for the departure of their husbands and to adjust to their absence once again. I refer to this work of preparation and adjustment as "getting used to," which is how I translate "masanay" and "mairuam," words the women used to refer to what they did to adjust to their husband's departure.

One said that the departure of her husband disturbed her physiological balance: "Di ka makaturturog, haanka makapangpangan inggana a haanmo mauray tawagna." (You can't sleep, you can't eat until he's called.) Normalcy was restored by her husband's first call after departure. Another wife described her husband's departure as involving a "break," a temporal and spatial cutting off of the process of bonding. Another wife described hers as a stoppage (as in road traffic) of a life together. A fourth wife described what she always felt like when her husband goes as "kaslang mapugsat man amin nga angesen. [. . .] ay hindi talaga ako natuto" (it's like all my breath is being cut off. [. . .] I never really learn).

One woman has gotten so used to her husband's going away that she described it as an "ordinary a pasamak" (an ordinary event). Staying behind, during at least the time of her husband's departure, has been relegated to the mundane. Yet this particular wife readily acknowledged that the husband's departure was associated with negative feelings. For most of the wives, while their husband's return was anticipated with excitement and generally looked forward to with positive expectation, their departure was met with justification: necessity, sacrifice, the good of the family: "Mailiw-liwagto manen; para iti masakbayan ti ubbing kunak met. Sakripisyo lang." (You'll get over it again; it is for the children's future, I say. Sacrifice.)

We have already mentioned a couple of wives who sometimes wished their husbands were away on account of their unruly behavior. Also, when husbands were home, families relied on saved money. Once this was depleted, and husbands were still unable to go, they begin to accumulate debt. Except for the chief engineer's wife, all the wives did not want their husbands to stay too long because they did not have any income while their husbands were home.

> "Oh, it's tough. You think about what it is going to feel like when he goes. But what choice is there when you have piled up debts again, like that. You think about that again. [. . .] What you will eat."

This particular wife who can now talk of her husband's departure as an ordinary event has adjusted over time to his absences. Some wives whose husbands have also been seafaring for many years but who still feel "separation pangs" talked of emotional preparation and practical activities to help with the transition.

For most of the wives, their most common way of adjustment was through *tungtong*: neighborly group chats. Such activity eased their situation as it involved interacting with other people, including going to their house, which also tightened social relationships. The ritual departure of their husbands is repeatedly, momentarily kept at bay so that wives are not always reminded of them (husbands are "forgotten") until such time they have again gotten used to their husband's departure and absence.

There is another dimension to "getting used to." For a number of wives, there was a certain limit to how long their husband's stay was enjoyable and welcome. Some wives did not like their husbands to stay too long because they did not want to get used to their presence too much, which would then make their adjusting to their departure and absence more difficult. As one explained:

> "I prefer that, for example, if he comes home today, next month he goes back. I prefer it that way. [. . .] If he came home today and goes back after seven months, it's going to be very difficult for myself to get over it. It's like my body has gotten so used to him being around."

The physical presence of husbands then had temporal boundaries set by the emotional and psychic reserves of wives, effectively determining their "tolerance" level for their being at home. Their desire for their husband to be around was tempered by this "internal limit" harbored within this very desire for their presence. Beyond this time limit, re-adjusting to the absence "became more difficult" ("Narigrigat ngamin nokua"), as one wife explained. To be sure, this determination of how long their husband's stay was positively experienced cannot be dissociated from the financial fortunes of the family for indeed they subsisted on savings, which were limited. It can only be replenished by the departure of the husbands, which is one of the temporal markers (return being the other) that frames the rhythmicity of their lives. Equally crucial, this departure hinges on what wives have accrued over time, that is, their ability to get used to their husband's absence which is compromised or weakened when husbands "overstayed."

This "transition period" meant the resumption of their own routine, that of being on their own again:

> "Oh it's another adjustment again. You really have to adjust again. It takes about a month because you have to go back to your routine, your routine when he was [away] [. . .] You adjust and once you've adjusted yourself again, everything becomes all right."

The routine of wives therefore had a quality of cyclicality to it, and by routine here I include the rhythmicity of the socio-material and psycho-emotional practices that underpins their lives as seamen's wives. They got used to this cycle but "getting used to" actually involved a lot of physical, material, and emotional work.

Time heals, so the cliché goes. But the condition created by spousal absence inadequately rendered affectively and visually by the word "missing" is not completely sutured. Adjusting to this absence particularly to the time immediately after the husband's departure is both a means of dealing with the "wound" of separation and proof of the recurring presence of "pain" (a cut, a gap, or a break). Thinking about the promise of life that this separation brings forth makes this "sufferance of pain" or sadness, however fleeting, to some bearable, justifiable, and meaningful. It is therefore simply not the passage of time that heals (for this metaphor might be appropriate to things we would want consigned to the past and not to what is a fact and part of the "present" of wives) but the psycho-material practices and activities performed by wives in order to "understand" the rhythmicity and chronicity of parting.[9] What these wives are effectively describing is a deferral of lives to the exigencies and contingencies of a "greedy job" that is inextricably linked to the global; hence the adjustment in order to resume it. "Hindi talaga ako natuto" (I never really learn) suggests that adjusting is an active process of learning, of teaching one's self to deal with the situation that cannot be left alone to the passage of time. Time heals because it is made to.

ROUTINE, HORIZON, AND INTERSUBJECTIVITY

Mothers saw routine as cumulative (Adam 1995; Davies 1990; Maher 2009) and having a future orientation to it. Routine accordingly is not just repetitive, the boring and mindless kind or one associated with the "commodified rationalized clock time of employment relations" (Adam 1995, 95). Acts of bathing, feeding children, for example, though repetitive are actually geared toward physical development, growing up, and maturing. As one mother said of his son: "He can now be on his own, I just give him instructions. [. . .] I train him so it is not too hard on me. [. . .] If I see that he has not done it properly, I make him do it again." As children grow, they are expected to be able to care for themselves, if not for their siblings.

This repetitiveness is training geared toward independence. It demonstrates that the doing of chores, for example, is not simply about getting those chores done. They are inextricably bound up with other rhythms of life: becoming old enough to do certain things, becoming responsible. There is hence a pedagogic dimension woven into these daily rhythms of life. For many of the mothers, they did not only have tasks to do; there was meaning to what they were doing. Children were not only a source of "work" or responsibility which in turn structured their routine, but also that there were corporeal, emotional, and psychological components of the temporal trajectory of their work. One mother with four sons (three of whom became seamen themselves) and one daughter credited her routine of prayer and church service as a critical part in the upbringing of her children. She explained that her children growing up in the word of God ("*gapu iti pannakangkangngegda iti sao ti Apo*") helped her in no small measure in instilling in them discipline and a sense of responsibility. She is convinced that had it not been for her faith that included prayer and fellowship in their daily and weekly routines, not only would raising five children have been so much more difficult but also that her five children could have taken life paths different from what they actually had.

My discussion of women's routines resonates with the idea of "provisioning." Neysmith and Reitsma-Street (2009, 383) define provisioning as "the work of securing the resources and providing the necessities of life to those for whom one has relationships of responsibility." It refers to:

> a range of specific activities that are never finished, must be performed regularly, and require energy and attention. These activities cannot be isolated or separated from the context of social relationships because provisioning consists of those daily activities performed to ensure the survival and well-being of oneself and others. Both the activities and the relationships may be voluntary or prescribed. The point is that these activities are necessary, without them people would not survive. (Neysmith and Reitsma-Street 2009, 238)

The homework and care work invested into these "maternal times" (Adam 1995, 95) linked everyday time with the life time. Thorne (1999) notes that the terms "growing up" and "raising a child" not only reveal the intermingling and interpenetration of a multiplicity of temporalities but also the future orientation of routines of care work. Their trajectory is both physical growth and social maturation. Thorne (1999, 9) writes: "These paired terms allude to a mix of daily, cyclical time (get up, get dressed, eat breakfast, pack lunches, head for school and work) and the sweep of cumulative time entailed in the passage from child to adult." Time, Tronto (2003, 123) points out, "assumes a different aspect from the standpoint of care. Time spent caring is not about mastery and control but about maintenance and nurturance." Feminist analyses of the diverse temporalities of care work (Davies 1990; Deutscher 2006; Maher 2009; Silva 2002) have shown that although care work might be repetitive, circular, fragmentary, "the organizing principle," as Maher (2009, 239) has noted, "is the desire to accumulate well-being; in the child, the family, the self." Maher also draws attention to the need to incorporate this sense of progress, of cumulativeness, in women's repetitive, cyclical, and seemingly endless routines of care work (238). The time of the seafarers' wives could be conceptualized as a spiral to capture how they invest their routines of "repetitive" care work with the sense of progress and growth (Davies 1990; Maher 2009).

The women's performance of routines of care work demanded in many instances their reliance on the help of kin and affine relations thereby tightening ties of reciprocity and obligation (see also Herd and Harrington Meyer 2002, 675). This is illustrated by the case of Jennifer whose routine I presented above. Women who lived with their natal family did not have as hectic a routine as Jennifer's because their parents and siblings were always there to rely upon to provide the care the women's children needed while the mothers attended to other responsibilities. Whether recipient or giver of care, either role underscores the women's relational and intersubjective contexts that add a significant dimension to their gendered subjectification.

Although seafaring is a job that might be seen to tighten the link among "husband," "father," and "provider," on the one hand, and "wife," "mother," and "home," on the other, it is also a job that exposes the mutability and contingency of gender practices as embodied in the performance of housework and care work. The demands that seafaring puts on both men and women help to engender an environment that arguably is conducive for both husband and wife to institute "a new moral economy for gender relations" (Gutmann 1996, 261) and to do gender differently (Coltrane 1989; Connel 1995; West and Zimmerman 1987). The state of "bukodmo amin" became, to borrow from Lieba Faier (2009, 8) "a relational site of subjectification" that became the condition of possibility for the negotiation of gendered tasks and practices between husbands and wives, and how these renegotiated gender practices shaped the intimacies of power between the women and their husbands, as well as the gendered subjectification of the women (and their husbands, too). The practices of surrendered tasks and shared tasks are ways of "undoing gender" (Deutsch 2007), that is, reducing the difference between what the women and their husbands did in terms of the gender of the tasks they performed to look after and care for their families. In this sense, the subjectification of the women is a relational and "a dialogic process" (Faier 2009, 8) occurring in their lived and quotidian experiences within spousal and family relationships. Practices of gender negotiation are tied with the "exchange of understanding" (Hochschild 1989) or "economies of gratitude" (Coltrane 1998). Both husband and wife recognize that they are making sacrifices and although wives bring in less or no money at all (with the husband the main or sole breadwinner), there is recognition of the importance each contributes to the family's welfare. This "exchange of marital gifts" (Hochschild 1989, 139)—the understanding and recognition that they are both protagonists performing different roles—help at least reconcile gender ideologies and strategies (Hochschild 1989). The couple's modes of surrendered tasks and shared tasks embody a negotiated practice of domestic life and show possibilities for changing conventional domestic politics precisely because they are underpinned by practices of subjectivities that blur the masculine-feminine gender dichotomy. Tensions remain, however, in how some husbands spent their leisure time, which the women saw as having negative consequences on their family's finances and on their husband's health.

CONCLUSION

I examined here the link between the women's gendered subjectivity and their routines, looking at routines within a social conception of time (Adam 1988, 1995; Hassard 1990; Nowotny 1994; Young 1988; Zerubavel 1979, 1985a, 1985b). Doing so located not only the women's routines but also the women themselves in space: their lived and inhabited times were spatial. The performance of their routines also drew on kin and affine relations, which embedded them in ties of reciprocity and indebtedness. Just as routine helped them to structure and organize their lives, so did these relations provide them with resources to fulfil their work. The women's routines demonstrated their gendered subjectivity, one that is centered on the work of mothering. The women's routines embodied their mothering responsibilities and activities in the context of the timeframes that bracket their lives: when their husbands are home, when they are departing again, and when they are away. Their routines were not just habitual, everyday activities but rather ones that they imbued with a future orientation. They linked their routine activities and practices of care with their children's well-being, growth, and flourishing. Equally important, their routine was a vital part of their moral pedagogy, that is, in disciplining and bringing up their children to be good and responsible. Both aspects aimed at shaping the future of their children.

When husbands depart, it is not just wives who have to live this departure and absence. There are children, many of them still very young, who must grow up not seeing and living with their father for longer periods than they actually do. Many of them have in fact grown up in this kind of family set-up. And part of the routine of wives is to help their children also adjust to their father's constant leaving, to make them understand and appreciate why they constantly have to depart until such time these children can appreciate by themselves that these departures are their umbilical cords to a better life. For many, if not all of them, their future rests on and is guaranteed by this absence. The women's performance of these routines of care work would show that their gendered subjectivity is not only relational and intersubjective. Particularly in the context of their practices of "time out," it is also inseparable from the people they have responsibility for. In others words, their subjectivity and agency are shaped and defined by and within these maternal and spousal relationships. Their "time of care" for others becomes part of their selves, which in turn becomes inextricably bound up with those they have responsibilities for. Their time, including their leisure time, becomes intimately identified with family relations.

Finally, to be able to give even a partial description of the everyday lives of the wives when their husband was away and plot the ways they inhabited this time, we need to bear in mind that their experience of the everyday depended not only on a structural location but also equally on a future horizon. This, I argue, informed and attended how some of the wives moved within the timespace denoted by their husband's absence. There is no doubt that being in waged work or being a mother particularly of young and/or still dependent children provided the content and structure of their time as well as determined the amount of their work. An awareness of how their routine and quotidian activities could be used to help bring up their children guided the way the women organized the temporality of their family lives. Prayer and church attendance were not only daily or weekly activities but also ways of instilling moral character and discipline.

A number of feminist scholars, specifically those looking at care work within the broader discourse of provisioning (DeVault 1991; Neysmith and Reitsma-Street 2005, 2009; Power 2004) have conceptualized unpaid care work as part of civic engagement (Herd and Harrington Meyer 2002). For Herd and Harrington Meyer (2002, 674), unpaid care work "provided within families, like other traditional civic activities, fosters the attributes of democratic citizens." Viewing routines of care work as vitally involved in civic participation reconceptualizes the home as not simply a space denoting the private domestic sphere, which is mostly associated with women, but brings to the fore the interpenetration of the public and the private spheres. Daly (1996) also points out that the women's coordination of the temporal organization of the family plays a vital role in the socialization process that children go through to develop "time awareness" that "prepares their children to meet the socially imposed temporal imperatives and constraints" (Daly 1996, 161 citing Le Feuvre 1994). As Blunt (2005, 510 quoted in Meah 2014, 674) has written, "the home itself is intensely political, both in its internal intimacies and through its interfaces with the wider world." In the next chapter, we look at how communication activities, admittedly necessitated by the absence-presence of husbands, were part of the ways by which wives negotiated distance and separation in order to reproduce family intimacy and ties in the context of transnational or international labor migration, and how these communication practices of intimacies were shaped by "the wider world."

CHAPTER 5

COMMUNICATION AND IMAGINED COMMUNION

Seamen's wives know absence very well. Their lives are striated by it. They prepare for and live this absence and its consequences. It is in this sense that I talk of the intimacy of absence in their lives. This chapter attends to this absence by looking at the ways by which these women have tried to lessen its presence and the means that have helped them ameliorate it. In so doing, it relocates these women from "home" to a space of *imagined communion*. I look at this space, which incorporates both their home and their husbands' ships (which is both their home and place of work), as one that has its origins in the home (or in making home) but which is not, however, analogous to it. It exceeds the physical, temporal, and spatial boundaries of the home in that this space extends to that which is outside of it, but which it attempts to incorporate and so in a sense domesticate and embrace. I dwell here on the wives' activities that bring their husbands home and that bring "home" to their husbands. These activities enable them to become intimate despite the absence, separation, or distance, and to make the absent present. This space of *imagined communion* then becomes the locus of the reproduction of family and of affective ties and is itself the result of these emotional and material activities.

This chapter investigates the communication practices of the seafarer families achieved in this absence and separation, and which produce that sense of home in an "elsewhere." I examine communication designed to foster family and affective ties, including father-children relationships, in the context of this separation. These are communication events and practices in and through which husbands are made "present." I also examine how intimacy is mediated by communication technologies and focus on how wives and husbands remit affection to each other. The women are the central figures in these "affective practices" (Walkerdine 2010) that bind the family together in the context of distance and separation. I therefore focus on two interrelated aspects of the women's lives and experiences that shape their gendered subjectivity. First, how they reproduce and foster family life and relationships in a transnational context from which we clearly see how these communication activities are linked to their mothering work. Second, how women ease their physical and sexual longing for their husband through the possibilities of expressing and communicating longing and intimacy offered by available communication technologies. As women who stay behind, their sexual subjectivity becomes a vital component of their gendered subjectification. As women whose husbands are away, part of their gendered subjectivity is remaining faithful, enduring the long absence of physical and sexual intimacy, and dealing with it in ways that will not endanger their marriage.

Here I focus on communication enabled by and dependent on mobile phones, the discussion of which I frame within the context of the state of telecommunication in the Philippines more broadly, and in San Gabriel more specifically. I also briefly look at the wives' use of prepaid phone cards that, together with the mobile phone, have made communication between the women and their husbands affordable. This contextualization shows how mobile communication has helped them overcome many of the limitations obtaining in the unevenness of the distribution of telecommunication infrastructure and facilities in the country. Moreover, this will help us better appreciate the role played by mobile phones in the lives of transnational families as illustrated by the experiences of seamen's families.

FRAMING MOBILE PHONE COMMUNICATION

Internet penetration in the Philippines in 2014 stood at 40 percent of a population of 100 million, with connectivity concentrated predominantly in urban areas leaving rural areas largely underserved (Freedom House 2015). In contrast, mobile phone penetration in 2014 reached 111 percent, suggesting that some users have more than one device. By the third quarter of 2014, the country's two biggest telecommunications companies, Philippine Long Distance Telephone Co. (PLDT) and Globe Telecommunications, had a combined 110 million mobile phone subscribers (Freedom House 2015). This scale of penetration of the mobile phone has been attributed partly to Filipinos' "strong cultural orientation for constant and perpetual contact" (Pertierra 2006, 1).

Rather than attribute the Filipinos' need to keep in touch to an essentialist cultural trait, it makes more sense to see it, among other factors, in the context of migration, and hence in the separation of family members and relatives. This would put the Filipinos' need to communicate within a more historicized political-economic context. The pervasiveness and (the now) mundanity of migration necessitates communication and the exploitation of the technology that allows them, in the most affordable way, to maintain family ties and relationships. I therefore take the position of Manuel Castells and his colleagues (2007, 125) who have argued that "[p]eople shape communication technology, rather than the other way around. Yet, the specificity of the technology reflects onto the way in which people conduct their lives" (cf. Arminen 2009; Horst and Miller 2006; Miller and Slater 2000; Wilding 2006). This position offers a sounder and more nuanced way of looking at the social consequences of new communication technologies than the perspectives provided, for example, by Ito et al. (2005), who have argued in the context of Japan that mobile telephony leads to individualization and atomization at the expense of sociality or social relationships. Rather than see new communication technologies as giving rise to brave new worlds, it makes more sense, as Wilding says, to see how they "have been incorporated . . . into the familiar, ongoing patterns of everyday social life" (2006, 126). We turn below to a historical contextualization of the mobile phone's place in the lives of Filipinos.

The Liberalization of Philippine Telecommunication

The deregulation of the Philippine telecommunication industry, which gathered momentum during the administration of Pres. Fidel V. Ramos (1992–1998), opened up to at least eight other players in a sector that had hitherto been a monopoly of the Philippine Long Distance Telephone Company (PLDT)—which, despite its name, was a private business whose majority stake was "owned" by the family of Antonio Cojuangco. In 1992 around 800,000 Filipinos, 75 percent of them in Metro Manila, were waiting for a telephone line. But "instead of expanding its network to meet service demand," PLDT, which had over 90 percent of the entire country's telephone lines (Bernardo and Tang 2008, 18), spent heavily to protect its market share (Tiglao 1993 cited in Bernardo and Tang).

In 1995 only 1.4 million telephone lines were available. By 2000 the number dramatically rose to 6.9 million, which improved telephone density—the number of fixed-line telephones per 100 population—from 2.01 in 1995 to 9.12 in 2000. However, there was a heavy urban bias to the roll-out of telephone service. Metro Manila, where only about 14 percent of the Philippine population lived, had 47 percent of the total, equivalent to 3.2

million lines. Countrywide, by December 2001, only 844 of the 1,609 towns and cities (52.4 percent) had fixed line coverage. Only 654 (or 40.6 percent) had cellular phone coverage (Salazar 2007, 280–82).

The liberalization of the Philippine telecommunication industry was pursued following a Service Area Scheme (SAS), which divided the market into eleven areas that were distributed to eight international gateway and cellular telephone operators. Each operator was assigned a profitable and an unprofitable area "to ensure both operational viability and the provision of rural telephony" (Salazar 2007, 243). Rural telephony, however, seemed to have been condemned from the beginning since operators were directed, at minimum, to install one rural exchange line for every ten urban lines installed. Moreover, there was a decline in the demand for telephone line connections precipitated by the 1997 Asian financial crisis.

With the decline in incomes and the consequent instability of the economic and financial situation of many Filipino households, prepaid cellular phones became the alternative, which had the advantage of mobility (Salazar 2007). Text messaging, introduced in the Philippines in September 1994 by Globe Telecom, which has made communication cheaper (Lallana 2004 cited in Pertierra 2005) and therefore more accessible, has become a defining feature of the Philippines' mobile communication culture. Estimates indicate that around 10 percent of global SMS volume is generated in the Philippines (GSMA Intelligence 2014, 7). Moreover, "messaging accounts for 37% of operator recurring revenue (high by regional and global standards), highlighting the 'texting culture' that has grown in the country" (GSMA Intelligence 2014, 7).

The access of low-income groups to mobile phones reversed what initially was the trend in 1991, when only those in high-income groups could afford a mobile phone. In 2013, there were 49.2 million unique subscribers compared with 3.15 million fixed telephone subscribers. Mobile phones, due to their affordability and accessibility, became a rational and logical alternative to fixed line phones (Salazar 2007).

Table 5. Mobile Cellular Unique Subscribers Philippines, 2011–2014, in millions

Year	Subscribers
2011	44.0
2012	46.8
2013	49.2
2014	50.9

Source: GSMA Intelligence (December 2014)

The mobile phone's penetration into ordinary Filipino lives may also be accounted for by how its cost was later built around the (weak) purchasing power of many Filipinos. Two marketing strategies, for example, of Smart, the country's leading cellular phone service provider, illustrate this point. The first, electronic load (or e-load) enabled users to purchase phone credit (or "load," hence the name "e-load") for as low as PhP30. Previously the minimum cost of a phone card was PhP300 (Nagasaka 2007). E-load enabled many Filipino users to acquire phone credits depending on how much they could afford at the time of purchase. The second, *pasa* load, enabled users to share (*pasa,* pass on) their phone card credit or load "to their friends' or relatives' cell phones by sending to a designated number their text messages that include the cell phone numbers of beneficiaries and the amount they want to give" (Nagasaka 2007, 103). Initially the minimum amount that could be "passed" was PhP10 but this was later reduced to one peso. Globe Telecom, Smart's closest competitor, later provided similar services: "auto-load" and "share-a-load" (103). I would argue that the business model for these two strategies was based on the Filipino *sari-sari*[2] store and the selling of goods through the *tingi* (retail) system. This further embedded the mobile phone in systems many Filipinos knew well because it was partly through these systems that they negotiated and transacted their daily lives.

To summarize this section, two fundamental reasons might explain the mobile phone's ubiquity in the Philippines. The first is its "leapfrogging" of the physical infrastructure that is the requisite of landline phones and the Internet. The mobile phone opened many remote towns and villages that were not attractive enough to the profiteering eyes of telecommunication companies owned by rent-seeking oligarchs. The second is its affordability not only in the sense of the cost of a mobile phone unit but also equally in terms of how its cost was adapted to the economic power (or weakness) of the general Filipino populace. The combination of these two factors enabled many rural and urban poor households to become linked to physically distant family and kin both in the Philippines and overseas. The landline phone, which previously had seemed so essential, became simply dispensable.

Telephony in San Gabriel

The mobile phone becoming an alternative to the landline phone might be demonstrated by the experience of San Gabriel. The town's first household telephone lines were installed in 1992. People who wanted (and had long waited) to have telephones at home recall with good humor the rush going to the municipal government office to have their names registered. Installation was initially limited to the *poblacion* (the town proper covering only 18 of a total 43 villages). According to San Gabriel's annual state of the local government report for 2009, only 30 percent of the town's 2007 population of 32,345 resided in this area. Later, three villages outside of the town proper but which were near the *poblacion* and lay along or was traversed by the national highway were included. Later still, a village farther from the *poblacion* (bordering the next town already, in fact) but which is bisected by the national highway was granted lines since enough number of households were going to subscribe and therefore justified the extension of the telephone area coverage. The telecommunications company manager whom I interviewed explained that enough people could afford to pay for the subscription since that village had many residents who were overseas migrant workers and even Hawaiianos, that is, Ilokanos who migrated to Hawaii and had become either permanent US residents or citizens but kept close ties with their families and relatives.

The telecommunications manager's explanation referred to the source of funding for these households, that is, an assurance that the monthly bill would be paid with money sent by the residents' relatives living or working overseas. The manager also identified the coordinates of this telecommunication. The telephone, it would seem, was meant to enable communication between residents from the village and their relatives who now lived in Hawaii or who are working in other countries more than communication between village or even town residents. This point resonates with Vertovec's (2004) argument that improvements in telecommunications infrastructure have significantly been driven and will continue to be driven by transnational migration practices.

Out of 6,289 households in San Gabriel, 765 or 12 percent had landline telephones. Of these, 720 or 94 percent lived in the *poblacion* (inclusive of the three adjacent villages) and 45 in the border village (including a neighboring village). Overall, 23 out of 43 villages (53 percent) had landline phone connections. The concentration of landline telephones in the *poblacion* was inversely related to San Gabriel's population distribution: only 30 percent of the town's population lived in the *poblacion*.

Residents who had no landline phones and no access to Internet at home had recourse to the mobile phone. Even those who had landline phones also had mobile phones. The mobile phone was particularly welcomed by those who lived in villages and who did not have landline phone connections either because they could not afford one or could not get one because their village was not covered by the roll-out. An antenna, with a 5-kilometer coverage radius built around 1998 or 1999 atop a hill has greatly improved mobile phone signal in San Gabriel, at least for subscribers of Smart. The situation in San Gabriel might be said to reflect the national situation as a whole. As of 2014, only 2.6 percent of the country's population had a fixed broadband subscription. Mobile phones are the main device for internet access, "with mobile internet adoption reaching 62 percent of total subscribers" (GSMA Intelligence 2014, 7).

Cheap International Telephone Calls and Prepaid Phone Cards

Steven Vertovec has written that processes of global linkage particularly "among non-elite social groups such as migrants" are facilitated more by "the boom in ordinary, cheap international telephone calls" than any other technological development (2004, 219). He noted that cheap calls, which enable and facilitate "everyday" transnational connectivity, have become these migrants' main connection to their social networks, particularly in their source communities. For Filipinos, of whom 40 percent or so live below the poverty line, these cheap international calls have been truly a windfall, if not manna from communication heaven. To illustrate, based on 1989 exchange rates, a three-minute landline call cost US$13.40, way beyond the reach of ordinary Filipinos who earned on average a daily wage of US$8.25 (Paragas 2009). The liberalization of the telecommunications industry both in the Philippines and abroad has considerably brought down the cost of a three- minute mobile phone call from the Philippines to anywhere in the world to US$0.50, or 5 percent of the 1996 average daily income of Filipino workers (Paragas 2009).[3]

In San Gabriel (and in the Philippines generally), however, not only did international calls become a lot more affordable, access to telephones has facilitated transnational connectivity and communication. Prior to the installation of landline phones in San Gabriel in 1992, residents relied on two public phone booths standing near the municipal government building (and one other in a village served by the national highway) if they wanted to make or receive phone calls. One can thus imagine the jubilation felt by those who had long waited for a landline phone when it finally arrived. Yet the arrival of landline phones excluded many, even those who could afford one, on the basis of where they lived. One interviewee who lived in one such village went to the extent of renting a house in the town proper just so she could get a landline and be better able to communicate with her husband. For the rest who did not have the financial wherewithal to do the same, it was the mobile phone that gave them connectivity—local, national, and global—as with many others in San Gabriel and in the entire Philippines.

All of the wives in this study used a mobile phone to communicate with their husbands, either through text messages or calls. Although only about seven have home Internet connection and a few others occasionally communicate with their husbands through the Internet at cafés or at a relative's house, the mobile phone is the most pervasive communication device they use. Most of those who have home Internet connection and a landline phone also have mobile phones. Only a few have home access to several ways of communicating with their husbands, such as video calls (Skype), chats, emails, landline phone calls, mobile phone calls, and social networking sites (such as Facebook). Access to these media is simply not available to most of the women. To many of them, the mobile phone is all they have. With their reliance on mobile phones, these wives have become consumers of another communication innovation, the prepaid phone card, which has made calls cheaper and hence contributed to the expansion of international communication through telephones (Mahler 2001; Vertovec 2004).

Of the 50.9 million unique mobile phone subscribers in 2014, 96 percent were on pre-paid subscription plans (GSMA Intelligence 2014). None of the wives in this study has a mobile phone with a postpaid plan. All rely on prepaid phone cards and many of them make extensive use of the ways by which mobile phone service providers have made it possible for phone card credit or "load" to be shared with others (such as through *pasa* load) or how a prepaid phone card's call time can be prolonged (such as through "unli-calls" [unlimited calls]). This suggests that many of the wives have found the mobile phone not only as the one available to them but also as the one that requires a financial outlay that can be flexibly suited around the financial needs and expenditures of the family. All that is required for wives to be charged the local rates for overseas phone calls (and text messages) is for their husbands to have a roaming SIM (subscriber identity module or subscriber identification module) card; however, a roaming SIM card does not allow husbands overseas to call or text at local rates. For example, whereas a wife is charged PhP1 for a text message she sends to her husband, the husband is charged PhP20 for every text message he sends.[4]

Phone cards are an important item in the family budget. The use of prepaid phone cards has given the women a sense of being in control of money spent on their mobiles as they always know how much phone credit they have left, and they can have a record of how much money they spend on phone cards. This is unlike using a postpaid mobile phone plan, which enables one to find out actual expenses only at the time when the bill for the month is received.

All of the seamen's wives recognize how mobile phones have greatly improved their communication with their husbands. Those already married during the "phoneless period" say that the mobile phone and other communication technologies now available have made them "lazy" at writing letters. To them the need to write letters to their husbands has lost its force of necessity. However, although writing letters is now a thing of the past, some "traditional" or asynchronous ways of keeping in touch have persisted, such as the sending of children's or family pictures, a request that husbands would text to their wives. These seamen's families show that their use of new technologies is contingent on their capabilities, needs, and the sophistication with which they can use these technologies.

All of the wives talk of how, because of better and faster means of communication, they are able to deal with separation more easily, specifically with worrying about their husbands' health and safety. Most importantly, family relationships have benefitted from constant or more regular and frequent, because cheap, communication. Yet, as Vertovec (2004, 223) has noted:

> For migrants and their kin in distant parts of the world, telephone calls can only provide a kind of punctuated sociality that can heighten emotional strain as well as alleviate it. This mode of intermittent communication cannot bridge all gaps of information and expression endemic to long-distance separation. Nevertheless, cheap international telephone calls join migrants and their significant others in ways that are deeply meaningful to people on both ends of the line.

In the following section we turn to a discussion of how telecommunication, particularly through the mobile phone, has enabled and shaped possibilities for (re)producing a real and imagined sense of family in the context of lives dominated by absence and separation.

COPRESENCE: BRINGING THE ABSENT FATHER HOME

To better appreciate how new communication technologies have facilitated and fostered family relationships, this section begins with a discussion of husband-wife/family communication prior to the mobile phone becoming easily available in San Gabriel. Succeeding parts provide a short description of the dynamics of communication between the seamen and their families and the ways wives have utilized communication to help their absent husbands experience an absent presence (Gergen 2002; Licoppe 2004) in their families.

Wives aged at least 40 years old at the time of the interview describe communication with their husband through the postal system as excruciatingly slow. One wife, who has always lived in San Gabriel, some 500 kilometers away from Manila, where all letters bound for and sent from the Philippines first make their stop, recounts that in one year she received four letters only from her husband. This, she clarifies, was not due to her husband's lack of interest in writing back.[5]

It might be argued that wives and husbands communicated "about the past." This is due to the nature of letters as a communicative practice and to the postal system's unreliability and slowness. What was recreated was a sense of, for example, what happened during the previous month, events that husbands would get to read about with even more time lag because, as the wives put it, of their having to move from port to port. Letters narrated events that had "long" happened and therefore removed any sense of immediacy from their narration. Laura, for example, looks back and compares her letters before her husband became a chief engineer to *telenovelas*, a popular television genre known for their extremely convoluted and drawn-out plots. The comparison is to the length of her letters because in the intervening time she would have accumulated so many things to share with her husband. Husbands and wives were thus at a spatial and temporal remove from these events.

In contrast, because of instantaneous communication, a few of the wives say that it is as though their husbands were with them. Arlene states: "Kasla every day kam' met lang nga agkadkadua, every day a tawag, text, email. Kasdiay." (It is like we are together every day, calls every day, text, email. Like that). Dina also talks about this sense of presence.

> "Now that there are cell phones, we have communication anytime, you are not that . . . you update each other, so communication between the two of you is there. It is like he is beside you."

This sense of copresence is a consequence of husbands and wives being able to get in touch quickly, share news, and for the husband to even take part in family activities despite being physically absent. It is worth bearing in mind, as Bloor (2016) points out, that contact may not be possible "every day" for all seafarers and all wives. The "every day" the wife refers to here pertains to the period when the husbands are able to pick up signal, and this happens when husbands are in coastal waters. Furthermore, some companies will offer limited internet access and/or satellite phone access.[6]

This copresence was not possible when wives and husbands relied on letters. In contrast, telephone conversations enable the family to "share affects and emotions, allowing their non-present partners access to the experience on the spot" (Arminen 2009, 98). Through these new telecommunication devices, Filipino seamen and their families not only "retain a sense of collectivity" (Vertovec 2004, 222) but also negotiate relationships in new ways. Through them, as Sarah Mahler has said about transnational Salvadorans, although "they are still physically distanced . . . they can now feel and function like a family" (2001, 584).

Fostering Father-Children Relationships

When wives and husbands talk on the phone, wives make sure their husbands also talk to their children.[7] Bearing in mind that many of the wives gave birth without their husbands around and that they saw their children for the first time when the latter were months, if not years, old, wives make a conscious effort to "introduce" father and child to each other. Or, because their husbands are not around to see their children grow, wives try to establish emotional ties between children and their father so that when they are home they already have something to start with. Equally importantly, wives do this so that children will not see their fathers as strangers. As to why wives ask their husbands to speak to their children, Maricel explains:

> "So that even if their daddy is not here, it is not their closeness but their communication, at least they can hear his voice so that when he comes home, they know . . . it's like they are close . . . like that."

Wives also show the children pictures of their father to reinforce their phone talk. Despite this strategy, the wives know that the emotional bond a child has with his or her father cannot be forged through voice and aurality; there is no substitute for the physical, tactile, aural, and visual presence. Rosario talks about how pained she was during the first few days of her husband's coming home when she saw her children behave toward their father like he was alien to them. Yet the wives know that without those phone conversations mediating their relationships, ties between father and children would be so much more fraught with estrangement and awkwardness.

Maintaining or developing father-children ties through communication technologies is a complex undertaking. Most of the wives, however, share how they have been able to forge these relationships mainly through mobile communication. Wives, particularly those with young children, talk about how fathers are pleased and buoyed by their phone conversations with them (with some children even singing to them). Others, such as Maricel, coach their children to tell their fathers not to sleep with other women. Some wives point, however, to the impossibility of catalyzing father-children emotional bonds particularly from children. Their experiences show that communication cannot always fully bridge the physical and emotional gap caused by the separation. Gina shares that although her husband wants to talk to their children, the children find it difficult not only to express warmth but also, more fundamentally, to even want to talk to their father:

> "the children are not that [close] to him . . . . I have to really insist otherwise they would not talk to their father. It is difficult, the ties. . . . Because they've gotten used to it since birth. I have to force them since they are quite distant."

However, Gina clarifies that it is different when her husband is home. Although it takes time for the children to adjust to their father's presence, because the husband would do things to win their affection, the children eventually warm up to him. Nevertheless, this does not lead to warmer phone conversations later on. Josefa shares her husband's comment that their daughter would take the initiative to talk to her father only when she fancied something, which she would then ask him to buy for her.

Wives are aware that distance and separation can have negative consequences on relationships (Fortunati 2002; Sahlstein 2004). They use the affordances of communication technologies to ameliorate and mitigate the negative consequences of this separation, consequences that have implications for the work they do as mothers and wives. For those whose situations have been more complex and circumscribed (by factors such as whether their children were already growing up before the era of affordable mobile phone communication in San Gabriel), even the inadequacy of telecommunication technologies to facilitate warmer father-children ties still communicates to both wife and husband the need to do something about these strained relations. In this sense, communication conveys its own limits. Although there are mothers who have not facilitated warmer father-children relationships through communication technologies, more mothers in this study say that their children and husband have succeeded in having meaningful emotional relationships through mobile phone communication. Mobile phone communication has enabled fathers to lessen the emotional gaps caused by separation due to migration (cf. Aguilar 2009, ch. 11).

Creating a Space for Husbands in the Lives of Their Children

One of the ways by which wives bring a sense of home to their husbands is by keeping them updated with their children's activities and accomplishments. For husbands whose wives gave birth without them around, stories about their babies they have yet to see enable husbands to "see" the growth of their children. Husbands ask whether the baby is already eating solid food or walking, has grown teeth, or is beginning to utter words. For husbands with school-going children, such updates enable them to imagine a place for themselves in what is going on in their children's lives and make meaningful attempts at inserting themselves in these moments. By knowing what is going on or what has recently happened, fathers can engage their children beyond formulaic "how are you" questions. By knowing what their children are up to, husbands, according to the wives, feel as though they are home. And because they learn of these things quickly, sometimes while these are happening, fathers are afforded more meaningful participation. These phone conversations help "in generating a strong sense of shared space and time that overlooked—even if only temporarily—the realities of geographic distance and time zones" (Wilding 2006, 133). They allow husbands to "bilocate," that is, be on his ship yet also experience a sense of being home.

Mildred's husband, apprised of the fall in his children's school quarterly marks, told his children of his disappointment:

> "Why are your grades low? he said. That is all I am asking of you, he said, and you could not even give it. Everything you want, I buy it, he said. Even if it is expensive, I buy it. You, that is all I want from you, you can't give it. So the children will not say a single word. So he talks to them. Give your best, see your father is upset, I would say. We are giving our best, mama they would answer."

Her husband then devised a reward system to motivate them to apply themselves harder.

> "If you get a perfect [score in a quiz, homework, project], I will pay. So they have many, they collect and keep them. When he comes home, they bring them out and he pays them. The children like it very much, so they have many perfect scores. How much, Papa? Their father would say, one hundred pesos each. How they love it, when their father is home, they have plenty of money."

When wives make their husbands aware of what is going on at home particularly with respect to their children, they make it possible for them to become more involved in their lives. Michael Billig (1995) has advanced the concept of "banal nationalism" to refer to the routine and everyday practices in which people express, practice, and experience nationalism and national identity. We may speak of a banal sense of family and intimacy arising from the wives' attempts to apprise their husbands of what their children are doing. These frequent telephone conversations enable fathers to make their presence felt not only through establishing emotional ties with their children but also, as Mildred's case demonstrates, in disciplining their children. In the next section we turn to a discussion of how fathers are involved in disciplining children.

Disciplining from a Distance and Vitiated Authority

When couples talk, the wife "reports" to the husband their children's misbehavior and asks him to talk to them. Wives thus enable husbands to exercise parental-paternal authority from afar. However, although communication devices help these fathers exercise what Pertierra (2005) has called "a post-corporeal agency," this authority is vitiated by the fathers' absence.

When talking about husbands' involvement in disciplining children, we need to have a firm grasp of the nature of the disciplinary issues raised by the wives. These issues are age-related or linked to stages in a child's life. The first is behavior associated with growing-up children, that is, when children become more difficult to handle and the problem is exclusively behavioral and part of growing up. This situation allows fathers to simultaneously exercise authority and tighten emotional bonds with their children. Because husbands are away, wives say that their husbands tend not to scold their children but to talk to them in a tone that is gentle yet firm and in a manner that strengthens their relationship. Teresa, for example, says that sometimes it is not just her voice but also her blood pressure that is raised by her son's stubbornness. Her husband, who would ask their son if he had been spanked by his mother (who had in fact told her spouse she spanked the child), would tell him, "maybe you are just very stubborn otherwise your mother would not get angry. In order that you can also help her, be good. That's all you have to do to help her."

These children will say yes to their father, promising to behave better. But because they are young children, their mothers say they go back to being stubborn once the conversation is over.

The second type of discipline-related issue poses more challenge in terms of how fathers exercise their authority to discipline their children, particularly in instilling in them a sense of responsibility. This concerns adult or approaching-adulthood children whose behavior is a worrying concern because of its consequences for their future and the situation of the entire family. Dolores, for example, recounts one conversation between her husband and their eldest son:

> "Be good, my son. Do not drink too much, like that. Work hard, help yourself . . ."
>
> "Do your children take heed?"
>
> "'Yes, yes,' they would say. My God!"

"'Yes, yes,' . . . My God!" makes it clear that this paternal advice is not really taken to heart. Without the father being physically there, his recalcitrant children can say one thing to him and do another. In trying to discipline children, fathers can only advise and encourage their children. They can perform the role but not exercise authority to ensure that what is said is also done. To be sure, even in families where fathers are around, grown-up children may still misbehave. Compared with fathers who are physically present in the home, seamen-fathers arguably are more constrained by their distance because they do not want to strain further their relationships with their children, which are already affected by their absence.

Breaking and Withholding News

For seamen who are away from their families, relatives, and other kin and social relations, knowing what is going on in their lives and in their neighborhood, village, and town helps them retain, as one interviewee puts it, a sense of "still being there." Consequently, they will have little difficulty participating in family, neighborhood, and village "talk" and affairs when they are back home. Most importantly, knowing about what is happening to their families gives them a sense of still being responsible for the family, and it is also an expression of the respect due them as husband, father, or family member. Precisely because they are a member of the family and an important one, being given access to news and information countered any feeling or sense of being excluded, which would have heightened their separation.

Breaking news

Most of the wives prefer to tell their husbands positive news about their families or about their children's activities. As much as possible they do not want to give their husbands any cause for worry. When they relay news of illness or death, it is mostly about neighbors and other people, which wives think will not impact negatively their husbands' well-being while onboard a ship. However, one wife says that she does not keep things from her husband because the less she tells him, the more worried he gets. For a few others, telling their husbands eases whatever burden weighs on their minds. However, they assure their husbands that it is not something they could not handle and so the husbands should not worry. Two other wives assert, however, that there simply is no point in withholding something that their husbands will eventually know about.

For those who regulate the news they share with their husbands, there are instances, however, when they are impelled to break bad or serious news about their families. These instances involve them dealing with certain dynamics that shape the breaking or embargo of news. Some wives tell their husbands what otherwise they would have withheld, worried that their husbands would ask why they had not been told right away. This suggests that husbands believe they have the right not only to be told of these things but also to be told of them right away. Others do not want their husbands to know of these things from other people—which their husbands dislike particularly—something that, because of available telecommunication devices, wives cannot monitor, let alone control.

News Embargo

For many of the wives, it is precisely their husbands' living and working on a ship that sometimes make them hesitant to break certain news to them. Some wives fear their husbands might think of jumping off their ship, a fear reinforced by reports of their husbands' behavior upon hearing about family circumstances. These reports reach them through vacationing seamen with whom their husbands work on the same ship or through these seamen's wives. To be sure, most of the wives say that their husbands prefer knowing everything to being kept in the dark. Some wives describe their husbands as "becoming restless" (*maburiboran, di makatalna, di makaidna*) when they are told something happened but only get bits and pieces of information. Sketchy news makes them suspect that something more serious than what they have been told has happened. Some husbands, knowing that their wives choose the news they share, in fact ask their wives to tell them about "bad" news. Of forty wives interviewed in 2010, only one, Maricel, has "instructions" (*bilin*) from her husband, with whom I also talked informally, not to tell him anything about incidents or illnesses "that are not that emergency" (meaning serious). If she can still deal with them on her own, then it would be best that she keep the news from him so he can concentrate on his work. When the situation is serious, and wives are duty-bound to let their husbands know, such as when a child is in the hospital, wives resort to lightening the severity of the situation. In such instances, wives intend to give their husbands the full version once things improve. Dina's case demonstrates this dynamic.

Dina's son suffered from a kidney infection and was in the ICU for eight days. She merely told her husband that their son was in hospital. Whenever he called to inquire about him, she simply said that he was getting better. It was only a month after their son's discharge that she told her husband what really happened. She explained that she did not want him to become too worried that he might injure himself while working. Although the husband understood her concern and conceded that his son's illness would have distracted him, he insisted that she should have told him everything from the start.

It is not just wives who try to spare their spouse of worry. Janet, for example, learned about her husband falling ill only by asking her husband's work mate about how he was. She also knew about the injury he had on-board ship through this same person. She knew her husband did not want to add to the things she had to think of, but as his wife she expected her husband to tell her of these things.

MISSING HUSBANDS

The preceding sections have looked at wives as agents using communication devices to facilitate family ties. This section focuses on spousal ties. It begins with a discussion of quarrels, and then moves on to how wives and husbands encourage each other. Although the section heading points to an absence (that of the husband) and alludes to issues of intimacy, I am expanding the semantic field of intimacy to encompass spousal arguments conducted over the phone. Although they are arguments, they nonetheless produce the sense of proximity and dynamic characteristic of couples who live in the same house. Although they are not "positive" intimacies narrowly defined, they speak to the strains of separation and the ways lives are negotiated and conducted across different space-time locations. Finally, I discuss briefly intimacy between separated couples.

In Good Times and in Bad: Phone Spats and Encouragement

Living apart exacts a toll and it is during telephone conversations (and even in text message exchanges) when tensions, which have lain dormant, can erupt. In these events pent-up emotions and fears get ventilated. A single word, uttered in a particular way, can be taken by the other as implying more.

Or a question, intended as a joke, albeit expressive of one's insecurities, can be interpreted as "fishing for something" and become a source of an argument, resulting in a period when couples do not speak to one another.[8]

Josefa and Raquel recount phone quarrels caused by their questions about other women, which the husbands took as accusations of infidelity. Three other wives say they do not like their husbands' questions about where they put their money, offended by what they perceive as accusations of profligacy. One wife's phone arguments with her husband stemmed from his "jealousy." Because of the time she finishes work, she gets home late and sometimes gets a ride from her male officemates. For her part, Leonora recounts a phone argument in which she gave free rein to her anger, repeatedly calling her husband "useless" (*awan serserbim*). About to give birth at the time of this recounted argument, she explains that she was under a lot of stress: she had not received any allotment for at least two months and she worried about how she was going to pay for a likely caesarean delivery. Finally, Aida, who has a successful commercial business but one that has taken so much of her time and energy, admits that she is, at the time of the interview, not in good terms with her husband: "we are not friends" (*saankam nga agfriend*).

> "When he calls, that is also the time when I am very sleepy. So he slams the phone. He'd shout at me saying, 'It's only now that we can talk and you are already sleepy!'"

Although they sometimes exchange harsh words, couples do encourage each other. Acknowledging her fault, Leonora, cited above, apologized to her husband for having seen her own predicament only and forgotten her husband's own situation. Reminded that at least she was surrounded by family and relatives whereas he did not have that kind of immediate kin and social support, she encouraged him to be strong and bear his situation with perseverance. Karen helped her husband, who had wanted to come home even before his six-month contract ended, to endure the separation. Indeed, he even extended his contract for two and a half months.

Sometimes, wives encourage their husbands by communicating to them both a sense of their obligation and their central role in the future of their family. Rosa provides an exemplary illustration. She says there have been times when her husband has come close to giving up.

> "And I would be close to crying. I tell him to endure because our children are still small. It is going to be hard to send them to school if we did not have any money. No one is going to help us except you, I tell him.

> [. . .] That's why I just keep on encouraging him to be strong. I try to make him laugh."

Husbands also give their wives emotional and moral support. Most of the wives say that when they tell their husbands of their difficulties, their husbands encourage them and are sorry for not being with them during such times. Lilia and her husband talk about trusting each other, with Lilia emphasizing that just as she exercises self-control so does she expect her husband to do the same. Finally, Lourdes and her husband, both devoted Christians, have drawn courage and fortitude from their shared faith. Lourdes says that they always encourage each other through, and find strength in, prayer.

The Intimacy of Absence

When couples encourage each other, they are simultaneously expressing and communicating concern and love for each other. They are invested with their selves and made to conjure up their physical presence. The words they utter and the text messages they compose and send to each other substitute for what they lack in physical intimacy. To the extent that what they say is also meant to convey themselves, their words simultaneously evoke their absence and presence.

Intimate Conversations and the Joy of Text

Understandably, most of the women are quite hesitant to let me "listen in" to their spousal conversations.[9] When I asked Norma, in her mid-forties and the owner of an Internet cafe, about how she tells her husband she misses him, she replied: "LOL, yun na lang!" (Laugh out loud, that's all!). However, a few do not mind giving me an answer. Lourdes readily says that her conversations with her husband always include him asking her never to lose heart, followed by expressions of his love for her. She narrates that he says "I love you, too" even though she has not yet said anything. Similarly, Rosario recounts her conversation with her husband a week after Valentine's Day, an occasion widely observed by Filipinos. Having failed to greet him, she asked him what he did, to which he responded: "Awan a. Inim-imagine ka" (Nothing really. I imagined you).

Rosario's response to my question—"If you miss your husband and he calls, what do you say to each other?"—allows us to have a glimpse of how husbands and wives who are apart may have intimate moments of conversations:

> "Well. What are you doing? There are times [my husband asks me] where are you? What are you wearing? [laughter] . . . 'What are you wearing?' he'd ask. Naturally, I am wearing shorts because it is very warm [explanation for my benefit]. 'I am just going to imagine you then.'"

Rosa, whose house does not allow for much privacy, says that when she talks to her husband through webcam, she bravely says she misses him a lot despite everyone else in the house overhearing it. "Even if they all hear it" (*uray dengdenggenda latta*), she says.

The mobile phone is considered "the communicative instrument that, potentially more than any other, can influence the traditional management of intimacy and distance" (Fortunati 2002, 48). Given the physical space available in many of the wives' houses, which frequently precludes intimacy between wife and husband, the mobile phone has enabled the couples to "strengthen personal intimacy inside family intimacy" (50). Raquel, for example, shares that her husband sends her naughty and sexually charged text messages that, she says, "excited her" (*mai-exciteak met nokua*). Text messaging, more than phone or voice calls, enables wives and husbands to express longing for each other, expression constrained by speech and physical environment. The orality and aurality of the expression of intimacy for many of these couples are replaced with visuality: rather than said and heard, it is read. Communicating spousal intimacy contrasts with wives' efforts to foster father-children intimacy, particularly between father and children who have not seen each other. Whereas facilitating father-children intimacy utilizes voice calls (orality-aurality) and visuality (mothers show children pictures of their fathers), spousal intimacy within family intimacy relies on what cannot (or must not) be overheard: the written. Intimacy thus becomes "textographic" or "scribed" (Pertierra 2005). Mobile phones not only enable mediated intimacy but also "discursive intimacy" (Pertierra 2008).

The Persistence of Absence

The long absences of their husbands require the women to deal and live with their longing for them.[10] A few of the wives give indication of their sexual longing and recognize that those whose spouses are away are closer to "temptation." As Leonora said:

> "Yes, because we are only human beings. [laughs] . . . that desire is there. I say, 'I am going to commit this' [laughs]. . . just to [satisfy] what you are feeling. But you have that fear, God strikes you with it. Because those who [have affairs] are mostly those who are left behind, I haven't done it. And I

> am not going to allow it to happen [laughs] because it is hard if you destroy your family."

How then do the wives cope?

Displacing Longing: From Eros to Agape?

When asked, "What if you longed for your husband?" (*no ngarud mailiwka kenni lakaymo*?), three wives say they busy themselves and use work to deal with their longing for their husbands. Maria, one of these three, combines work with going out, which I understand to mean as going to neighbors for chats and visiting her relatives who live in another village. On the other hand, fifteen of those who have children say they forget about their husbands by focusing on their children. Agnes's response encapsulates what these women say:

> "Nothing, I kiss my son. Nothing, it is my son who I hug. That is what I do. It is to him I express my longing. If my husband calls, then it is to him I express my longing. Of course, I have no other outlet except my son. I focus my attention on him."

How do children ease these wives' longing? Two wives may offer illumination. Linda looks back to when she did not yet have a child:

> "You cry. But when we had our daughter, we did not have to wait long for a child. My attention for my husband went to our daughter. When we did not yet have her, I missed him terribly, but now I am used to it. My attention is focused on the child."

Alicia, who fostered a child without first discussing it with her husband, provides a description of how children may serve as conduits for rechanneling feelings and emotional needs meant originally for their husbands to meet. She also clarifies how children can be both a source and recipient of material and practical work—care work—that keeps her busy and occupied. This also generates a relational context in which the act of caring (including the emotional investments it entails) enables her child to become someone who can both love and care for her.

> "You can deal with your longing for your husband more easily because you have a child to look after. If you are finding your husband's absence difficult, well you've got the child. After doing housework, you take care of the child.

> You go to neighbors with her. It is those things, you still miss your husband, but you have your child to . . . ease your longing for him. There is someone to hug you, kiss you [laughs]."

These women's physical and emotional longing for their husbands are rerouted and "translated" and the children are the medium through which this work is accomplished. They are also its recipients. Yet, Alicia also indicates that this only helps to ease her longing for her husband; it does not make it go away completely. Lilia talks about how she expects her husband not to gratify his needs with other women because she, too, has to control her own.

My discussion of what wives do to deal with their physical and sexual longing for their husbands relies on what these wives could realistically share with me, given personal, cultural, and various other reasons. Despite the limitations in my access to how wives and husbands expressed intimacies toward each other, the women's answers point to some of the ways by which the women dealt with their physical, emotional, and sexual longing for their husbands. Because I interviewed most of the women in their houses, there is reason to believe there was little possibility for mediated sexual intimacy (cf. Aguila 2008/2009; Pertierra 2006). Besides, only seven of the wives had home Internet. Also, just as Leonora's case demonstrates, there are spatial requirements for it. It is more likely that when husbands and wives do share to each other their longing, it is in the manner suggested by Raquel whose husband sends her sexts. The reality of separation has necessitated—and communication technologies have enabled—the exploration of mediated sexual expression and agency (cf. Pertierra 2007). In this, the mobile phone is particularly vital as it has provided a means to privacy. The mobile phone becomes a space to which only the owner has access (cf. Pertierra 2006, 77–95).

CONCLUSION

With over ten million Filipinos living and working overseas, separation has become warp and woof of the fabric of many Filipinos' lives. It is a paradox that what connects Filipinos with many others is this shared experience of separation due to migration. With international communication becoming more affordable and accessible to many Filipinos through mobile phones, separation has become easier to deal with. Mobile communication technology and also Internet-enabled communication, such as video calls, emails, chats, and social media (Facebook), have enabled those separated from their families to experience virtual copresence in place of physical copresence.

Filipino seafarers and their wives and children have tremendously benefitted from these developments. Compared with land-based Filipino workers, however, communication between seamen and their families is less frequent, affected by the movement and geographic location of the seamen. Nevertheless, seamen's wives have benefitted from the affordances particularly of mobile phone communication. It has made it possible and easier for them to foster ties between them and their husbands despite absence, separation, and distance. It has enabled husbands to experience copresence, and wives have facilitated the possibility for their husbands to experience meaningful interactions with their children. In this wise, we can see how mobile communication has enabled coordinated presence (Aguilar 2009) and connected presence (Christensen 2009; Licoppe 2004). It may be argued that no longer are these seamen mere disembodied voices, which their children hear only so often. Because mobile phones have made communication a lot more frequent (which partly accounts for intimacy), although wives and children still experience the seaman husband and father as a voice, his talk might be said to be experienced with a sense of his physical corporeality. Thus, seamen can have more than "spectral presences" (Rafael 2000) especially in the lives of their children.

Through instantaneous communication events facilitated by mobile phones, wives and husbands are now able to experience intimacy despite being away from each other. Encouraging each other, for example, is a vital work performed by husbands and wives. It is a work that constitutes part of the intimacy they are able to demonstrate to each other. Nevertheless, a life of separation is never easy and is always fraught with anxiety, tension, and misunderstanding. Telephone conversations (and even text message exchanges) are not simply communication events through which family members may be drawn closer together. These are also times when the messy aspects of maintaining a family become visible and audible. Wives and husbands can now have "domestic spats" in real time. Mobile phone communication has enabled Filipino seamen's families to create "narrative and imaginary spaces" (Pertierra 2005, 26) that help reproduce family and affective ties. Seafarers' families demonstrate how separation and distance no longer preclude the involvement and participation, particularly of the seamen, in the daily lives of their families. In this sense, as Pertierra (2008, 176) has argued, these communication technologies are *techne* in that they are "a way of dealing with others in the world" and in that they enable "new ways of being in the world."

Communication technologies have enabled family relationships to be reproduced outside of the confines of domestic physical togetherness. Seamen's families have used this technology not only to bridge space-time differences but also to build human relationships despite differing geographies and locations. For seamen's families, these opportunities for intimacy have enabled them to actively imagine communion. This has implications for how the link between intimate relations and the domestic is conceptualized. As McNay (2000, 71) has noted, the domestic sphere has predominantly been the site for the reproduction of intimacy among family members. Consequently, intimacy is unbounded (McNay 2000).

Lives defined by separation and the absence of one spouse vitally constitute the sexual and gendered subjectivities of the women who stay behind. When the women talked about their lives and experiences, they frequently drew on a discourse of "sacrifice." While they did not specifically refer to their having to endure the absence of sexual intimacy, I submit that this is part of the sacrifice they have to make in order for them to have a better life. In this sense, we might say they worked through the absence of physical and sexual intimacy by subsuming their sexual needs under their *maternal* and *parental* obligation to provide for the lives and future of their family or children, while also having to deal with the social burden of a "woman whose husband was away." They, particularly the younger ones, were frequently perceived as vulnerable to temptation and could easily become the subject of moral surveillance.

CHAPTER 6

DIBERSYON AND *ISU PAY*
Gossip and the Morality of Mobility

The seafarer wives negotiated an environment in which their morality became dominated by the need to keep their reputation as faithful wives intact. As women whose husbands were away for long periods of time, they were seen as vulnerable and susceptible to temptation. In this chapter, I examine gossip's impact on the women's lives, focusing especially on their spatial mobility which gossip moralizes. I draw exclusively on the experiences of women who were not in paid employment and who, in order to engage in leisure activities to help them survive the absence of their husband and deal with boredom, translated work into recreation, which they referred to as *dibersyon*.[1] The women's *dibersyon* enabled them to relax and "work" at the same time. For women who were not in paid employment, and who, as a consequence, might have felt or been made to feel had no "socially acceptable" reason to go out every day, *isu pay* provided the justification for their activities that enabled them to engage in activities that provided relief from the absence of their husband.

I look into how their *dibersyon* is underpinned by the Ilokano concept of *isu pay*. *Isu pay* is an expression used in a variety of contexts. It may refer to acts of not wasting anything, as in the expression "*sayang, isu pay.*" It is expressive of an attitude geared toward making the most out of one's time, that is, what one can accomplish given time demands, as in the expression "*isu pay ta maubrak*" (it is one more task I can do) or "*isu pay ta malpasko*" (it is one more task I can finish). A wife who learned to fix a broken faucet spoke not only with pride at having learned to do it but also came to appreciate it for pecuniary reasons: "*Isu pay ta pagbayadko.*" (By fixing it myself, I save some money since I don't have to pay somebody to do it). *Isu pay* may thus be seen as oriented not only toward saving and making money or responsibly looking after resources but also making the most out of something or a situation. I therefore develop *isu pay* as an Ilokano sociocultural category that references a certain way of thinking and, as such, a mode of practice, geared toward not only the proper management of temporal, material, financial, and other resources but also their maximization.

The women's reconceptualization of livelihood and economic activities as leisure is a strategic move that enables them to simultaneously engage in recreation and counteract gossip's constricting impact on their mobility. I develop *isu pay* here as the legitimizing concept for their undertaking of livelihood and other economic activities. I argue that although the women cited what their activities contributed to their family's financial situation, the monetary gain was secondary to how these activities improved their spatial mobility without compromising their perceived morality.

MALE EMIGRATION, GOSSIP, AND WOMEN WHO STAY BEHIND

Studies of gossip have looked at its function, following on Gluckman's (1963) assertion that gossip strengthened group unity (Stewart and Strathern 2004). For Gluckman, rumor and gossip reinforced norms as well as policed individual conduct (Stewart and Strathern 2004, 37). Gluckman has been criticized for taking gossip only as negative slander (Mohl 1997) and for taking the community, rather than the individual, as the center of analysis (Paine 1967). For Paine, gossip advanced the interests of the individual doing it, denigrated others and catalyzed social process (Stewart and Strathern 2004, 37). Others have pointed to the socially constructive aspect of gossip (Mohl 1997) and to its "democratic or subaltern potential" (Herriman 2010, 725), that is, its capacity to articulate and become a vehicle for resistance particularly by those at the bottom of the socio-economic hierarchy (Herriman 2010). Accordingly, gossip has the "power to mobilize crowds and to spread subversion" (725). Still others have looked at gossip as a means of social control focusing on its disciplinary power (Brennan 2004; Mintz 1997; Van Vleet 2003; Wolf 1972). Because gossip "carries moral evaluation, and it can stigmatize those who step outside the boundaries of what the community deems appropriate behavior," it is an effective way to "reinforce cultural norms and values" (Feeley and Frost 2014, 9).

The migration of their husbands puts wives under strict moral surveillance (Carling et al. 2012; McEvoy et al. 2012; Mahler 2001; Skolnik, Lazo de la Vega and Steigenga 2012). Aside from the close supervision of these women by family and kin (Gulati 1993; Mahler 2001), gossip is another important mechanism of policing women's morality and mobility, which are inextricably entwined. Transnational migration "generates and amplifies the role of gossip" (Skolnik, Lazo de la Vega and Steigenga 2012, 31), and women's fear that gossip about their moral and sexual behavior (whether true or not) might reach their husband is fertile ground for controlling women's behavior and mobility (Chant 1997; McEvoy et al. 2012; Skolnik, Lazo de la Vega and Steigenga 2012). The context of these women demonstrates that gossip is particularly gendered (Brennan 2004; Dreby 2009; McEvoy et al. 2012; Menjivar and Agadjanian 2007; Skolnik, Lazo de la Vega and Steigenga 2012). Gossip about these women center on moral issues (Dreby 2009), a morality tied to their sexual fidelity to their husbands that affirms their suitability as wives and mothers (McEvoy et al. 2012; Skolnik, Lazo de la Vega and Steigenga 2012). Hence, women took "more preventive actions to avoid being gossiped about" and were "more negatively impacted by the effects of transnational gossip" (Skolnik, Lazo de la Vega and Steigenga 2012, 12). For men, gossip about their faithfulness, or lack of it, to their wives did not bring about the threat of abandonment (which the women faced and feared) so long as they continued to provide for their families (Dreby 2009; Menjivar and Agadjanian 2007).

Within these asymmetrical impacts, gossip reinforces traditional gender ideologies and relations. McEvoy et al. (2012) have noted that research on migrant-sending communities in Mexico and Central America has found that women who stayed behind had fears about gossip reaching their husband and what it could lead to. To avoid being gossiped about by their community, they stayed at home and avoided social activities. The women's limiting of their movement in order to protect their honor highlights the contradictions this policing brings about in terms of the stay-behind women's morality and mobility. The association between the women and the domestic sphere (as safe haven and as their "proper place") is strengthened (McEvoy et al. 2012; Skolnik, Lazo de la Vega and Steigenga 2012). Because of the out-migration of their husbands, these women faced tension created by, on one hand, the absence of their husbands and, on the other, the tasks they had to take over, which forced them to venture into a public sphere, consequently exposing them to gossip. Because of the threat gossip posed to their marriage, women dealt with the conflicting consequences of their husband's absence by restricting their movement (Skolnik, Lazo de la Vega and Steigenga 2012).

Aside from restricting stay-behind wives' mobility, gossip prevents them from breaking gender ideology and practice (the potential for which is presented by the restructuring and reconstitution of families through migration [Parrenas 2005]) and therefore enforces existing gender relations in these migrant-sending communities. The findings of McEvoy et al. (2012) and Skolnik, Lazo de la Vega and Steigenga (2012) on Mexican communities resonate with what De Haas and Van Rooij (2010) have written about the role played by gossip in keeping women within socially sanctioned gender roles. Going against the norms is met with hostility, expressed through social criticism and scandal mongering, which could "endanger their respectability and, hence, their social security" and "lead to social exclusion the consequences of which can be disastrous in times of economic hardship" (de Haas and van Rooij 2010, 59).

> Gossip, in particular, is a powerful social instrument that prevents villagers from breaking too overtly with the prevailing cultural norms on gender roles. The widespread fear of gossiping prevails in all the research villages and maintaining the good name of the family preoccupies the minds of villagers in social interaction.

Gossip is hence an important factor that shapes gender relations and structures, and which affects the lives and experiences of women who stay behind. It does not only police their morality and curtail their mobility, it also blunts the potential for positive, empowering, and even emancipatory changes to gender ideology and relations.

Studies of transnational gossip (Dreby 2009; Drotbohm 2010; Lang and Smart 2002), particularly those that have looked at its impact on wives who stay behind (McEvoy et al. 2012; Skolnik, Lazo de la Vega and Steigenga 2012), have not paid attention to women whose husbands work in the global maritime industry. Seafarers do not live in the same kind of communities that land-based migrant workers do as seafarers live and work on a ship. Because they work anywhere from three to twelve months with other seafarers sourced from other countries and who they will most likely not work with again, seafarers do not have the dense social networks that land-based workers develop, ones that link them and their families transnationally and through which gossip can travel to the migrant husbands. The accessibility of communication is also more difficult for seafarers and their families because of the mobility of their ship, which means that they do not always have mobile phone signal. Internet on-board ships has become more available than before, and this has improved communication between seafarers and their wives/families but only for those who have access to internet at home. Mobile internet has become more accessible in San Gabriel and follow-up interviews with wives showed that a number of the women have availed themselves of this technology.

KASLA AGREKREKKANG A DAGA MASAPULNA TI TUDO: WOMEN "LIKE PARCHED EARTH IN NEED OF RAIN"

As mentioned in the previous chapter, the absence of physical and sexual intimacy with their husbands became part of the sexual and gendered subjectivity of the women and a defining context of how others saw them as women-wives-mothers tied as it is to their virtue and honor. As such, this condition shaped their social lives and relations. A number of the women were forthright in saying they have unmet sexual needs and, as such, were, as one wife said, "closer to temptation" but that they were not going to seek to gratify them with other men. They did everything they could to avoid being suspected of sexual impropriety that would certainly make them the subject of gossip. Rosa, 21 years old, married for three years and with two children, said that when she went to the capital city to do her groceries, she almost always brought along a companion or her two-year old son (even if bringing him along made the task more difficult). She was worried that people would think she was up to no good if she went out alone. Also, she said she wore very simple clothes and used no make-up or lipstick as her prettifying might be perceived as being done for someone, that is, "draw attention to herself to attract men" (*ipagarup danto pay adda pappapintasak*). This was echoed by another wife who said that even if she was not doing anything improper, her actions might be interpreted differently, if not maliciously, since "she could not control how others think" (*di mo makontrol ti panagpanunotda wenno panagipagarupda*). The younger research participants particularly felt that they existed in and moved around an environment in which they were seen as vulnerable women, ones who, because of the absence of their husbands, would more easily succumb to seduction. To demonstrate stay-behind wives' careful negotiation of gossip, I will present the case of Marissa, who elaborated on her experience. She is 30 years old, has been married for 11 years and has two children (aged 10 and 8).

Marissa said that men looked at women like her as "easy-to-get" because she thought they saw her as "like parched earth in need of rain" (*kasla agrekrekkang a daga masapulna ti tudo*). Her perception of men's perception of her was based on her experience of receiving text messages and mobile phone calls from men propositioning her.

> Marissa: Yes, I will admit. There are men who will really [try to exploit the fact that] some women do not have their husbands around. They have the impression that you, the woman, they think you can be tempted easily. They probably think I am like parched earth in need of rain.
>
> RG: Do you tell this to your husband?
>
> Marissa: Of course. There was one time he was here, he was home. And my cell phone, I leave it anywhere. But I never expected it to be that way. There was someone who had been contacting me and he texted, "Well, now that your husband is home," he said, "what about us then?" But I had no relationship with that man. What he probably wanted to do was to destroy me because I did not succumb to what he wanted to happen. Before my husband came back, he [her husband] would sometimes ask me who I spoke to on the phone, who I exchanged text messages with. And I said, "oh there are many." But I never thought he [the man who wanted a sexual relationship with her] would be so serious [as to send her such a text message that suggested they had a relationship]. But I said, before my husband came home, "there is someone who is doing this." I only wanted to protect myself from what might happen. There was one time that, "I heard your husband is now back, what now then?" he said like that. "Why, what is this?" my husband asked. "Reply to him," I said. So my husband replied to him and what he said is "I don't need you for now since my husband is here, when he is gone, then it will be the two of us again." And they texted each other until the man admitted we did not have anything, there was nothing. Stupid man. I told my husband about it so he was not going to think anything.

Marissa protected herself by pre-empting the gossip that she knew would find their way to her husband. She already had an inclination that her husband was getting "news" about her when her husband asked her "who she was talking to or exchanging text messages with." Why would her husband ask her such a question? Marissa suspected that it was her husband's relatives who were her neighbors who might have "planted" the idea to her husband; the informant should at least know his mobile phone number, and this limits the usual suspects to his relatives or even mother-in-law. Marissa suspects that gossip about who she was in contact with was spun around her being seen with male and female classmates in a care-giving course she took in the capital city. That someone was so persistent and brazen in his propositions to the extent of sending her the said text messages seemed only to confirm her husband's niggling suspicions fuelled by gossip that reached him while he was still out at sea.

Marissa's act of informing her husband while he was out at sea about a man who was propositioning her is strategic in that it responds to what Marissa was convinced as gossip reaching her husband. By also showing the text messages to her husband, she prevented them from becoming the source of arguments between them and staunched the potential damage it could have brought to their marriage. Her husband's willingness to engage in a text conversation with the man propositioning her would also seem to indicate that the gossipmonger had been successful in planting a seed of doubt in Marissa's husband's mind. His message to the other guy, "I don't need you for now since my husband is here, when he is gone, then it will be the two of us again," was not only written as though it was Marissa who was replying, it also seemed designed to trap someone.

A few other wives shared that gossip about them behaving improperly had been spread by their husbands' relatives. They believed the gossip was meant to cause a rift between them and their husbands. The wives knew that eventually the gossip would reach their husbands either while they were out at sea through text messaging or when they came back. The wives said that their husbands' relatives would pretend to be merely informing their husbands of what they have heard. Like Marissa, these wives told their husbands of these gossip to forewarn them of what was being spread against them. Thus, mobile communication, particularly text messaging, played an important role in the spread of gossip. Mobile technology enables information and gossip to circulate instantly (Horst and Miller 2006). The relatives' improved facility to communicate with the women's husbands has thus led to the increased surveillance of the women (Horst 2006). While these wives were understandably worried about gossip, Maria, 51 years old, mother of four children and whose husband has been seafaring for 13 years, in contrast, took a belligerent attitude toward being the subject of gossip. She said that the final judge will be her husband: "A man would know if 'it' had been used. What has not been used for a long time tightens [*agserra*]."

The women took care to be above any suspicions of sexual impropriety. They, especially the younger ones, were concerned that people who knew their husbands would talk about them being seen with a man who was not their relative and that stories would be spun around it. As one interviewee said, with the sophistication of mobile phones now, it was easy for someone with malicious intentions to take a picture of her talking to someone and send it to her husband. In contrast, older wives were less bothered by gossip not only because they have proven through many years their faithfulness to their husbands but also because, as one said, "who would be interested in me at my age?" Such statement suggests that the potential for being gossiped about for sexual infidelity was greater for younger women.

The ease with which the young wives' being seen with a man was framed within illicit sexual relations was demonstrated by the initial concern made by the owner of the snack house where I was going to interview one wife while she waited for her son to finish school. As it was still quite early in the morning, the snack house was just getting ready to open. I spoke to the owner if she could already let us in. The interviewee was known to the owner as she and other mothers went there to wait for their children. The alarm on the owner's face, the questions she asked, and what she said made clear to me that her initial hesitation arose from not wanting her snack house to become known as a place where adulterers had their trysts.

Gossip not only made women vigilant about their practical behavior and who they were seen with. When they had problems, they chose to keep things to themselves rather than seek the comfort and wisdom of others as they have sometimes been betrayed by their confidantes. Finally, gossip had consequences on the women's mobility particularly with respect to leisure. Perversely, the women relaxed by busying themselves with more work. I turn below to an examination of how gossip's moral surveillance of these women played a role in translating work into leisure.

DIBERSYON: WOMEN WHO RELAX BY DOING MORE WORK

Mobility refers to "the movement of people from one place to another in the course of everyday life . . . the daily rounds of activities such as paid and unpaid work, leisure, socializing and shopping" (Hanson 2010, 7 quoted in McEvoy et al. 2012, 371). I will look at how concerns about gossip, particularly in relation to infidelity, interacted with the absence of financial and other economic infrastructure in San Gabriel, which engendered the specific form the women's mobility and leisure took. Finally, I will look at how these women's relaxation is imbued with economic justification and used not only as a way to deal with boredom but also with missing their husbands. Such a rationale provided a moral justification to their activities that responded to questions about the implication of their mobility on their morality.

San Gabriel does not have a bank and at the time of my first fieldwork in 2010, had only two ATMs (automated teller machines) or cash machines, both inside the municipal government building, despite the considerable number of families who had members living or working overseas and who therefore receive remittances. The absence of these banking facilities is not due to the town's economic status but to its proximity to the provincial capital city. Its *poblacion*, the more urbanized area, is just seven kilometers away, about 15 minutes by jeepney, the most common public transport. The town immediately to the north of San Gabriel has one bank despite having the same income classification as San Gabriel. This bank branch serves the other northern towns, which are much farther from the capital city.

The absence of banks or inaccessibility of financial facilities in San Gabriel meant that women have to go to the capital city to withdraw money for their family's needs. The dependence of San Gabriel on the capital city's financial and commercial infrastructure—banks, cash machines, grocery stores, restaurants, fastfood establishments, shopping stores, etcetera—necessitated women venturing not only out of their homes but also out of town. Also, a number of the women lived in villages where San Gabriel's town center, although closer in terms of distance, was actually less accessible in terms of available public transportation. They therefore preferred doing their groceries and attending church service in the capital city as it was more convenient and cheaper to do so.

These Filipino seafarers' wives were more mobile than the wives depicted in Skolnik, Lazo de la Vega and Steigenga (2012) and McEvoy et al. (2012), whose mobility was severely restricted by the gendered binary between *casa* (house) and *calle* (street), which respectively stood for the private (domestic) and public (world of work) spheres. These seafarers' wives' mobility was not defined by the same strict gendered delineation of space. Indeed, nine of the research participants were in full-time paid employment who faced no social criticism for being in the world of work. Their working neither put the masculine identity of their husbands as provider in question. One wife, however, shared her husband's wish for her to give up working because he did not like the fact that she often had to get a ride home from one of her male colleagues, especially when they finish work late and there is no longer public transportation available (around 7 p.m.). A husband I had an informal conversation with shared that he did not want his wife, a full-time mother, to work because he was concerned she might be courted by male colleagues.

Wives who were not in paid employment, particularly the younger ones, made sure that they had a companion when they ventured out of their homes in order to avoid being suspected of anything inappropriate. When they went to the town's *poblacion* or the capital city, their reasons were related to the provision of care to their families such as getting money from the bank, the purchase of food and clothes, etcetera. None of them went to the capital city to see a movie (there is no cinema in San Gabriel) or for the sole purpose of leisure. For married women, especially mothers, leisure is a problematic concept (Bittman and Wacjman 2000; Davies 2001; Forman 1989). Messner has noted that "women's time spent in visiting, parties, outings, or watching television is certain to contain some obvious work, in preparing, serving, and putting away dishes." He concludes that much of this "'free time' is also *work*" (quoted in Forman 1989, 3; emphasis in original). Messner points to the work inherent in these leisure activities.

The seafarers' wives' *dibersyon* represents a different conceptualization and practice of the relationship between work and leisure. They transformed work into leisure. One wife explained she did not want to be just sitting down doing nothing. For many of these wives, filling in their "empty time" meant finding something "meaningful" to do. Some raised pigs, chickens, or goats. Others tended to vegetable gardens. A couple of mothers farmed. For most of the wives, this was a pleasant distraction. As Maria, one of the wives who farmed, explained, her farm was something she could visit (*napia lang nga adda sarsarungkaran*). Many of the wives, particularly those who were not in paid work, said that they rarely went out. By this they meant going out in pursuit of personal recreation or leisure. When Maria said "you go out," she meant going to her neighbors she was really close with,

Figure 1. A seaman's wife's corn harvest

especially another seaman's wife. When they did go out, it was to perform a responsibility associated with their being a mother, looking after their family, or with activities that are considered proper for a married woman whose husband was away or which affirmed their morality such as going to church once a week. A wife considered the time waiting for her son at school as her leisure time since it enabled her to hang out with other wives she has befriended.

The women's economic activities made it possible for them to enjoy more sociality. They enabled the women to venture much farther from their homes in ways that were socially acceptable and hence did not elicit suspicion. They widened the women's social contacts as they became known to people through the food products they sold. A neighbor who was helping the two women who partnered together to make and sell food items suggested they include their mobile numbers in the packaging of their products so that they could more easily be contacted for orders. The wives did not like the idea, explaining that what they were doing was merely a *dibersyon,* something they did to occupy their time. They did not want it to grow too big for them that it would dominate their lives. Also, they did not want to expose themselves to people who will contact them for reasons other than making an order. They immediately recognized the risk of giving away their contact numbers. There was thus a limit to how far the wives were willing to take the social possibilities of their business activity, of the social becoming the backdoor to the sexual. But they welcomed how it provided a distraction to what they oftentimes described as a boring life. They thus relaxed but their activities also simultaneously involved work. Indeed, they transformed work into leisure. Leisure, paradoxically, was to be found in work.

Dibersyon might be understood another way. Maria explained that she made herself "forget" her husband, that is, dealt with missing him by distracting herself with work. She raised pigs and farmed. Maria's farm was located on the other side of the river, which was not far from her house and she used a bamboo raft (*rakit*) to get there. To quote her on the link between work and missing her husband: "I deal with it through work. I deal with it through work. [. . .] That's how I deal with it. Work so that my mind is taken away from my husband. Just work." Maria used these forms of leisure-work—farming as well as raising pigs in addition to her care work for her children and elderly parents—to sublimate her sexual longing. This rechanneling of her sexual desire enabled her to simultaneously relax, protect her morality, and enjoy more mobility.

Figure 2. A *rakit* that a wife used to cross the river to get to her farm.

DIBERSYON AND *ISU PAY*

The women's leisure-through-work activities not only occupied them and filled their empty time. There was also a financial justification to their activities. Those who raised animals and grew vegetables had something to sell or had food for the family, thus saving them money. "Rather than buy them" is how one wife put it. Another wife said, "*isu pay*," referring to the money saved from having to buy them. Some women, particularly those who sold processed food items such as sausages, tapas, tocino (a form of cured meat), and who originally intended what they were doing as *libangan lang* (just for recreation or amusement) to occupy themselves with and to relieve them of boredom came to see what they were doing as work that generated a return they did not simply call profit (*ganansiya*) but rather as income (*sapul*). They thus effectively framed their leisure or recreational activity within work. The wives not only produced goods that saved them money but even more significantly, earned them some, which gave them much to be pleased about as, according to them, it was the fruit of their own labor (*bukodmo a nagbannogan*). This made them proud as it enabled them to see themselves not as women financially dependent on their husbands but as contributing to their family's financial well-being, albeit modestly.

Interestingly, the women did not explicitly talk about their *dibersyon* activities in the context of the insecurity of their husbands' employment. This may well have been part of their motivation to engage in such activities, but what was emphasized was the relaxation and sociality they enjoyed. The money they made was not big and their activities were tailored around their other responsibilities. The two wives who partnered to make and sell food stuff have abandoned their business activity, as reported in a follow-up interview in 2015. The decision to discontinue it was made when the woman who did not have a child when the business was started finally had her daughter and the caring responsibilities she had for her gave the mother something to do. Another wife, who did not have a child but who looked after her parents-in-law, had a *sari-sari* store that only broke even but which she continued to have because it gave her something different to do. Another wife who did not have a child and who admitted to losing money from selling lingerie, cosmetic, and perfume products persisted in what she was doing because it gave her a reason to not "just stay in the house."

Figure 3. "Awan Utang/No Credit": The *tianggi* (store) of a seaman's wife.

Different cases indicate that the overriding motivation for their *dibersyon* was to counter the boredom and tedium of waiting, which consigned some of them to the house and its immediate environs. Further, the additional money they made, the *isu pay*, provided a rationality to what they were doing that easily obtained social approval and which consequently countered gossip's negative consequence on their movement.

Dibersyon is an adaptive strategy, a socio-cultural practice that enables the women to bargain with patriarchal gender relations and practices (Kandiyoti 1988). Although they do not radically unsettle the ideology that underpins these gender relations and practices, they nevertheless extend and expand their mobility without compromising their morality. Paradoxically, *dibersyon* loosens and tightens the link between morality and mobility in the women's lives. The women's negotiation of the power of gossip to police their morality and mobility reveals a creativity to work around the gender ideological and normative boundaries that gossip enforces for wives who stay behind.

The conversion of work into leisure resonates with but is not quite the same as that propounded by critical theorists of the Frankfurt School. Adorno and Horkheimer noted that "amusement under late capitalism becomes the prolongation of work" (1979, 137). Workers seek amusement "to escape from the mechanized work process and to recruit strength in order to cope with it again." Further, "mechanization has such power over a man's leisure and happiness, and so profoundly determines the manufacture of amusement goods that his experiences are inevitably after-images of the work process itself." Whereas for Adorno and Horkheimer amusement becomes an extension of paid labor, the stay-behind women engage in activities not simply because of the absence of work since many of them are mothers whose caring responsibilities kept them busy. Especially for those who had no children, there were huge blocks of time that needed to be filled. They engaged in activities that could be reconceptualized as work or framed within work in order to legitimize them and gain social approval. To the extent that these activities provided distraction to them, that is, enabled them to enjoy more sociality and acted as a balm to their monotonous lives, their work are leisure activities. Their conversion of work into leisure demonstrates that although they are able to engage in activities that they found pleasurable, their choices were circumscribed and constrained by the gendered moral politics created by male emigration and which gossip enforces. Gossip structured their mobility; indeed, it functioned as a "structure of constraint" that vitally organized their lives (Clarke and Critcher 1985, 46).

CONCLUSION

Gossip shows that women "bear the moral burdens of family separation" (Dreby 2009, 34). The women's negotiation of gossip responded to ideology. Stewart and Strathern have said that "[f]or words to be harmful,

[. . .] they have to be spoken in contexts of ideology that are congenial to them" (2004, 30). They could not simply shrug off the slanderous gossip that could be spread about them because their character and actions were being framed by discourses and representations about the behavior or imagined misbehavior of wives who stay behind. Thus, it is "the ideological and historical context rather than the words themselves that ultimately produces the effects" (Stewart and Strathern 2004, 30). They established their moral propriety by enjoying a mobility that entailed the transformation or translation of work into leisure—*dibersyon*. In the concrete lives of the women, it also means "distraction," a way of diverting their thoughts and feelings into something else. Thus, as a form of amusement or relaxation, the activities helped to distract them from the empty time that they had to confront as well as helped them to "forget" their husbands. Of course, the women missed their husbands and they needed activities to help them deal with their physical and sexual longing for them. Such activities enabled them to go out farther and more frequently because what they were doing were morally acceptable. Their invocation of *isu pay* helped them give their work-leisure activities—their *dibersyon*—social legitimacy.

How women relaxed was mediated, if not limited, by stage in the life course (mothers with school-going children used their waiting time to socialize with other mothers), socio-economic standing (where and how often they and their families can enjoy outside meals), and gendered social and moral norms. None of the wives would ever contemplate going to a disco or some other form of night entertainment. Not only would they have to go the capital city and leave their children in the care of others (for mothers) but availing themselves of such leisure activities would have met criticism. Even going to a cinema on their own potentially risked their reputation. Drinking at home with friends remains mostly a male activity. Clearly, there are socio-cultural limits to what women can choose to spend their "free" time on. How they relaxed increased their spatial mobility, but they made sure that this gain did not lead to a loss in their reputation. The stay-behind women not only are responsible for the work and labor needed to sustain and reproduce the family in the absence of their husbands. Those who were not in paid work performed this while having to ensure their honor and faithfulness to their husband were not put into question. Because of their fear of gossip and its consequences and despite what they achieve through their *dibersyon*, they inadvertently help to maintain gendered conceptions of morality and mobility, conceptions that themselves shaped their sexual and gendered subjectivities. In the next chapter, I will examine how women in paid work or who were earning a living through business activities used *isu pay* in order to continue with their work, hence incorporating work as a vital component of their gendered subjectivity that is framed within spousal and family relationships and responsibilities.

CHAPTER 7

WOMEN WORKING
Isu Pay and Moral Rationality

Isu pay informed how women who were paid in employment constructed their spousal and maternal obligation to their family. *Isu pay* enabled them to resist pressure from their husband to quit their jobs and focus instead on becoming full-time wives or mothers. It provided moral justification for the particular mothering that they insisted on performing, one that combined caring and working and, in one case, even prioritizing making money over care work. To justify being in paid work, and in one case, engaging in a number of profitable business activities, the women linked *isu pay* to the insecurity of their husbands' employment. *Isu pay* here means doing everything they can to contribute to the financial resources of their family and thereby help ensure its stability and security. In this chapter, I examine the women's use of *isu pay* as a framework for their construction of their gendered subjectivity and identity by putting it in dialogue with the concept of "gendered moral rationalities," which I consider in the context of male emigration's consequences on the labor force participation of women who stay behind.

MALE EMIGRATION, WOMEN WHO STAY BEHIND, AND PAID WORK

Two perspectives on the impact of male emigration on the employment of women who stay put in developing countries are most relevant to the aims of my discussion here. The first links a decrease in wage work among these women to changes in the family's financial resources and the time-labor demands that the absence of husbands put on their wives. A number of scholars have noted that greater household income from the women's migrant husband's remittances is linked to women's decreased wage work (Acosta 2006; Amuedo-Dorantes and Pozo 2006; Cabegin 2006; Lokshin and Glinskaya 2009; Mendola and

Carletto 2009; Rodriguez and Tiongson 2001). Remittances lead to a rise in individual reservation wages making them higher than market wages (Binzel and Assaad 2011). This makes being in wage work less appealing. In addition to this, Wang (2013) argues that the need to replace migrants' labor at home explains the shift from paid work to unpaid work by Mexican women whose spouses are working in the USA.

The second perspective links women's limited, or lack of, participation in wage work to existing gender relations in which there is a clear division of labor between men and women. Ennaji and Sadiqi (2008) note that in rural and semi-rural communities in Morocco, women who stay found it difficult to work outside the home because doing so undermined the social role and image of their (migrant) husbands as breadwinners. Ikuomola (2015) reports in his study of Nigerian women from Edo State that those who worked to complement their husband's remittances were met with resistance and criticism expressed through accusations of infidelity. Women who did not want to remain dependent on their husband's family for support were cast as women "looking for freedom." This tactic polices and maintains gendered boundaries (by casting questions on their sexuality and fidelity). This association between "home" and "mother" finds strong resonance in the work of Manohar and Busse-Cardenas (2011), who write that the migration of the husbands of working-class Peruvian women led the latter to give up the advances they have achieved in their role as wives and mothers. In order to secure their spouse's loyalty to them and keep the remittances flowing, they focused on looking after their children, which meant giving up working outside the home. Their devotion to their children demonstrated their being good mothers which in turn attested to their being good wives.

Gendered Moral Rationalities

Simon Duncan and Rosalind Edwards first developed the concept of "gendered moral rationalities" in their study of lone mothers' orientation toward mothering and employment to account for the varying ways these mothers justified their decision to work or not (1997, 1999). The founding insight on which the concept rests is that "economic rationality may be determined by nonmarket criteria about what is socially right, and may change according to the social context, where these ideas are negotiated, modified and changed with others" (1997, 32). Hence, this rationality will be "collective and gendered, rather than individual and gender-free." Thus, "gendered moral rationalities":

> were gendered because they fundamentally dealt with notions of mothering, they were moral in providing answers about the right thing to do, and they were rationalities in providing a framework for taking decisions about participation in the labour market. They were also negotiated and maintained within social networks in particular socio-spatial contexts. (Duncan et al. 2003, 313)

The concept has also been applied to the case of partnered mothers. Duncan et al. (2003) have concluded that the partner's presence or absence had little impact on gendered moral rationalities women had concerning how motherhood and paid work ought to be combined.

Duncan and his colleagues developed the concept as an alternative conceptualization of family behavior particularly around decision-making on caring responsibilities and work commitments (Barlow and Duncan 2000; Duncan and Edwards 1997, 1999; Duncan et al. 2003, 2004; Duncan and Irwin 2004). The concept responds particularly to the two theories that have dominated the way family behavior has been understood (Duncan and Irwin 2004). First is the "new household economics" (Barlow and Duncan 2000; Duncan and Edwards 1997, 1999; Duncan et al. 2003, 2004) and second, the individualization of gender relations in late modernity (Duncan et al. 2003; Duncan and Irwin 2004).

As argued by Duncan and Irwin (2004), new household economics, propounded in, for example, Becker (1996) and Ermisch (2003), utilizes neoclassical economics' concept of rational choice to explain family behavior and practices. This rational choice is embodied by the figure of the "rational economic man." The rational economic man approach is premised on the conceptualization of a person as an individual, that is, as a separate economic agent "whose 'preferences' or 'tastes' are already given and do not change, make cost-benefit analyses in order to maximize their utility. Such preferences are taken to be independent of the behavior of everyone else, and of past behavior" (Duncan and Edwards 1997, 33). The approach "retains as fundamental the idea that preferences are stable, individual, and exogenous." Applied to gendered divisions of labor, "new household economics" posits that couples benefit from mutual dependence, one based on each performing different and specialized roles: women focusing on domestic work and men on paid work (34). Duncan and Edwards (1997) point out the obvious inapplicability of the notion of trading (or the rational exchange of labor) on lone mothers since they simply do not have someone to do this with. Even among partnered women, the negotiation of what they and their partners did or the allocation of housework and care work occurred in ways that defied the logic of economic rationality that was supposed to underpin this exchange in order to optimally divide and distribute labor within the family (Duncan and Irwin 2004). As Duncan and Edwards (1997, 35) have written: "Certainly there is little empirical support for Becker-type marriage trading models, and women's specialization in domestic work can result from coercion, or gendered social expectations, more than from 'rational' trading."

The individualization of gender relations in late modernity is the second influential perspective on family behavior that the concept of gendered moral rationalities flags up as inadequate. Duncan et al (2003) locate this process within developments in the West described and theorized by Ulrich Beck (1992), Ulrich Beck and Elizabeth Beck-Gernsheim (1995), and Anthony Giddens (1992) as individualization and destandardization of life. They note Beck's argument that the process of individualization of gender relations partly derives from women's increasing participation in the labor market, which leads to the commodification of their labor and the weakening of the male breadwinner model, both vis-à-vis the increasing insufficiency of a single income for a family's survival. As this model is replaced by the adult worker model—with both partners working in order to co-resource the family (Irwin and Bottero 2000)—women find more reason and justification to be in paid employment. Women's participation in paid work is thought to enable more equitable relationships between men and women (Giddens 1992). Thus, individualization, the thinking goes, provides women with what is supposedly the environment and opportunity for self-construction, for rethinking and building their choice biographies rather than simply following socially prescribed and conventional roles. Individualization, as McDowell and colleagues (2005) have pointed out, is also seen to free women from class and gender strictures. In this environment of destandardization, work then becomes a vital component of the women's new self and identity (Duncan et al. 2003; Duncan and Irwin 2004). Consequently,

> [c]ouples are no longer tied together in a complementary domestic and market specialization. Rather, couple relationships are increasingly governed by, and contingent upon, ideas of mutually satisfying intimacy. [. . .] Traditional gender relations and 'the family' are destabilized, and the constitution of late modern family has to be individually negotiated. (Duncan et al. 2003, 324)

Duncan and Irwin (2004) argue that both "new household economics" and "individualization of gender relations in late modernity" posit an individualized and standardized rationality (see also Duncan et al. 2003). As such, they fail to capture adequately, and indeed misrepresent, family practices—what families actually do and what actually happens within families. Individualization disregards the significant role played by social ties and socially negotiated gendered moral responsibilities in shaping the division or allocation of labor between couples (Duncan et al. 2003, 325). Others have pointed to the potential of individualization to lead to the retraditionalization of gender relations (Adkins 2000).

As opposed to the "rational economic man" who, as a separate individual, makes cost-benefit calculations about work in order to maximize the gains of working, gendered moral rationalities point to how decisions about working are very relational undertakings. While the rational economic man approach focuses on individual characteristics such as "human capital (education, training, experience), individual resources (for example, income) and constraints (for example, number and age of children)," the concept of gendered moral rationalities, in contrast, considers social imperatives as fundamental. It "focuses on collective negotiations and understandings about what is morally right and socially acceptable" (Duncan and Edwards 1997, 30):

> It is "gendered moral rationalities"—social and cultural collective understandings about what is best, and morally right, for men, as well as for women—that provide a basis for individuals' economic-decision making within families, including lone-mother families. Calculations about perceived economic costs and benefits will be important once these understandings are established, but are essentially secondary to such social and moral questions. (35)

The concept of gendered moral rationalities underscores the making of family decisions not only as being morally framed but also negotiated in particular social and geographic contexts. As such, decision making is variable in contrast to being uniform as posited in new household economics and individualization (Duncan and Irwin 2004). "Moral rationality" is attentive to the importance of context and specificity (Duncan and Irwin 2004, 398).[1]

Local Conditions for Gender Negotiation

As will be demonstrated below, the Filipino women's choice to work or their attitude toward working is shaped by various factors, including the availability of jobs, the capacity of their husband to obtain a new contract, and their husband's ideas about what their proper roles and responsibilities are.

Their consideration of these multiple factors in making what to them are both moral and rational decisions dovetails with a fundamental argument in the literature on gendered moral rationalities. It is that women consider both their "ideological orientations towards caring with a knowledge of differential command over resources and assets" (McDowell et al. 2005, 231).

People in San Gabriel do not see the home as the only proper place for women. In a town where more than 40 percent of the population is unemployed, and where many of those not in the category of unemployed are self-employed (farmers, tricycle drivers, and jeepney drivers who have meager and unstable incomes), families take a generally pragmatic attitude toward women working. None of the women I interviewed held the view that they should not be in paid work or earning some money through informal economic activities because earning a living is a job reserved for men. Most did not work because there simply were no jobs available. What emerged as crucial was the husbands' attitude toward their wife's choice to work, which reflects their gendered views about what men and women ought to do. While a few of the women were asked by their husbands to stay home or concentrate on caring for the family, many more women were able to continue working.

There is variation in husband's commitment to gendered separate spheres. Pingol (2002) has also noted this flexibility in her study of migrant wives and househusbands in another Ilocos town. She showed how a number of house-husbands seriously took their role of looking after their children, reframing their role as responsible fathers as a demonstration of their masculinity rather than an emasculation of their manhood. They countered the social perception of their emasculation. In contrast, in her study of women participating in paid work through subcontracting in the agricultural economy, Dungo (2007) noted how some women were able to convince their unemployed husbands to let them work only when they assured their men that their paid work would not interfere with their housework. Thus, while there is a social expectation about what men and women are supposed to do, what enable men and women to transgress boundaries are, one, the flexibility of the husbands about their wives being in paid work and, two, the resilience and persistence of the women in making a living in the face of spousal opposition.

THE FIGURE OF THE HUSBAND: THREE IDEAL TYPES

From the women's stories of their husband's responses to their being in paid work or engaging in the informal economy, three ideal types of husbands may be constructed: the unable to compromise, the able to compromise, and the enabler. The unable-to-compromise type insisted on the wife staying at home to give her full attention to family care. The able-to-compromise type asked their wife to give up paid work but who, when their wife did not, respected her choice. The enabler type includes husbands who encouraged their wife to pursue economic activities in the informal economy, did not discourage their wife from being in paid work, supported their decision to stay in paid work after the birth of a child, and encouraged their wife to undertake overseas migration ready to take over the care responsibility. I elaborate on each type using cases in order to show how the women's working or earning a living intersects with various issues that informed the negotiations and decisions made, as well as the rationalizations offered.

The Unable-to-Compromise Husband

Irene's husband: Guardian of gendered spheres

In 2010 when I first interviewed her, Irene was going through a difficult patch in her marriage. Her relationship with her husband was suffering from the strain of the meddling of her mother-in-law and a husband still heavily influenced by his natal family. Furthermore, Irene felt oppressed by her lack of financial independence, which made her feel frivolous when buying personal items (see also McDowell et al. 2005). She wanted to work overseas, which her husband opposed arguing that he provided well for the family. He saw her decision to working as putting into question his masculine identity built on being the breadwinner. Irene explicitly referred to her husband's ego being offended. Although his refusal to let her work overseas is reasonable, his invocation of a discourse of the good of the family built around the mother being there to look after the children consolidated his claim to being the family's sole earner. Irene's husband rejected her appeal to him to let her have a small stall to sell goods at the town's public market. This she could have accommodated into her family's routine especially because she lived with an adult sister who acted as her helper. Her husband had practically decreed that her place was in the home.

Interviewed again in 2014, Irene, now with a second child (she had a two-year old in 2010) and no longer living with her older sister, said that having a seller's stall at the town's public market has become practically impossible to do. Her relationship with her husband and in-laws has improved, which has helped her feel better about staying put and becoming a full-time mother. She says that when her children are older, she might pursue selling goods at the public market despite her husband, whom I also interviewed in 2014, not having changed his position on the matter.

Donna's husband: Memories of maternal care deficit

Donna's husband had made known his wish for her to give up working even before they got married. When they did, however, she negotiated to continue working until they had a child, explaining that working would help her cope with his absence. Her parents, however, had encouraged her to continue working even when she already had children, advising her that she and her husband take a pragmatic view. With how difficult life has become and with local jobs being very scarce, they said she was lucky to have one and should thus hang on to it. They offered to look after her children when they arrived. Although Donna agreed with her parents, she had to reconcile what she, her parents, and her husband wanted. Donna said that her job was important to her because it enabled her to help her natal family. As the eldest child and because she had a job, her parents expected her to provide financial assistance to them. Although helping her family was very important to her, she also wanted to look after her child full-time. As she said, "there is nothing like a mother looking after her own children." Although she gave up her work, she is still able to help her own family as her husband had promised to help her continue to do this.

Donna's husband's wish that she devote her time to caring for their child springs from his own experience of not having had enough maternal care. Donna shared that he grew up without his mother, who had worked overseas as a domestic helper when his father became too weak to farm, work which his mother did in his place for a time until the needs of her family became too great to be supported by her farming alone. The absence of his mother deprived him of the care and attention of his mother, and Donna's husband vowed that when he had a family, he would make sure that his children had the full attention of their mother especially because his work as a seafarer meant he was away for long periods of time. The abundance of available care resources for his family—his own mother, who has come back from overseas work and with whom they live, his wife's parents, and his and his wife's siblings—could not change his mind. Both Donna and her husband recognized each other's needs: for her to be able to continue helping her family and for him to have his children looked after by their own mother, his wife. The decision they made reveals how each took into account their responsibilities, ones that unfortunately could easily map onto a gendered division of labor.

The Able-to-Compromise Husband

Rosa's Husband: Hesitant pragmatist

Like Irene, Rosa said that her husband did not let her work because he saw himself as the family provider. Yet, he had to compromise and be pragmatic when he was out of work for eight months. Having miscalculated the amount of time he needed to get a transit visa, he was not able to join his cruise ship in Europe. Within a short time, they used up their savings and Rosa insisted she look for work. At that time she was still breastfeeding her small son. The first job she got was as a sales assistant, working for 12 hours from 8 a.m. to 8 p.m., standing most of the time, and earning PhP100 a day. She lasted only one day. Having earlier worked at fastfood chains when she was still unmarried, she quickly found work in one where the shorter hours and shift duties were easier. While Rosa worked, her husband looked after their son. During that time, therefore, a reversal of roles occurred.

Rosa's insistence that she find work while her husband was home unemployed was motivated by her not wanting to be a burden to her mother with whom they lived. She also wanted to show that, as adults, they were capable of providing for themselves. She did not want her neighbors to think that they were depending on her mother. Rosa's strong position is indicated by the expression she used: "patartaraken," from "taraken," an animal raised as livestock or pet. Rosa could not accept the position of being fed like an animal dependent on its master or owner. By working to remain independent, she also showed her husband that gender order does not have to be rigid, that there are alternative, if not better, gender arrangements.

The Enabler Husband

Mildred's Husband: Ready to take on caring role

A few of the women had husbands who were already finding it increasingly difficult to get a job for reasons of diminishing health (see Bloor 2011). Mildred, whose husband is already facing career-threatening health problems, shared that her husband had been telling her that when he stopped going to sea, it will be her turn to go abroad. Her husband has several siblings in Italy whose migration he financed. She herself desired to work and to work abroad especially since there were no jobs for her locally. If she goes, her husband will look after their children. Interviewed again in 2013, Mildred shared that her husband did not go to sea for three years (he was home in 2010 when I first interviewed Mildred), during which he had a heart surgery to repair a valve. Unable to wait any longer for financial assistance from the Philippine Charity Sweepstakes Organization, Mildred's husband sought the help of his siblings in Italy, who quickly pooled resources together so he could have the life-saving surgery. He has since fully recovered and on his very 44th birthday boarded a ship. Although Mildred's husband has been the family's breadwinner, his masculine identity appears not to be inextricably bound up with it. He does not subscribe to a strict gendered division of labor; indeed, when I interviewed Mildred in 2010, he voluntarily prepared his family's lunch when it became apparent that we were not close to finishing. He enables his wife to entertain the possibility of becoming the breadwinner herself and finds no problem at all at the prospect of him becoming the carer.

Agnes's husband: Man who's got his wife's back

Agnes gave up work when her son was already a few years old. She had hired a helper to look after her son so she could go back to work. Agnes's husband respected and supported her decision to remain working even after the birth of their son. When her son's developmental problem was diagnosed, she quit her work, a decision made in consultation with her husband who remained sensitive to her commitment to a professional identity. Although working was very important to her, she gave up her professional life for the sake of her son.

As the primary parent (her husband being away for long periods of time), it fell upon her to make the moral decision to give up work so she can give her son the care he needed. The decision is pragmatic and Agnes said that even her parents thought that she should give her son her full attention. Giving this attention included being able to relocate where the medical and other professional expertise necessary for her son's care was available. As one of her colleagues said of her decision to quit, "of what use is all the money she has if she can't give her child the full attention he requires. If he was all right, she could go on working." Unlike Donna, Agnes had a husband supportive of her working. It was the combination of her son's condition and the unavailability of facilities and expertise in the Ilocos that her son needed that made her quit in the end.

In this section, I analyzed the vital importance of the seafarer-husband's gendered views on the roles of men and women in the possibility and actuality of the women's participation in paid work or in the informal economy. The cases of Donna and Agnes, who both gave up paid work in order to care for their children full time, demonstrate the various considerations and the factors that shaped the making of gendered responsibilities and moral rationalities of care. Donna's decision to quit working was made not only in the context of her spousal relationship but also in wider kin obligations, as well as how biographical experiences of care and nurture inform paternal attempts at parenting practices that have vital consequences on what mothers/

spouses are expected to provide. Biography and memory are implicated in efforts to rewrite the generational provision of maternal care in order not to allow what the previous generation suffered to be visited upon the next. Such efforts, however, to ensure the provision of "proper" and sufficient maternal care unwittingly relies upon, and leads to, the perpetuation of traditional gender relations.

Agnes's decision to become a full-time mother highlights how a geography of uneven development and inequality in the distribution and provision of health resources helped determine her decision. People living in predominantly rural regions do not have easy access to specialist medical facilities and professional expertise, which are easily available in such big cities as Manila where they are concentrated. In Mildred's case, her husband's broaching the idea of her working overseas and his corresponding readiness to become the carer is vitally and inextricably bound up with what he sees as the depletion of his "health capital" (see Bloor 2011) which, given the neoliberal logic of a highly globalized maritime industry, renders him a "disposable body" (Rodriguez 2010).

The discussion of different cases was built around the three ideal types of husband I constructed from the wives' description of their experiences negotiating combining care responsibilities and earning some money. Only four of the men could be categorized as of the *unable-to-compromise* type. They wanted their wives to stay at home and be full-time mothers (one said he did not want his wife to work for fear that she will be courted by her male co-workers). Just as these men would not be moved to show some flexibility, a good number of women resisted their husband's wish that they give up working or engaging in business activities that occupied them as if it were a full-time job. One of these wives is married to one who is *unable-to-compromise* and her continued engagement in money-making activities has been the source of serious spousal conflicts. The rest are married to *able-to-compromise* husbands. These are men who, despite their traditional views on gender relations, did not impose them on where their wives ought to be (at home) and what they are ought to be doing (caring for the family). They listened to the women's rationalization of their continued working. The women's reason for doing so emphasized more the good it did for the entire family than for their personal or professional identities. Their justification is unassailably rational, and to the extent that their continued working is intimately linked to the provision of financial security to the family, such a choice is also simultaneously moral.

ISU PAY AND THE MORAL RATIONALITY OF WOMEN EARNING A LIVING

Seven of the nine women who were in paid employment had been encouraged by their husband to give up working. Only one did—Donna, discussed above. (Agnes, also discussed above, was never asked by her husband to quit.) Except for two women whose husbands received pay while not at sea, these women who combined working and mothering said that their work was a source of income—fall-back income. To be sure, many of them had thought of becoming full-time mothers but the experience of relying on saved money when their husbands were home and the uncertainty their husband faced in getting their next job convinced them to hang on to their jobs.

In response to my question of why they continued working despite their husband asking them to quit, their answer was a variation of *isu pay*: *"Isu pay ta masapulak." "Isu pay ta nayon ta paggastomi." "Isu pay, daytoy a rigat ti biag."* All of these statements mean essentially the same thing: *isu pay* points to the maximization of resources. *Masapulak* comes from the word *sapul* which refers to the act of looking and result of looking or searching for something, in this context, earning a living. What the women "find" in the act of looking (working) is a resource, financial resource. Similarly, *nayon* means "additional" or "extra" money intended as reserve for when the husbands are not earning. The extra money they make extends their capacity to survive their husband's unemployment ("nayon ta paggastomi"). The last makes a direct reference to how hard life is (daytoy a rigat ti biag) and that being in work alleviates their condition. Their income was vital especially when their husbands were off work and not earning. Given the contractual nature of their husband's work and the time it takes for them to get their next contract, the women argued that giving up working was not in the best interest of their family. Giving up work would therefore be both a wasteful and an irrational thing to do.

In this sense, the women's strategic recourse to a discourse of *isu pay* resonates with the idea of the strategy of "co-resourcing of households." Irwin and Bottero have noted that "there has been a decline in the relative sufficiency of male earnings and an increased importance of female earnings across the life course of individuals and families" (2000, 274). With the increased significance of female contribution to the financial and economic well-being of families, they say, the idea of a male breadwinner is increasingly becoming modified especially where women's earnings are vital to the financial security of families. The growth in importance of female employment to the survival of families has led to the development of such "co-resourcing of households." In the case of seafarer families, the importance of women being in paid work is even more significant to the "resourcing of households." When their husband was home/out of work, the women became the main family earner, if not the only one with an income. Also, since most of their salary was unspent and therefore formed a big part of their savings, it could be said that it was the women's salary that ensured that their families had money to tide them over. They would not have to face the prospect of having to borrow money and accumulate debt, the payment to which would consume the first few months' salary of their husband, as happened to some of the women who did not have work.

Isu pay therefore is a strategy of providing financial stability to the family especially when the main earner is out of work. The survival of the family is a fundamental aspect of care and casting away the means to secure it is both irrational and immoral. Men whose wives were in paid work have seen the value of their wife's continued working, and the discourse of *isu pay* has been vitally important in convincing them to stop asking their wives to stop working. The case of Dina, a teacher with two children (12 and 6 years old), proves this point. Her husband, 38, who had been going out to sea for 12 years at the time of my first interview in 2010, had not been able to go back to sea since that year for health reasons. At that time, he was only taking a much-needed break after nine months of being on a ship. In a follow-up conversation in 2014, Dina shared that her husband had not been able to go back to sea. When he went for a medical check-up in 2010 to get certified fit for his next contract, his chronic health condition was discovered. Now with the family relying only on her salary, Dina said that the quality of their life has suffered. Unlike before, they now struggle to buy things that they want and allocate money only for very essential ones. Fortunately, she said, she did not listen to her husband when he first asked her to give up work: "Where would we be now if both of us did not have a job? Thank God I did not resign from my work! At least we have something, albeit small." A wife went back to paid work after a number of years caring for her elderly parents, a decision impelled by her husband's failure to get further shipboard work.

Women who combined paid work and caring responsibilities were able to do so because they could rely on the help of mothers, siblings, relatives or paid help. The availability of kin and other people to provide this care while they were at home eased the guilt that mothers of small or young children felt because they were working. As discussed in Chapter 3, when they were home, they tried to do as much mothering as they could. They tried to provide more care work and spend more time with their children during weekends, which also helped them combine the demands of their domestic and working lives. The point here is that these women in paid work saw working (or the provision of financial stability to their family) as an integral part of their moral responsibility of mothering (see also Duncan and Edwards 1997). One woman, Aida, who was focused more on making money than on taking care of her children, faced the continued disapproval and resistance from her husband. Aida looks at making money or financial provision as the more important aspect of her being a married woman-mother. Aida is a "worker" who "give[s] primacy to paid work for themselves as separate to their identity as mothers" (Duncan and Edwards 1997, 72).[2] What is remarkable about Aida is that she is not in paid work; she has business activities to which she has devoted her attention as if she were holding a demanding full-time job. She also is married to a man who belongs to the unable-to-compromise type of husband.

Aida as provider-worker and her presentation of herself

Aida's business activities so consumed her time that despite her claims to the contrary, her priority as a married woman with children was not to provide mother care but to make money. Her case is instructive in that she was concerned about being seen (at least by me) as someone who did not neglect her children. I asked her what her daily routine was like:

> Aida: **I take care of the children.** Because I have a business venture, when I get up in the morning, I get the list [names of people and their transactions] ready. Then I go out to collect, come back to the house, go out again, it's like that. When I get home, we eat, I take a short rest then I will have plenty of people to attend to. Those who are . . . I will just tell you, those who are renewing [loans], like that. I release money. I take a nap at around three o'clock. Around four or 4:30, I get up, 5 o'clock I take a shower and go out of the house again to collect. Rest. Then 10:30 in the evening, at 10:30 in the evening, I come back home. Because I also attend to my other business activity [Aida has three stalls selling 'empanada,' a popular local foodstuff sold mainly in the evening], there [fronting the public market].
>
> [. . .]
>
> RG: At what time do you get up then?
>
> Aida: 6:30.
>
> RG: You get the children ready for school or it's your mother?
>
> Aida: No. They know that I am very tired. Our helper does it. She wakes them up, gives them a bath, changes them to their school uniform and takes them to school. **But I supervise and follow up on them.**

The interview extract above shows how Aida has framed, for the purpose of the interview, her income-generating work as a businesswoman in a relational matrix with caring. In other words, she was concerned to present herself as engaged in earning a living but without neglecting her caring responsibilities for her children. Yet both structure and substance of her answer indicate she does very little care work. Her claim that she does is stated at the beginning ("I take care of the children"). This is then followed by detailed descriptions of her work activities. Her narrative of her daily routine is dominated by her work, and her claim to taking care of children is contradicted by her last statement: that the work of getting her children ready for school has been delegated to her helper and the children understood this because they knew she was always very busy and tired.

Aida's case demonstrates the social pressure on working women to still perform care work as part of their moral responsibility as mothers. This social expectation became evident in the way Aida tried to construct a moral self and identity capable of performing her responsibilities under the strain of the competing claims of working and caring. I would argue that how good she was as a mother, at least privately for her, was not determined by the amount of care work she did for her children. The structure and content of her response suggested that providing for her family (including her natal family especially her elderly mother) was a far more vital part of her moral responsibility as a mother than performing care work. How she chose to respond to my question reveals the "force of domesticity" (Parrenas 2008a), that is, how women's roles and identities are constructed by and through the private sphere embodied by the house, a private self that she did not necessarily subscribe to and actually live yet which she felt compelled to publicly assert to be performing. Aida might have seen me, a male researcher who she knew is himself a father, not only as an individual but as a representative of a certain set of ideological, socio-cultural, and gender expectations. As such, and not knowing exactly where I stood on this matter, she strategically slotted me as a conservative. I do not see Aida as lying (as being inconsistent and hence her answer unreliable) and the content and structure of her answer "betraying" her. On the contrary, it is the inconsistency of her answer—or what I prefer to call the tension between the structure and content of her answer—that is most significant. My "awareness" of the internal dynamic of her answer, of the external dynamic of the interview (how I might not have been just a male researcher but a particular kind of man and audience), and of the broader social and cultural dynamic pertaining to "mothers" that Aida might be said to be engaging enables me to see the mechanisms involved in her construction and presentation of herself. We could see how Aida's identity is socially implicated, how the self she has cultivated is asserted in relation to her past and to people around her, and to how it is presented to others such as me, according to how Aida thinks it strategically appropriate to present it.

Aida's construction of herself as a mother being bound up with work is linked to her past, to a vow she made as a young woman oppressed by poverty and by others because of it. For ten years she worked as a domestic helper first in Singapore when she was only 19 years old then in Hong Kong, where she met her husband. To earn some extra money, she sold small items to fellow Filipinos and cleaned the flats of expatriates in Hong Kong. Even then, she said, she had always been driven to work, to extricate herself from an abject existence. Before, her very own relatives did not want to have anything to do with her and her family because of how poor they were.

> Before, he just passed by, in his car, not saying anything to you because of how impoverished we were. [. . .] They now greet you because you have something. [. . .] Those who treated us badly, they now even come here to our house. Once, my mother went to them to borrow some rice but they never gave her any. They even said, 'why, is this a rice mill where you could borrow rice from? Go ask at the rice mill.' [. . .] I now have plenty of relatives, plenty.

The "history" of Aida's desire to work helps us better appreciate why her being and becoming a mother and her identity as a woman might be defined less by the actual work she did to take care of her children than by providing for them. This is a specific aspect of motherhood that comes into conflict with the more traditional aspect of performing care work and which has also posed some problems for the quality of time she can give her husband. More importantly, her insistence that she make as much money as she did, if not more than, when she was a migrant worker in Hong Kong, that she make use of her time not doing anything at home to make money has made her relationship with her husband conflict-filled. Her view that she should profit from her time is her version of the employed mother's conception of their salary as back-up income. What is more, Aida's version involves profiting from the circulation of her money, circulation that involves her engaging in commercial and business activities that demand that she is out of the house a lot and at times that can be gruelling (10:30 p.m. every day to supervise her food retail business). Working up to such late times, she said, is what she wants and needs to do; as a workaholic, she needs to be busy. She said she found just being at home doing nothing unbearable.

THE RATIONALITY AND RELATIONALITY OF *ISU PAY*

Provided with moral justification through *isu pay,* the women's continued working, set against the insecurity of their husband's employment, turns the gendered moral issue of mothers being in work on its head. In their case, the proper question becomes: "how could we not work?" *Isu pay* points to multiple relationalities at play between the women and their husband; their working and caring; and *isu pay* and the discourse of "the good of the family."

Isu pay and the negotiation of gender relations

Isu pay is a form of argument, a rationalization that the women creatively and strategically use to remain working and earn a living. By emphasizing how the money they make functions as back-up income, the negotiation of gender relations particularly around their working is re-oriented as about the collective good of the family rather than about what husband or wife should be doing. Hence, the issue becomes more than just what responsibilities properly belong to each based on a gendered division of labor. Resource provision for the entire family is a cause around which wives have a good chance of rallying their husbands (see also Chant 2003). Paid work, which takes the mother away from the home, is reconstituted into a form of care provision, a process that also underlies how migrant mothers have justified their absence due to overseas migration (D McKay 2007).

Isu pay and the negotiation of caring and working responsibilities

Isu pay links to women's notion of giving their families some financial security by hanging on to jobs that provided them with a monthly income. This income is set against the insecurity of their husband's employment. Their contractual work left them with months of relying on saved money since during these months the men were unemployed. The impact on the family of not having any other source of income is severe and families could end up accumulating debts. *Isu pay,* therefore, is a strategic and moral imagination, of reckoning the horizon and ensuring that especially during the time of their husband's unemployment, the family did not unnecessarily get plunged into difficulties. Women in paid employment used this sense of *isu pay* to formulate and justify a gendered moral rationality for hanging on to their jobs despite being asked by their husbands to give them up.

Closely related to this sense of *isu pay* as strategically oriented is its sense of the temporal. It is about anticipating the future, toward ensuring that certain things are prevented from happening, events that have vital consequences on the family. If families, for example, are left in debt, it sets the family back in its desire to advance economically, to move up. Debt means a temporal delay in many of their plans such as finishing building their house or some other important undertaking.

Isu pay as a discourse of family well-being

It is quite clear that the strategic use of *isu pay* to negotiate gender relations and to reconcile women's responsibilities by providing a moral rationality to their choices points to a broader social discourse within which *isu pay* is in fact put to use. Above, I referred to how *isu pay* reframes the issue of the gendered roles of men and women in a family into one about provision, provision that is principally about ensuring the security and stability of the family. To be sure, this made the women important because although their husband was the family's main earner, they, too, were also depended upon. Their identity and sense of self-importance engendered by their work, however, simultaneously derived their salience from how this work functioned for the family. In this sense, the personal is at once familial.

CONCLUSION

From a moral rationality perspective, I examined how the cultural discourse of *isu pay* constituted the women's moral rationalization of, one, their active participation in earning a living and, two, their negotiation of spousal expectations about what they should be doing as wives and mothers. How working women deployed *isu pay* reveals their conception of their self as at once and simultaneously social; their sense of self points to a mode of practice that is always relational. They justified continuing in their work by framing it within an obligation to protect and ensure the welfare of the family. For example, they cannot engage in preparing for the future of their children when they are too preoccupied with the family's daily needs and paying off debts as a result of giving up work and the husband's unemployment. The women's use of *isu pay* as moral rationality is oriented toward breaking a cycle of relying on borrowed money, of living off debt. One cannot invest or have enough money left for huge expenditures such as college tuition fees for several children if all that can be guaranteed is the present.

Providing for the present and future of the family is not just the task or responsibility of men as breadwinners. With no recourse to public resources (such as unemployment allowance to tide them over), which in the first place are not available, *isu pay* enables the women to make up for the absence or lack of state assistance in the survival of families and the reproduction of family and broader social relationships. Giving up their steady source of income was something the women, except for one, could not countenance as it constituted a dereliction of their duty as wives and mothers. For these mothers who work or are earning a living, being a parent-mother and a worker are not two oppositional and irreconcilable roles (Garey 1999) and *isu pay* enables the women to "weave" together "home" and "work" (14). It points to a move away from gender dichotomy toward gender complementarity (Tsing 1993), one in which the women develop a gendered subjectivity that enables them to be both wives-mothers who care and who earn. *Isu pay* could be seen as both a moral and strategic justification that interrogates the allocation of spousal and parental responsibility according to masculinist gender ideology. It becomes a powerful justification for reorienting the issue of women being in work away from being merely about what husband and wives do in separate spheres to an issue concerning what both husband and wife should be doing jointly and collaboratively.

CHAPTER 8

PANAGBUKBUKOD AND RELATIONAL AUTONOMY

Being a wife is not just a status one assumes with the act of contracting marriage. Aside from bringing with it responsibilities and obligations, it also involves becoming part of a new web of relationships. These new, affinal relations need careful negotiation. Although in-law relationships with the wife's father (Nydegger 1986) and siblings of either spouse (Silverstein 1990) have also been characterized as problematic, it is the relationship between daughter-in-law and mother-in-law that is traditionally seen as conflict-filled (Brown 2004; Kandiyoti 1988; Vlahoutsikou 1997; Wolf 1972). Kandiyoti (1988, 279) describes as one of "deprivation and hardship" the experiences of a new bride in a patriarchally extended family in North Africa, the Muslim Middle East (plus Turkey, Pakistan, and Iran), South Asia (India) and East Asia (China). The new bride's subservience and submission to the authority of her mother-in-law will end when she herself becomes a mother-in-law who will impose the same asymmetrical power relation that had defined her life as a wife. Brown, who refers to a "mother-in-law belt" extending from the Mediterranean to the Pacific, provides the following ideal-typical description of the relationship between the two women: "At marriage the wife enters into a life of servitude and is expected to be obedient, submissive and stoic in the face of gratuitous mistreatment, both psychological and physical, until she becomes a mother-in-law herself" (2004, 168).

Kandiyoti (1988) has referred to the negotiation that women do to secure or preserve their positions and well-being within existing patriarchal arrangements as "bargaining with patriarchy." In the classic patriarchy that Kandiyoti examines, this entails women in patriarchally extended families internalizing patriarchal ideology as a strategy for achieving security in old age. Because such security is guaranteed through their sons, mothers-in-law work hard to ensure that their sons' primary allegiance is to them and in making their sons' love for their wives secondary (1988). In this account, the conflictual relationship that pits the two women in competition to secure their position is created in a system of relations and values where they are clearly subordinated. While they maneuver for individual power within the family, they entrench and perpetuate the system of gender relations that valorize male privilege and keep the women dependent on men (Shih and Pyke 2010). Marilyn Strathern (1988) rightly reminds us to interrogate assumptions that the gender identity "woman" is the position and perspective from which women will always speak (Tsing 1993, 33).

The seafarers' wives' project for autonomy provides a case that offers an account of how daughters-in-law, who reside virilocally, come to exercise authority, an account that differs from that provided, for example, in Kandiyoti (1988). The account provided here of how the wives become autonomous yet remain relational relies on a non-deterministic conception of the relationship between mothers- and daughters-in-law; that is, they are not characters whose actions have been predetermined by patrilineal ideology (Collier 1974, 92–94; see also Shih and Pyke 2010). This chapter highlights the empowering potential for daughters-in-law of the negotiation of the unequal relationship between daughters-in-law and mothers-in-law, which appears not to have been systematically examined as studies have primarily focused on how the conflict between the two women has served as a barrier to female solidarity (Vlahoutsikou, 1997). I frame my examination of the autonomy project of daughters-in-law within the quotidian, material, and affective practices of living together in order to explicate the dynamics of gender, generational hierarchy, family life, and kinship relations that inform the autonomy and agency that daughters-in-law achieve.

This chapter conceptualizes three major aspects that mark the process, indeed the project, of becoming autonomous, what the women referred to as *panagbukbukod. Panagbukbukod,* which means independence or autonomy, comes from the word *bukod,* the same root for *bukodmo amin* (or *bukbukodam*), the state of being on one's own overburdened with responsibility that I discussed in chapter 3. First, for some of the wives, autonomy begins with breaking their silence/talking back in the face of mistreatment from their mothers-in-law and in the context of a strong cultural injunction to respect one's in-laws. The second looks into how this autonomy is linked to their becoming their husband's recipient of his remittances, a dynamic shaped by how the Philippine state has regulated the remittances of Filipino seafarers. The last examines how the women's autonomy is linked to having their own house. Indeed, finding a voice and becoming the designated recipient of their husband's remittances might be said to find their concretization in having a house of their own. To that extent, it is the logical extension of finding a voice, of a voice finding its own dwelling and abode. Finally, by examining through the lens of kinship as relatedness how the women's autonomy project is embedded in intersubjective, particularly affine, relations, the chapter argues for retaining normativity as an integral part of the conceptualization of kinship as relatedness (Miller 2007).

SEAFARING, KINSHIP, AND WOMEN WHO STAY BEHIND

The women's location and experiences within their husband's family had been profoundly shaped by how Filipino kinship is established. It is bilaterally extended; that is, kinship is reckoned from both the mother's and father's sides following both vertical (e.g. grandparents) and horizontal (e.g. cousins) structures of accounting relatives. This system of reckoning blood relations is also followed in establishing affinal relations, which are extended to the entire kin group of the spouse: "the husband's and the wife's uncles, aunts and grandparents are *agabalayan* [in-law] to each other . . . the *agabalayan* relation has the weight of real kinship" (Jocano 1982, 41). Thus, when wives moved into their husband's family's house, they negotiated the structural and cultural implications of these relationships on their lives and behavior, particularly so if their husband was surrounded by neighbors who were his relatives. Although data from this study show a preponderance for virilocal residence (37 out of 60 women moved into their husband's family's house), in Philippine kinship there is no preference for either virilocal or uxorilocal residence (Go 1993).[1] Consequently, the rigid and hierarchical relations that characterize the mother-in-law/daughter-in-law relationship within patriarchally extended families (Kandiyoti 1988) do not have the force of an unavoidable social law in Filipino society since a new couple can choose to live with the woman's natal family.

In the Ilocos Region, a nuclear household is considered the basic socioeconomic unit. Couples are expected to establish their own household after marriage, although this may be delayed until after the birth of the couple's first child (Nydegger and Nydegger 1966). The composition of Ilokano households is flexible such that it is very common to have other consanguines and affines as part of the household (Jocano 1982; Nagasaka 1999). Due mainly to economic difficulties, couples are not able to establish neolocal residence soon after their first child is born and so continue to live with their families until they have built their own house, which could take years to achieve. Labor migration, specifically seafaring, has been the principal way for the research participants' husbands to realize this goal.

Seafarers' work—characterized by insecurity and long periods of unemployment in between contracts—has shaped the temporality and spatiality of the lives of the women. Their husbands' employment onboard ships in the international fleet meant that not only did the women live with their mother-in-law but also, even more critically, that they lived with her without their husband for long periods of time. The women therefore had to deal with the difficulties of living with in-laws on their own and without the help of the person they considered their ally. Their husband's period of unemployment between contracts, which could last for several months, has significant financial implications on their family's lives and capacity to save enough money to build their own house.[2]

As detailed below, while living with their husband's family and in proximity to many of his relatives, the wives were compelled by a strong socio-cultural norm to respect their in-laws. And as the one who moved into the house, they, particularly those who were not in paid employment, felt an expectation to serve their husband's family by, for example, being the first to get up in the morning to cook and clean. Most of the wives reported that their residential arrangement had their movement monitored and freedom curtailed. Some suffered mistreatment from their mothers-in-law whose actions included gossiping about them, verbal abuse, and attempts to ruin their marriage. Analyzing how this intimacy of conflict constituted the agency and autonomy of the wives not only shows how the wives suffered in unequal relations of power but also illuminates the ways that this conflict can be empowering as it provided the impetus for them to assert themselves. Framing it within kinship, particularly affinal relationships, will help clarify "the material and emotional ways that individuals are intimately involved with each other and the negotiated aspects of relatedness" (Van Vleet 2002, 568). It will also reveal the given principles (Miller 2007) that underpin this relationship and that constitute its negotiation, particularly the asymmetries (Van Vleet 2003; Vera-Sanso 1999; Vlahoutsikou 1997) that define and undergird it.

In his work on migration and cultures of relatedness in a Philippine village, a work firmly framed within Southeast Asian kinship, Filomeno Aguilar (2009a) points out an important insight made by Janet Carsten on how anthropological studies of kinship that have looked at it as structure have concentrated on its "positive and harmonious aspects," neglecting the fact that it is also about "disconnection and disjunction" (2000, 24) as well as "differentiation, hierarchy, exclusion, and abuse" (2013, 247). Carsten (2000, 1) writes that although the social, material, and affective connections of people to others "can be described in genealogical terms," there are other ways of accounting for how these connections are established and maintained. She conceptualizes kinship as cultures of relatedness (Carsten 2000, 2007, 2013). "Cultures of relatedness" looks at kinship as lived experience rather than as structure or system of classification (Carsten 2007, 3; see also Finch and Mason 2000, ch. 7). Kinship, as relatedness, relies for its construction on everyday practices—"small, seemingly trivial, or taken-for-granted acts like sharing a meal, giving a dish of cooked food to a neighbour, dropping in to a nearby house for a quiet chat" (Carsten 2000, 18). Looking at kinship as practices of relatedness highlights kinship's processuality (Aguilar 2009a; Carsten 2000). This is particularly salient for the Philippines, a country with over ten million of its citizens—comprising around ten percent of its population—living and working overseas.

The separation of family members due to international migration has significantly shaped the ways and practices that those who stay behind and those who are away sustain relationships. The performance of obligations and provision of care have to be adjusted with corresponding consequences on family and kin ties and relationships (Aguilar 2009a; Parreñas 2005). The separation also presents new challenges for members to face, exacerbates existing problems in marital or affinal relationships (see Pingol 2001), and provides or intensifies the conditions for problems in relationships to become more visible as the case of seafarer wives will show. This negative side of kinship can be attended to by conceptualizing kinship as relatedness as it pays attention to the practices and actions, both positive and negative, that people do to shape, sustain, assert, or even ruin relationships (Aguilar 2009a; Carsten 2000).

The conceptualization of kinship as process and practices, however, sets aside, as Miller (2007) has noted, aspects of relationships and how they are negotiated that remain dependent on norms, principles, and codes of behavior. Studies of Filipino family and kinship in the 1970s noted this processuality. For example, Mendez noted that "although there is a definite structural kinship pattern . . . in practice reciprocal behaviour and comradeship often determine the feelings of closeness" (1974, 65). Nevertheless, commenting on the impact of internal migration on family and kinship ties, Mendez notes the resilience of kinship structure as basis of relationships. "Geographical distance and consequent loss of face-to-face relationships is no barrier to spiritual, emotional, and financial ties. Family structure remains intact" (42). Studies of Philippine kinship particularly in the context of transnational migration that have used the prism of relatedness (Aguilar 2009a, 2009b) have not explicitly incorporated how sociocultural norms and principles continue to shape relationships and their negotiation (Miller 2007) despite them implicitly underpinning the analyses offered. Aguilar, the main proponent of looking at Filipino kinship as ties of relatedness, however, implicitly acknowledges the continuing salience of these norms in his more recent work on siblingship (2013). Nagasaka's study of the processuality, flexibility, and ambiguity of kinship in the context of the experiences of children from an Ilocos village growing up in a transnational family shows that "normative discourses on family, parent-child and mother-child relationships" remain important (2015, 22). As the experiences of the seafarers' wives will show, kinship retains elements of expectations of how one should behave toward in-laws such that their relationship with their mothers-in-law and the practices that informed it were shaped by normative understandings of daughters-in-law's "proper behavior" toward their mothers-in-law.

My discussion of relational autonomy and its negotiation within affine relations draw on the perspective of daughters-in-law, and especially those who lived with their mothers-in-law. It does not include the perspectives of husbands and mothers-in-law. My informal conversations with husbands revealed that their wife's relationship with their own mother was not a subject they were willing to discuss, excusing themselves by pointing out that they were away most of the time and "did not really know what was going on." Except in one case of a daughter-in-law and mother-in-law who had a warm and pleasant relationship, I did not talk to the mothers-in-law for ethical reasons. Interviewing both of them had the potential to further strain the relationship between the two women. It would have put the daughters-in-law in a difficult position. It was possible that they would think that what they shared would feed into my questions to their mothers-in-law. Furthermore, mothers-in-law would have probably also thought that my questions were based on what their daughters-in-law had shared with me. Clearly, the fact that the women lived in the same house made interviewing both of them extremely difficult and ethically problematic. Indeed, asking the women about their relationship with their mothers-in-law made them uncomfortable because we were in their in-laws' house. The interview took into account the presence in the house of the mothers-in-law who, despite not being within hearing distance, made the women feel uncomfortable talking about their relationship with them. Several times I was asked to assure the participants that what they were going to say would remain confidential and proceeded to talk in a lowered voice. Truly, the place of residence and the "haunting" presence of their mothers-in-law had significant consequences on the women's freedom of expression.

BREAKING THEIR SILENCE/TALKING BACK

> When it is genuine, when it is born of the need to speak, no one can stop the human voice. When denied a mouth, it speaks with the hands or the eyes, or the pores, or anything at all.
>
> —Eduardo Galeano, "Celebration of the Human Voice/2"

Every one of the wives spoke of a cultural expectation to show respect to their parents-in-law. Such expectation originates in the inculcation among young children of respect for parents, other older relatives, and generally any older person. Article 357 of the Civil Code of the Philippines, arguably a codification of Filipino social and cultural values, explicitly instructs children to obey and honor their parents and to respect their grandparents and old relatives (Pangalangan 1995, 21). In fact, many of the wives who lived with their in-laws stated that if they were taught since they were young to respect their parents and other elders, even more respect is to be shown their in-laws. They may disrespect their own parents but never their in-laws. This was cogently expressed by Jessica, 33 years old, who used to live with her in-laws but who now lives in a house that shares a wall with her in-laws: "Your in-laws mark the limits of your propriety and respect. You can talk back to your parents but not your in-laws. If you do not show respect to your in-laws, then you really are shameless."

Jessica's statement reveals the close affinity between respect and shame in Ilocos society. To show respect is to exercise *bain* (shame), that is, for one's actions to be guided by a deep sense of propriety (see also Torres-Mejia 2000, 141). When the women married, they (and their husbands) were fully aware of this cultural injunction and would have always treaded carefully not to disrespect or offend their parents-in-law. This was particularly true of wives who went on to live with their husband's family and came under the close watch of their mothers-in-law. Respect, and its inculcation, function as a disciplinary practice by which children and adults learn to police their own selves. It acts as a cultural and social force that makes people watch how they behave, what they say and the tone in which they say it. It is a way by which parents and elders could exercise authority and perpetuate hierarchy. This cultural premium placed on respect compelled the women to suffer in silence; indeed, it might be argued to be tacitly founded on a culture of silence. Many of the wives who lived and were living with their mothers-in-law endured mistreatment and initially suffered in silence. Gina and Marissa illustrate this.

Gina: "Bad Words"

"I just kept quiet. When it became too much, that's when I talked back. Super. I really had a row with her [mother-in-law]. I couldn't stop what came out of my mouth. They were really bad words, because I was just in my room, not saying anything. She even dragged in my family, saying things about my family. I have had too much, so I just, you know, even if my husband was there, it was good my husband was around. He tried to cover my mouth, 'that's enough!,' he said. Then he turned to her, 'it's your fault mama, she wasn't even saying a single word yet you kept on and on and on there,' he said."

Gina relates that living with her mother-in-law included suffering from verbal abuse, constant monitoring of her activities, invading her own life (her mother-in-law would shout to tell her to take her birth control pills and not to have too many children, which she found infantilizing—"as though I did not have a mind of my own"). She was, in her own words, being controlled.

Marissa: "I Became Shameless and Disrespectful"

"But I learned to talk back. [. . .] Then, I did not know how to talk back, I did not know how to fight back. But when I realized . . . why should I allow it, why should I be oppressed? Why do I not fight for myself when in fact I can? That's how I learned. You know, my behavior now, like I have become shameless. [. . .] I really don't want to be treated lowly. . . what I want is when something is said to me, I confront the person. [. . .] My mother-in-law, when she says something like that, I really talk back. Before, I was never capable of talking back to her. But because they themselves taught me. She tells me, 'you are shameless.' 'It's you who taught me,' I tell her. 'When I moved in to this house,' I say, 'did you hear me say anything? No. Did you hear me talk back? No.' [. . .] 'You are shameless and disrespectful.' 'I am shameless and disrespectful because of you. I learned to talk back because of you. If I don't fight for myself, you mean to say you'll just trample on me, you'll just step on me?' I said."

The sheer need to defend herself pushed Marissa to speak out. Yet, we can also see the force of the cultural injunction to respect one's in-laws in her characterization of her becoming assertive as turning into a disrespectful woman.

Talking back was a critical first step in the assertion and development of identity and agency and a crucial beginning in the women's exercise of power and in addressing the asymmetries of power relations in which they frequently found themselves. Gina's breaking her silence was a point of no return. It was this experience that made her want to move out of her mother-in-law's house where she felt she could not breathe (*para kang hindi makahinga*). Marissa's talking back was a defiant and belligerent act, shocking her mother-in-law by the force of her assertiveness and new-found confidence. Her mother-in-law could only say Marissa was *natangsit* (arrogant and disrespectful), thereby exposing an expectation for her to be meek. Both women demonstrate that there is a limit to their being respectful. From their talking back emerged a sound, the sound of the women's voice breaking the prison-house of respect and the splintering of an old self giving way to a new one. Experienced by the wives as liberating, talking back was a defiant act precisely because it meant becoming freed from an ideological and cultural doctrine that valued silence understood as obedience, submission, subservience.

BECOMING THE ALLOTTEE

After marriage, women, specifically those who lived with their husband's family, did not automatically become the recipient (allottee) of their husband's remittances (allotment). The Philippine state, through Executive Order Number 857 issued by President Marcos in December 1982, made it mandatory for overseas contract workers to remit regularly 50 to 80 percent of their income through the Philippine banking system (Aguilar 2003). Seafarers, however, had no choice since their salaries were paid by manning agencies based in Manila. This regulation compelled unmarried seamen to designate a beneficiary who, more often than not, was their mother. Both state and familial obligations ensured that the mother became the "legal" recipient of her son's allotment. Women who moved into their husband's family had to live with this arrangement in place. Six women who lived or used to live with their mothers-in-law waited for at least two years before they became their husband's beneficiary. This, however, did not stop their husband's financial support for their mother or natal family, which the wives perfectly understood.

Getting their husband to have them replace their mother-in-law as the allottee was, however, fraught with conflict. The women asserted that as wives, they should be the beneficiary and that this was an important component of their position within their own family and status as wives. As Gina said:

"Because in [my husband's] first and second contracts, it was they [who received the allotment]. He [her husband] himself decided to transfer it to me. But then still what my mother-in-law wanted to happen is I hold the bankbook but the account is in her name and her son. I hold the bankbook! [. . .] Seriously, who would agree to that? What woman will agree to such an arrangement?"

It is interesting to note how "allottee," the beneficiary or recipient of something, came to be translated as "alote," the object itself that was (to be) received. The person receiving and the object received became elided. However, the women I interviewed used the verb "nag-alote" to refer to their becoming the allottee; for example, "Idi nag-aloteakon" (literally, "when I became the allottee" or "when I started receiving the allotment"). When women said "idi nag-aloteak," they might be seen, at least symbolically, to be transforming a status or identity from one that is merely designated to one that is attained through a process of conversion. Viewed this way, there is a dynamic process by which the women identified with the money being received. They used "alote," a noun, to refer to the money but turned this noun into "nag-alote," a verb that might be argued to indicate both the process of their *becoming* the allottee and of their *being* the allottee.

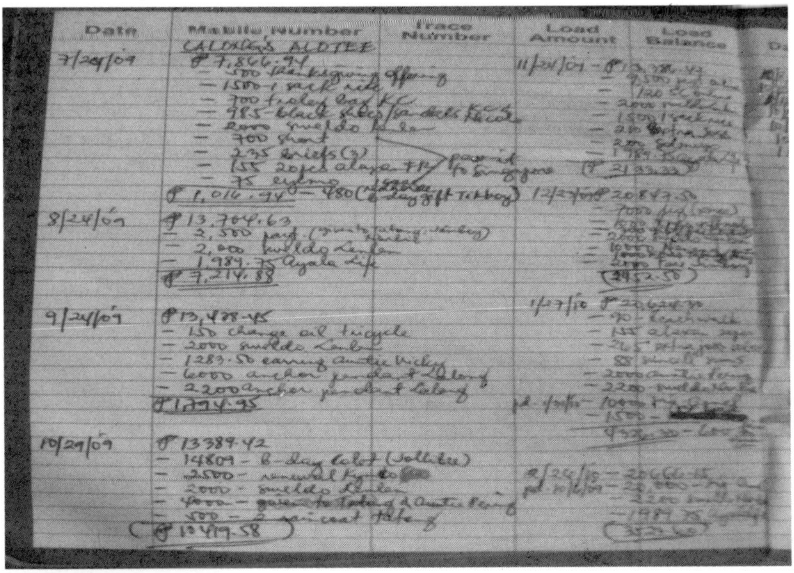

Figure 4. A wife's record book

The allotment was therefore as much about money as about what it symbolized. Aida, who did not live at all with her mother-in-law, shared that her mother-in-law, who has four other children working overseas, still asked for money from her husband. She recalled what her mother-in-law once said to other people and which reached her: that her son's affections were no longer hers. Aida's mother-in-law appreciated the money her son gave her not only on account of her financial need but also as proof she still had a place in her son's universe of affection. Most mothers, however, did not have other children to depend on and hence might have viewed their daughters-in-law as threatening their economic well-being.

Many Filipinos who take maritime-related courses come from rural and poor backgrounds (Amante 2005). They see working as a seafarer in the global maritime industry as a way to obtain a better life. If parents struggled through great financial difficulty to send them to school, it is with both a sense of duty and gladness that these seafarers support them once they start earning. Many of these seamen's mothers would have been unemployed and have only them to rely on especially in their old age. We can at least understand, however partially, why mothers would wish to remain as their son's beneficiary. It is also helpful to understand some of the husbands' initial hesitation to change their allottee from their mother to their wife within the context of *utang a naimbag a nakem* (debt of gratitude), which informs the sense of obligation these seafarers have for their parents, siblings, and members of their extended family. A moral character undergirds the sons' fulfilment of their kin obligations (see also Finch 1989). A seaman refusing to extend financial help to his family would be seen as neglecting or abandoning them. The seamen's wives knew this well and they themselves helped their families. The issue is they were at the mercy of their mothers-in-law.

Wives who lived with their mothers-in-law who acted as conduit for their husband's monthly remittances recalled how very little freedom they had even in the way they spent their money. Laura, for example, uses the word *pinapakialaman* (meddled with and dictated upon) to describe her experience. Marissa shared how her mother-in-law constantly reminded her how to spend her son's money. When she finally became her husband's beneficiary, her mother-in-law maneuvered to cause Marissa and her husband to separate. Even wives who did not live with their mothers-in-law suffered as a result of becoming the allottee. Nancy, who lived just across the street from her in-laws, recalled how her relations with them (not just her mother-in-law) progressively soured and became unpleasant when she started receiving allotment. Mothers-in-law's desire to be the recipient of their child's remittances has also been shown among men married to migrant women. Pingol (2001), for example, reveals how mothers-in-law fabricated stories against their sons-in-law to gain sole access to the fruits of their daughter's migrant labor. This not only ruined the relationship between sons- and mothers-in-law but also drove a wedge between stay-behind husband and migrant wife.

The wives becoming the allottee brings up the issue of the degree of control they had in spending their allotment. This appears to be bounded. First, they did not have to consult their husband when it came to money allotted for family expenditures: food, children's clothes, school expenses, and others that had anything to do with the provision for the needs of the family. However, a few women reported feelings of discomfort when it came to buying items for themselves. Some of the women, particularly those who were unemployed and were therefore completely dependent on their husband, said that the way they spent money was informed by the sense that "it is not their money." They absolutely had no problems spending for the needs of the family because it was not for them personally but really for the children. Also, they had clear agreement with their husbands that their allotment (or monthly allowance) is for the maintenance of the family. Women were also therefore uneasy when neighbors or friends borrowed money from them, particularly when it involved fairly large sums. Second, major projects and purchases were made in consultation with the husband or when the husband was home to make the purchase himself.

Women who were employed seemed to have greater say as to where money would go and, because they also contributed to the family coffers, did not feel frivolous if they bought items for themselves. However, once husbands had made up their mind about the purchase of, for example, a car, there was very little that wives could do to change their mind. Feminist analyses of the household indicate that how resources are allocated and who allocates them depend on cultural notions of gender (Busby 2000, 187). For the seamen's wives, it is the fact that in all but two cases, the men were the main or sole earners, which consequently gave them more power to determine where to spend the money. Although most of the women said that their husbands did not interfere with how they spent for the needs of the family, this tends to demonstrate the gendered association between the women and the responsibility of looking after the family. Two women who earned just as much as or more than their husbands did exercise considerably more control of and authority over the family's finances. My empirical data would thus suggest that a factor that informs the dynamic governing the management of resources, the allotment, is the level of direct financial contribution the women made to the family's finances.

Notwithstanding the dynamic that underpins the freedom the women had to spend their husbands' remittance, becoming their husbands' beneficiary gave the women a sense of control, one that gave them both symbolic and material purchase on power. This boosted their position in a house in which they felt under their mother-in-law's authority. Becoming the recipient of their husband's allotment peeled away one layer of the structures of power they had to negotiate. Their mother-in-law ceased to exist as the mediator through which their monthly financial support passed. It made it untenable for their mother-in-law to tell them how to spend their son's money. It confirms and affirms the primacy of the conjugal relationship over that of the parent-son bond (Vlahoutsikou 1997). Becoming the allottee therefore restructured the ties that bound them, ties both hierarchical and affective that strengthened and reinforced spousal relationship. Mothers-in-law might have perceived this as marginalizing them both affectively and materially. This demonstrates, as Van Vleet (2002, 578) has noted, how the "affective and economic relationship between a mother- and daughter-in-law is intertwined with the structural relationship and more general system of values that shapes the relationships between parents and children." The restructuring of the relationships between parents and children, specifically adult children no longer coming under the authority of parents is established most clearly by the married couple having their own house (see also Aguilar 2013).

THE SOCIAL AND INDIVIDUAL SIGNIFICANCE OF A HOUSE

The social and individual meaning and significance of a house has been widely examined particularly in anthropology. As Aguilar (2009a) has summarized, much of the literature has focused on how the house and its construction is the focal point of kin and social relations, how it validates and strengthens social and individual identities and statuses and affirms filial obligations (Aguilar 2009a, 2009b; Carsten 1995; Carsten and Jones-Hughes 1995; Grigolini 2005). This section broadly shares this concern, but my strategy highlights the social significance of the house by underscoring how it matters especially to daughters-in-law who moved residence virilocally. To get a better sense of what living in their own house meant to women who lived with their in-laws, it is instructive to first briefly look at what owning and living in their own house meant to women who lived with their natal family.

The House as Declaration of Independence

Two women who lived with their natal family yet have begun building their own houses cited as reason their desire to be independent for doing so. One explained that living in her own house would teach her what it is like to be a wife, to be a mother, to be in charge. She wanted to experience what it was like to be concerned with what was missing in the house and not have her mother do the worrying for her. Maribel explained that having her own house would enable her and her husband to know what it was like to have and raise a family of and on their own. So while her children were still young and had fewer things to worry about, she and her husband have begun what for many is a long process of building a house. They knew that once the children went to college or university, money was going to be tight and building a house much more difficult.

Men, even more so, wanted to prove their capacity to be "padre de familia," one that is boosted by the fact that they were earning well. A wife who initially lived in her husband's family house but later on had a small house of their own built on her husband's family's compound said that her husband refused to build a more permanent and bigger one where their house now stood. She shared that if her husband was to build one, it would have to be on a piece of land he owned. Her husband not only wanted to avoid future problems arising from the division of property when his parents died. He also wanted to prove that in due time, he would be able to buy his own piece of land. Her husband linked his notion of independence from his parents not only on having his own house but also on building it outside of his parents' property and on his own. Men who moved into their wives' family also felt that they could not move and act freely. As Lilia said of her husband, he had their house built so he would have the power and freedom to do as he pleased.

The House as a Tangible (Sign of a Better life)

In contrast to the women and man discussed above, Dolores was not concerned about independence since she lived near her husband's family, not with them. Her house was not a declaration of personal independence; it was more invested with social significance.

Dolores, her family, and her mother used to live in a small hut, its walls and floor made from bamboo slats, its roof from palm leaves. The house they presently lived in was built by dint of her own determination. She recalled telling her husband that she wanted to have their old hut replaced with a concrete house and that he asked her how could she when there was no money. By that time, however, she had scrimped long enough to have set aside enough money to have it built. This surprised even her husband. Dolores was (and is) understandably proud of her achievement; she herself helped build the house. She said that her children liked their father more because they saw her as tight-fisted and he, generous. But as she said, had she not been tight-fisted, they would not have their house.

For Dolores, her family's house did not only stand as a concrete manifestation of her frugality. For her, it was important that the money her husband made be put to something concrete and tangible. This philosophy to use money for something tangible (*tapno adda pakakitkitaan*; literally, so you have something to see it in) is common among people in San Gabriel. For Dolores, too, the house was her way of showing that they had a better life, one provided by seafaring. The house is a living and inhabited memorial not only to her frugality but also to her husband's labor. Occupying a place of honor in her living room wall was a framed picture of her husband and his ship.

Nancy, whose biographical narrative opened chapter I of this book, attributes the start a harmonious life for her and her family to her husband's effort to start building their own house. Where before her husband was a womanizer and a profligate, the project of building a house set him to the straight and narrow path. The "housing project" made him a better and more responsible husband and father, a transformation that coincided with him becoming better at husbanding his earnings. Rather than waste money through drinking, gambling, and extramarital affairs, the money was invested into something tangible that physically and figuratively symbolized their family's more settled status.

Lilia, whose family initially lived on their own in her family house, explained that living in her own gave her a sense of security, peace of mind as well as pride in that their house was the product of their own hard work.

The House for the Oppressed Daughter-in-Law

In the first section of this chapter, I talked about women finding their own voice, a voice directed against their mother-in-law and about how it was the beginning of a process of self-assertion. Before discussing what having their own house meant to women living with their mother-in-law, I wish to discuss first how the women described living with their mother-in-law.

Of the 37 women who used to live or are living with their in-laws, the case of Ruth is exceptional. She lives with her mother-in-law, Josefa, who herself is married to a seafarer. They used to live in separate houses in the same village but decided after facing some life-changing circumstances to live together. It was Josefa who asked Ruth to move to her house that was still being built. The relationship between the two women is characterized not by conflict but by interdependence. I interviewed Ruth in 2015 with Josefa around who would contribute every now and then to the conversation. Josefa also agreed to be interviewed but eventually became shy and nervous so I only had informal conversations with her. People who know Ruth and Josefa also commented on their close relationship, noting how they have helped each other. As the teacher who referred Ruth to me said, "agkadkaduada latta," that is, "they are inseparable, always together."

I asked Ruth if the fact that they were both married to seafarers was a factor in how they have built such a healthy interdependent relationship. Ruth acknowledged that this helped them to understand many of the things that they are going through but also explained that her mother-in-law, despite the many years, still finds being alone difficult. She prefers having a companion. This is not to suggest that Josefa had not developed a sense of self-efficacy necessary to survive the life of a stay-behind woman for she has successfully raised a family during which her husband was away most of the time. Her children had given her companionship and provided a center of her life that steadied her, but this center is gone as her children have started their own families. Josefa herself alluded to this when she said that living with Ruth and her children was better than being on her own and that it enabled her to help look after her grandchildren. Ruth acknowledged that Laura provided, aside from care help, financial assistance when Ruth was financially tight, as well as a house to live.

For most of the women, however, living with their in-laws was generally unpleasant. Marivic shared that she would just keep quiet when her in-laws spanked her six-year old son even if she felt it was not their place to do so. She described her mode of living with them as "agpapaigid," that is, staying at the margins or not being in any one's way. Grace, who described what she felt like when her husband was coming home, effectively described her life with her mother-in-law:

> "You are excited it's like you will now have an ally. [. . .] You'll feel comfortable because he's there, you can smile really beautifully. You will be able to laugh. But if he's not around, nothing, you'll be very quiet. It's as though even your breathing is not free, like it's really hard to breathe."

Grace's use of the word *kakampi,* ally, alludes to conflicts in the house. Living with her mother-in-law is like living with enemies. Her husband's return meant she could smile again, that she could breathe freely again.

House and Freedom

Women who lived with their in-laws saw having their own house as giving them the possibility and actuality for self-determination, the ability to control things in their families that otherwise would have been difficult to do had they continued living with others.

"You can cook and eat what you want."

For some of the women, living with their in-laws meant a re-education of their palates. As the *naikamang* (the one who moved in to the family) and as a daughter-in-law, some of them felt obliged to help cook. This was particularly the case for women who did not have a separate arrangement for cooking; in other words, they were not a separate household. If they cooked and ate from the same pot (*agkakabanga*), then the women would have offered to cook. This meant they had to learn to cook the way their in-laws did. Getting their *templa* (how they wanted their food to taste) was very important. This was both a time and process when wives adjusted their own taste buds, if not "re-educated" them. In some cases, women adjusted not only to how food was prepared but also to the preferred food of the family. This limited their preparation of their own preferences.

"You can control your expenditures better."

A number of women cited the strain put on their budgets by living with others. This was true also of women who lived with their own natal families. For women who lived with their in-laws and who already had the issue of allotment to contend with, expenses for food and utility bills added to the things they had to carefully manage. When women tightened their belts according to their financial situation, their mothers-in-law made negative remarks, which reached them through other people. This was what happened to Grace, and her mother-in-law's gossiping about her "not buying adequate food" motivated her to have separate cooking arrangements. Becoming a separate household was a first step toward having more control of how much the family spent. This mattered a lot to the women because it also meant that they could save more.

The time their husbands were unemployed between contracts loomed large in their horizon. Jessica's mother-in-law's remarks about her not buying enough food for everyone (which Jessica took as a veiled accusation of her not including his husband's natal family in her groceries) motivated her to put pressure on her husband to build a small house that shared a wall with her mother-in-law's house. Mothers-in-law who have ceased to be their son's allottee might be seen to use gossip to compel their daughter-in-law to share resources. The gossiping indicates tensions in the relationship between the two women and mothers-in-law resort to it to maintain or gain access to material resources. Thus, gossip is used as a way of continuing to exert influence (Wert and Salovey 2004) over spending or money that mothers-in-law used to have more power over.

"You have more privacy."

Many of the women appreciated a certain amount of privacy, particularly those who lived with their in-laws and who shared a house with the families of their husband's siblings. Indeed, there were a number of women who lived with two or three other families aside from their in-laws. Grace's description of her living arrangements illustrates what usually happens when multiple families or households live in a single house. Grace said that the only space her whole family could consider "their own" was the room where they slept. However, it did not have a door; all it had was a flimsy curtain which she herself had put. The children of the other couples freely went in and out of the room, even when she would have wanted to rest or have a *siesta* with her children.

Certainly, these women's desire for more privacy arose from the fact that they shared the house with other families. There were many people and situations to deal with as well as dynamics of relationships shaped by differing ages, hierarchies, personalities, and temperaments. Misunderstandings, tensions and conflicts were built into this kind of situation. Their own room, which many of them considered as their only place of refuge when a particularly difficult situation happened, could not even be completely closed off to others. Having their own house ensured their privacy and, although their rooms would have doors, there would not be as compelling a need to have a door with which to signify that that space was theirs and theirs only. They could just leave it open.

"You can do as you please."

Living with in-laws gave the women the feeling that they were monitored. As Grace said, "it's like someone is watching your every move, [. . .] like you are being monitored." Living in a house that was not theirs limited the freedom they enjoyed. They said, for example, that if they did not feel like washing the dishes just yet, they could not put off doing it. They felt compelled to behave according to "expectations," imagined or otherwise. As one wife said, having her own house would enable her to do as she pleased. Another said it would enable her to breathe. The women saw having their own house as their means of having the freedom to do as they pleased. As Mildred said: "if you had your own house, you could do what you want. If you lived in somebody else's house, you are embarrassed to even rest. You can just be idle if it was your own house. You can sleep if and when you want."

Related to this constraint on the sovereignty they had in terms of physical movement and in how they used their time is the freedom they had to entertain their own family members and friends. The feeling that they did not own the house affected how comfortable they felt regarding this issue. Marissa not only endured being treated badly by her mother-in-law but also seeing her own mother and sister disrespected. Her sister had helped her look after her children when she did her care-giving course.

> "When my sister came here, she [mother-in-law] told her to leave and to never come back. [. . .] I told my older sister, let it be but when I have my own house, I will try to utter those words to her so she will experience what I am going through, how it hurts to be told those words, I told my older sister."

Grace referred to how this freedom had liberating effects not only on her movement but also on her body: "Nothing in you tenses. . . . Because it is yours, you can move freely. You can do what you want to do."

A HOUSE OF THEIR OWN

For women who lived or were living with their in-laws, all of the experiences discussed above contributed to their desire to have their own house. Living in their own house was the beginning of these women's self-determination, when finally they were not dominated by their mothers-in-law. Women employed various ways to realize this. For example, Linda left her husband's family house where they had lived with her in-laws and did so while her husband was at sea without telling him. She had found living with her mother-in-law without her husband around simply unbearable. She vowed never to live again in San Gabriel unless it was in her own house. She had agreed to go back to her in-law's house because her husband was on leave but, more importantly, her husband had agreed to build their own house.

Linda's action was defiant but she still showed respect for social values since leaving while her husband was away and without knowledge of this decision effectively absolved him of the conflict between her and her mother-in-law. Linda hence left open for him the role of restoring frayed relationships. When the husband came home, he had to fetch her and their daughter.

Ill feelings that remained were temporarily set aside in this rite of restoration. Her mother-in-law could not refuse her because it meant refusing her own son. This rite of restoration, however, was only transitional since Linda had in fact used her decision to leave to demand that her husband build a house she can make into her own home, albeit one that was going to be just a few steps away from her in-laws' house. Although the husband remained the agent for restoring things, she nevertheless positioned herself to re-order structures of authority and respect. At the time of the interview in 2010, Linda was waiting for the blueprint of the house for construction to commence.

Figure 5. A seaman and his wife's unfinished house.

Although Linda did not exchange words with her mother-in-law, her action spoke louder. There were a few women, however, like Grace, whose voice remained muted: "of course, sometimes it really hurts, there's nothing I could do except cry." She, however, directed her voice to her husband, a voice insistent in its demand for autonomy. Linda summed up the women's desire to live in a house of their own:

> "[Y]ou never know what sin you are already committing. You think what you're doing is okay. To them it is not. If you're not feeling well, if you're living in someone else's house, you are forced to do your chores. If it was your own house, you can say, 'that can wait. I am going to just sit down, I have a headache.' You can always do so. You really have to be on your own.

It is different when it is your own, you can really be independent. The house you see as a symbol of your independence."

Building one's own house has of course financial implications. Money was not always available so a house became a long-term project, finished over many years. It was a process adapted to the financial situation of the family, moving in-sync with the family's life course. With children going to college or university, resources had to be prioritized and so the building and completion of the house was done little by little, in modular fashion. As Luz said, their house evolved as a series of extensions, emerging from work done when there was money saved for it. Their house grew as their children grew up. For Grace, convincing her husband to build her even only a basic house was not easy. The availability of money was not the only issue. Her husband's indecision to build one for his own family had to do with kinship structure. As the youngest son, he will inherit the family house and building one for his family therefore seemed a misuse of money, which Grace herself understood. She was, however, desperate to move out of her mother-in-law's house. It did not matter to her that the house was only a basic structure and that it was unfinished. She would take charge of getting something done little by little.

I have examined in this chapter the autonomy projects of Filipino seafarers' wives in the context of the "intersubjective relations of kinship" (Carsten 2013, 249) through an empirically grounded conceptualization of the dynamic and texture of the women's relationship with their mothers-in-law in the context of the absence of their husbands due to labor migration. Male emigration and their co-residence with their mothers-in-law led the women to desire and indeed seek improvements in their agency as wives and daughters-in-law. This is a sense of agency that affirmed both their autonomy and their interdependence with others. It freed them from the controlling authority of their mothers-in-law and strengthened conjugal bond. Admittedly, although such a project increased their agency within her own family (of procreation) and the wider web of affinal kinship, the "patriarchal bargain" (Kandiyoti 1988) is that such agency is contingent on the husband remaining the main, if not, sole, provider. Although this indicates their family's financial dependence on their husband, it also points to interdependence. The women's contribution to the maintenance and welfare of the family in the absence of their husband was different and no less significant. Indeed, the women, whether employed or not, pointed to the immense work they performed keeping the family intact in order to make their husband's labor migration a viable strategy in obtaining a better life.

For the women, this better life meant not only improving the family's financial security but also gaining autonomy. Their autonomy project did not mean turning away from familial and kin obligations. Indeed, autonomy, for the women, was fundamentally relational. The argument for the relationality of autonomy, Mason (2004) has noted, goes against how agency and autonomy have been conceptualized in the "individualization thesis" that has become influential in social theory and sociological research. Beck and Beck-Gernsheim (2002, 22–23), influential proponents of this idea, have written that "[t]he choosing, deciding, shaping human being who aspires to be the author of his or her own life, the creator of an individual identity, is the central character of our time." The individualization thesis has been extended to the study of intimate relationships but as Mason (2004, 163) has pointed out, the analysis is questionable in the face of research that has found how "individual identities and life projects mesh with the connectivity of kinship and interpersonal relationships."

Autonomy meant being able to exercise a sufficient degree of self-determination the exercise of which would give them a position in which to view their social location and their participation in it in more positive terms. Oppression and maltreatment intensified their desire for it while giving it a new slant and nuance. Women who lived with their mothers-in-law and whose mothers-in-law received their husband's allotment felt the absence of this same freedom in how they spent their money. They were told by their mothers-in-law to spend it appropriately. Such meddling by mothers-in-law, combined with other forms of mistreatment, taught them to talk back.

As Alampay (2014) has written, a number of scholars (e.g., Chao and Tseng 2002; Ho 1993) have noted the affinity of Filipino family relations to East Asian cultures that emphasize hierarchy, filial piety, and obligation. Filipino relationships, however, are built upon a relational conceptualization of self and other (Enriquez 1992) rather than Buddhist and Confucian values to which Chinese and Japanese sense of harmony and collectivism has been attributed (Alampay 2014). The relationality of Filipino interpersonal interaction has been conceptualized through the Tagalog concept of *kapwa* or fellow being (Enriquez 1992). *Kapwa* denotes a mode of relating to others (*pakikipagkapwa*) that is underpinned by a recognition that one's self is inextricably bound up with others while simultaneously remaining differentiated (Alampay 2014, 108; see also Guillermo 2009; Ileto 1979). One's identity or autonomy is thus affirmed by its relational existence with others. *Kapwa* and *pakikipagkapwa* resonate with the autonomy projects of the women. How they related to their mothers-in-law, how they asserted themselves, and deferred to their authority were informed not by patriarchal ideology alone but also by a strong sense of shame that went along with a culture of respect for in-laws, a respect that was intensified by co-residence with them.

Reared in a culture that puts a premium on respecting parents and elders, these women began the process of asserting their self and identity with answering and fighting back. They were not merely redefining their relationships with their mothers-in-law but also changing the terms of this relationship. For by answering back, that is, in facing their mothers-in-law, these oppressed daughters-in-law were questioning, that is, turning their back on, the cultural and social ideology that has taught them to suffer in silence. Their "faculty of voice" (Appadurai 2013 drawing on Hirschman 1970) enabled them to break free from the limits imposed by cultural ideals of "respect for elders, especially in-laws" and to become vitally involved in a process of fashioning themselves as individuals with identities and capacities that needed to be respected and recognized. They began to demand and practice a more horizontal, rather than vertical, exchange of respect, a demand that ironically became possible for them to make only by becoming "shameless" and "disrespectful." Their experiences intensified their desire for a house of their own, a space within which they could exercise freedom, for themselves and for their families. They linked their *panagbukbukod,* that is, their autonomy, identity and agency, to a house of their own. The house was the condition and space of possibility for them to have a life of their own. As Pauli (2008, 181) also noted of Mexican women married to spouses working in the USA, a house of their own is "an important expression of agency and creativity."

The women's desire for autonomy, which the house both symbolized and concretized, was also a desire for more equality, that is, more egalitarian relationships, between the wives and their mothers-in-law rather than ones dictated by hierarchy and subordination. This notion of more parity and egalitarian relationships is captured by the Ilokano concept of *pada,* fellow, which connotes being in the same position as in the expression *agpapada tayo amin* (we are all the same). Being in the same position connotes some shared experiences (*padas*) or enables one to share experiences with others, which then shape the experience and sense of fellow-ship or *panagpapada.* For the women, this relationship *with* others is to be experienced in their having their own house, which ends their relationship of being *subordinated to* parents or in-laws. But this sense of having attained more horizontal relationships in terms of their status as social adults continue to be shaped by notions of respect and devotion to one's elders.

The house "would appear to have become the topography of our intimate being," wrote Gaston Bachelard (1994, xxxvi). What a house meant to the women varied depending on their location in kin relations. Women who lived with their natal families wanted a house of their own to become independent, but this desire was not engendered by oppression. Indeed, they built their own houses near their natal family's house, which enabled them to be by their family's side in times when they or their natal family needed help. Like women who initially lived uxorilocally, those who lived virilocally also desired independence, which was vitally informed by their experiences of living with their mothers-in-law. Where wives lived with or near their husband's family and had good relations with them, owning a house may have meant independence but not with the intensity with which it was desired by women who lived with their mothers-in-law who made their lives unbearable. They described living with their mothers-in-law as akin to extinguishing the life out of them and saw living in their own house as life-giving. Many of the women said that having a house of their own would enable them to breathe, and to breathe freely. Living in their own house eased the tension between the two women. Indeed, Linda, who was waiting for the blueprint of her house in 2010 and who I re-interviewed in April 2014, reported improved relations with her mother in law as a result of living in her own house, an improvement also reported by those who have long ago built their own houses.

Having their own house did not mean that the women escaped their in-laws totally. Two of the wives who had difficult relationships with their respective mother-in-law were going to have their house built on a piece of land given to them by their husband's parents and within the family's compound. Their own house will give them self-determination but also locate them in the community of their husband's family and relatives and in proximity to the person who they wanted to stay away from. Kinship structure and the paucity of money, however, have made it more difficult for these women and their husbands to build elsewhere. The piece of land is their husband's birthright or inheritance; using it saves them money that could then be added to their budget for building their house.

CONCLUSION

The women's relationship with their mothers-in-law and the experiences it engendered would show that kinship is a "negotiated experience" (Miller 2007; see also Vera-Sanso 1999) and "constituted in relational practices" (Finch and Mason 2000, 164). The relationship between the two women, however, was shaped by a cultural code to respect one's in-laws. Also, the case of Linda, who fled her husband's house and who used this action to convince her husband of the necessity and urgency of having their own house, shows how the negotiation of affinity was shaped by what Schneider (1980, 26) calls "a pattern for behaviour" or "a code of conduct." Linda's fleeing triggered a series of actions, primarily done by her husband, to restore the peace between her and her mother-in-law. Linda's action and the "rite of restoration" that followed relied on long-established principles, which underpinned not only Linda's negotiation of affinity with her mother-in-law but also her renegotiation of the terms of their relationship. Further, the case of Grace, whose husband, as the youngest son will inherit the family house, indicated how her attainment of autonomy, which she inextricably bound up with having her own house, was strongly being shaped by established principles. Grace's having or not having her own house in turn shaped her relationship with her mother-in-law and her experience of affine relations. This demonstrates how affinal kinship is shaped by the interaction between, on the one hand, cultural ideals and, on the other, the interests and goals of different family members and how they influence both their everyday existence and relationships (Shih and Pyke 2010). Kinship is therefore relatedness shaped by "normative categories" (Miller 2007, 536) and this chapter shows how they shaped and structured the wives' relationship with their mothers-in-law and their negotiation of it.

The experiences of the women show the embeddedness of their autonomy projects in thick kin, especially affine, relations. The women's desire to have and live in their own house is an expression of the cultural ideal of achieving the status of no longer being and coming under the authority of their parents (Aguilar 2013) or parents-in-law. Such separation from parental or affinal authority, however, does not mean an abandonment of family obligations. This separation yet location in a group might also be captured by the word "cleaving." The English Oxford Living Dictionaries define "cleave" as "split or sever" but also "stick fast to, adhere strongly to, or become very strongly involved with or emotionally attached to (someone)."[3] Although their autonomy projects were forged in conflict and antagonism, they did not aspire to cut off ties from the people who made their lives difficult. Their life goals and meanings were defined by and derived from their belonging to a family, both their own and their extended ones. Their selves are at once intersubjective and their autonomy relational.

CHAPTER 9

CONCLUSION
Hopeful and Strategic Subjectivity

"Dumtengto latta. Saan met a puro rigat ti biag."

[It will come. Life is not all hardship.]

—Nora

Nora, who described her life as revolving around debt—*utang met laeng ti pagpuligosan*—said that a better life will eventually come. As she abundantly exemplifies, women do not only develop and come to possess the character and efficacy that enable them to endure the physical, emotional, and mental demands they face as stay-behind women. Equally crucially, they endure because of their abiding faith that the future holds something for them: a promise yet to be fulfilled. The sense of hopeful waiting and expectation that Nora evokes informs my discussion of what I call the women's hopeful and strategic subjectivity, which is a defining component of the women's migration subjectivity that I began to explore in chapter 2 and that I fleshed out in the succeeding chapters. I build this hopeful subjectivity on "waiting game," a concept that I develop to capture and account for the various strategies and practices the seafarers' wives employed to navigate their lives and experiences and their various spatiotemporal dimensions.

WAITING GAME

"Ata no diak met tenglen a nalaing, di nakibbutanakon."

[If I don't handle our money well, I will have nothing left (before the next allotment).]

—Teresa, 36 years old, with two children

The women employed various strategies to navigate their lives. Teresa, quoted above, spoke of her handling of money through the idiom of a Filipino game. *Nakibbutan* is a term used in *sungka,* a game played by two players whose goal is to accumulate as many cowries from the competitor's reserves (49 for each player) distributed equally at the start of the game into seven pits (see also Guillermo 2013). When one of the players loses all his/her cowries, then s/he is *nakibbutan.* The road to *nakibbutan* is frequently preceded by one of the players having empty pits (each must always contain seven cowries at the start of every round) so that if one player loses even just one to the competitor, s/he will have one empty pit called *puor,* fire (or gutted by fire). As both players move, they drop one cowry on each pit on their path, depositing one cowry in their "house" (the head pit located on the opposite ends of the *sungka*) every time they go past it. I found the wife's use of the idiom of a game to describe her family's situation (and by extension her efforts at financial management) suggestive of how she has to deal with outside forces over which she has very little control or influence and also of the ways by which she can distribute her "cowries" in order to protect her house from being *nakibbutan* (emptied) and ultimately gutted by fire.

In developing this concept of "waiting game," I draw on Sherry Ortner's conceptualization of "serious games." Ortner says that social life, viewed from a serious games perspective, "is actively played, oriented toward culturally constituted goals and projects, and involving both routine practices and intentionalized action" (2006, 129). Games "are built upon power relations at the micro-level" (151) but whose "ultimate purpose is to understand the larger forces, formations, and transformations of social life" (130). "Waiting game" vitally incorporates a sense of the strategic, that is, how women combined everyday forms of decision-making and rationality, doing, thinking, and feeling with the long-term trajectory of their lives.

I use "waiting game" to refer to how the women navigated their lives. It encompasses the various strategies used by the women to deal with experiences engendered by the alternating absence and presence of their husbands, their location in family, kin, and wider social relations, and the social and economic consequences of their husbands' insecure employment. "Waiting game" refers to a sense of timing, of knowing when to make a move, of acting because the women have reached the limits of their capacity. It connotes a sense of right timing, that is, of making demands or acting because "the right time for action has come." It involves awareness, for example, of their economic situation and a calculation of the right time to do certain things. It is meant to capture the strategy adopted by the women (and by their husbands, too, of course) of attaining goals over a long period of time such as the building of their own house.

Yet "waiting game" is not just about time, the biding of it; it is not just about the deferral of action, the calculation of when the women and their husbands would be in the best position to undertake something. Waiting game is also about place, the location of actions and activities that precede the "right time," the moment of action. In other words, "waiting game" also refers to the physical and social spaces where these women were located or which they occupied while they waited. The prime example of the spatiality of "waiting game" is the living or residential arrangements of the couples. While waiting for the time when they could afford independence, the wives (and their family) either lived with their natal or husband's families. Such an arrangement embedded women (or their husbands) in the social space of kin relations that served as a fertile ground for the development of the women's identity, subjectivity, and agency. Women who lived with their mothers-in-law were located in hierarchical structures that relied upon prevailing cultural injunctions to respect one's parents and elders.

"Waiting game" also refers to how women negotiated the spaces created by their husband's absence, that is, the discursive and ideological spaces to which they were positioned as women without husbands, women whose husbands were away or as one wife put it, "as like parched earth in need of rain." The gossip, for example, that was spread about them and the sexual advances from men to which some were subjected not only relied upon images of what women whose husbands were away are assumed to be but also reinforced these images. They had real consequences on how the women disciplined themselves (or how they were disciplined through surveillance by gossip) in that these women's mobility was curtailed. Worse, in some cases, many of the women themselves curtailed their mobility. "Waiting game" hence also applies to the concrete measures women took to deal with the absence of their husbands, for example, their modes of recreation that helped them "forget" their spouses.

"Waiting game" also encompasses the women's negotiation of various boundaries. The women's navigation of their temporal and spatial locations meant boundary work. Navigating time and space necessarily involved the creation, maintenance, crossing, transgression, or blurring of boundaries. While boundaries also functioned to position them (in this sense, boundaries "told them their place"), they are nevertheless porous and permeable (Cunningham-Burley et al. 2005; Jamieson 2005). Boundaries "clarify a range of interfaces from roles and gendered relationships within families and relationships to the relationship between families, family members, and wider social institutions" (Wassoff and Cunningham-Burley 2005, 263). Boundaries might thus also be conceptualized as *sites of passages*. Although work on boundaries and boundary making, particularly on work and life balance (e.g. Cunningham-Burley et al. 2005; McKie et al. 2005; Nippert-Eng 1996), has examined the important role they play in structuring women's lives and informing and shaping their sense of self, identity, and subjectivity, scant attention has been paid to how migration or the separation of members of families impacts on how women deal with boundaries.

An area in which the women undertook critical boundary work involved work and leisure. In order for some of the women to relax, they engaged in what has frequently been labelled as the informal economy. Selling food and clothing items provided a number of the women a legitimate reason to go out more often and farther afield, hence improving their mobility, albeit this movement was also seen as an extension of (domestic) work. Some other women farmed or raised livestock to distract themselves, helping them "forget" their husbands. The women might be said to have merged (domestic or care) work and leisure. This is not simply about some form of work involved in relaxation or leisure activities. Or that women had very little "pure free time," that is, "time 'uncontaminated' by family caregiving" (Lois 2010, 423). The case of these Filipino seamen's wives is different and more extreme in that work itself becomes leisure. They relaxed by doing more work and this work was itself justified for its potential to contribute financially to the family. Equally important, the women's *dibersyon* enabled them to counteract gossip's surveillance of their behavior and mobility. Such activities offered meaningful distraction from the absence of their husband and so could be considered as part of the "waiting game" of the women.

Another instance in which the negotiation of boundaries empowered the women was the relationship between them and their in-laws. Where the women lived with their mothers-in-law, negotiating this relationship did not only involve the demarcation of space but also, more importantly, the negotiation of hierarchy that was underpinned by cultural and social codes of respect. Shared residence, which meant the lack of privacy and the circumscription of the agency of the women to do what they would have wanted to do, was replete with invisible boundaries. Or it engendered attempts to draw boundaries. Boundary work was also involved in redefining and restructuring mother-son relationships, a task that involved their husband's allotment and which resulted in the transgression of boundaries between daughters-in-law and mothers-in-law. Where daughters-in-law transgressed, they expanded the space of their selves and agency.

Co-residence became a transitional phase and what Winnicott (1971) has called "transitional space." Transitional space has been conceptualized as a fertile ground for individual and cultural creativity (Aitken and Herman 1997). The case of these women, however, reveals that viewing the women's co-residence and their experiences in relation to it as transitional phase-space also makes visible the often abusive contexts and dire straits of these women's lives. Indeed, it was a period that might be said to have been defined by *ressentiment,* one of whose critical elements is "the sense of injustice based on the belief that one does not deserve to be in the subordinate position" (Rollins 1997, 265). *Ressentiment* refers not only to the hostility felt by those who are mistreated but also "toward those whom one feels unjustly have power or an advantage over one's life" (266). Nevertheless, this transitional phase-space was fertile ground for the growth and development of the women's sense of self and agency. In other words, the women and how they made sense of these experiences were directly linked to their social location, which was structurally defined.

A HOPEFUL AND STRATEGIC SUBJECTIVITY

As discussed, "waiting game" conceptualizes how the women linked their quotidian lives and practices to a future horizon, how the present is critically informed by goals or expectations that will be realized at some future time, that what women do in the here and now shapes this future, and that this sought-after future shapes their behavior and practices in the present. I therefore call the subjectivity of the women "hopeful and strategic." I will elaborate on this by examining the link between routine and horizon in the lives of the women, what Sennett (1998, 43) called the capacity of routine to "compose a life."

The lives of seamen's wives, and their subjectivity, might be characterized by a forward movement through recurrence. Time was not simply a background in the women's lives (something that passed) but was instead a vital element that shaped their lives and experiences, one that itself had to be navigated. Time was not abstract but lived, and lived because it was both an embedded and a structuring component of their existence. It might be argued that many of the routine activities of the wives, particularly those with children, were intimately braided with the future horizon, which functioned as the purposive context of their everyday or quotidian lives. The absence of their husbands and why their husbands have to be absent in the first place were justified and rationalized by a consideration of the future.

Routine therefore does not refer only to frequently performed actions that provide structure to the conduct of life. For the women, it must be taken to include those that do not happen daily, weekly, or even monthly. There are events in the life of seamen's wives that, because they happen repeatedly and at regular intervals in the course of their husband's career, become part of the routine of their lives. These events shape their life's structure, cycle, rhythmicity, and meaning. They include the alternation of absence and presence, departure and return, as well as the cycle of the family living on saved money when the seamen are home and have no income. The contractual nature of seafaring jobs had significant consequences on how the women spent money and on their money-saving practices so that they would not fall into debt. It is in this sense that I link routine and horizon. Horizon might be understood in other words as "lived future," which "refers to the future experienced as a constitutive element of the present, something without which there could not be a temporal aspect to experience" (Adam and Groves 2007, 123; also Frederiksen 2013; Nielsen 2011). Considering the horizon as "lived future" makes the future "neither empty nor abstract" but rather "a lived aspect of our experience that embeds us within a meaningful world" (123).

The women's routines not only embedded them in their present but also located them in a future. All of the wives knew that the time will come when their husbands could and would no longer get a job. The women and their husbands were investing in their future (through sending children to school, saving money, starting some business projects, buying property, etc.), aware that their husband's seafaring will come to an inevitable end, and they also knew that there was a real possibility that they will go back to a life characterized by "there is nothing but hardship." Migration as social navigation and the social navigation wives do help make possible that it is not only the present but also the future that is secured. Although all the women were married to seafarers, they and their families have attained different levels of social possibilities. They bear upon how the women and their families perceive time, particularly the future. And their perception of the future, of what potentially lies ahead for them, impacts on their experience of their present. How they spend money, for example, is linked to how they see their position in this future time. The projects they undertake in the present are bound up with their calculation, if not speculation, of the future.

Navigating the present by a consideration of the future, of prospects, bestows upon many of the women's (and their husbands') thinking of and acting upon their condition a certain amount of purposiveness. It does not, however, make the future less uncertain and precarious. Indeed, it is this awareness of the future that makes them acutely aware of the limit(ation)s and finitude of their possibilities for improving their life chances, a finitude that is tightly linked to the health and age of their husbands. This purposiveness helps give the women the mental and emotional strength that helps to make the present and the future more navigable as well as with the pragmatism (coupled with forbearance and longsuffering) that so often guided their decisions as couples. With limited resources, especially in the first few years of their married life, wives and husbands set priorities and work toward achieving them one after the other. The same limited resources, but also a sense of obligation to their families, drive wives and husbands to live with their natal families or in-laws until such time they have the financial capacity to build their own house.

In the women's "lived future," the past is something that has never really been left behind. A memory of their hard life was important in imagining their horizon. Many of the wives wanted their children to have a (deep) sense of their hard life for they want their children to have a sense of purpose and direction so that this hard life is not perpetuated. They do not always succeed but in attempting to do so they navigate future lives, not theirs, in which they will forever be implicated. They try to steer their children's lives (and their lives) by providing an anchor, a memory of their hard lives, or of what it used to be like. By doing so, children might be led to appreciate what they have and be encouraged and inspired to make their lives even better. Parents have also either encouraged or supported their children to undertake their own migrations, their search for better social possibilities. Their future is such that their horizon is somewhere across the sea. Their hopes are pinned on migration.

Agency might then also be understood not only to refer to capacity or ability to act but also to possibility (Vigh 2008). If agency as possibility denotes "to what extent we are able to act within a given context," then agency is also about overcoming constraints and limitations and therefore about furthering or expanding what is possible (11). If navigation is concerned with moving within the present (encompassing both time and space dimensions) with a consideration of the past and future or horizon (and with an acute awareness that this future cannot be fully known, let alone determined), then we have to reflect on how women "felt" about the future. What role did emotions play in the women's imagination of a better future?

One emotion that links the imagination and the future is hope. In different ways and in varying degrees, the women expressed feelings of hope.

To that extent, hope not only helped the women endure, to become durable; hope constituted how they perceived their and their family's future. Hope shaped how they cast their gaze on the horizon and how they imagined their prospects, however uncertain they might be. Considered this way, hope is not only emotion that resides or is generated inside a person, a feeling one has. It has materiality; hoping is action. It is an active and material labor that obtains in the concrete socio-structural contexts of these women. As Lois McNay (2008, 183–84) argues in her examination of hope in the work of Pierre Bourdieu:

> Bourdieu ties his discussion of temporal uncertainty to a discussion of the emotion of hope which itself is connected to social location. Hope is an emotional expression of protention defined as a practical sense of the forthcoming. [. . .] Although protention is a general feature of agency, an individual's capacity to experience hope is conditioned by the ways in which power relations shape the agent's expectations and orientation towards the future.

McNay further writes that "[e]motions emerge through practice and practice is both the product of power relations that have been internalized into the body and also of an active engagement with social structures" (185). She argues that the better positioned people are, the more hope they have.

But Nora, source of the statement "something will come, life is not all hardship," and a number of other wives did not have much in life, they did not have many options or alternatives yet they were filled with hope; they were hopeful. They had an unwavering faith that the future was not going to be as bad and as hard as the present. Indeed, faith was an important element of the hoping of these women. For many of them, it was not enough that they had inner strength, that they were resilient and tenacious. Their possession and exercise of these qualities or resources was linked to their faith in God. They spoke of the dangers their husbands were exposed to, of the risk that always accompanied their husband's departure. They contended with the possibility that their husband might not come back alive or that something bad might happen to them. Their husband's leaving entailed taking great risks and was a gamble they had to take (see also Aguilar 1998; Bankoff 2004; Mojares 1983; Rafael 2010). These things they cannot do anything about, they say, except to leave them to a higher power, thereby recognizing the limitedness of their capacity. By doing so, their hopes become more powerful and deeper, more vital to how they look at the future. Hope, as a constitutive element of the women's navigation of their social horizon, is also a navigational tool. It is a positive force and resource aiding them to maneuver around what have frequently been rough and turbulent times. It enables them to view their life, despite the difficulties and challenges, not with resignation and fatalism but with resilience and tenacity. It enables them to demonstrate a "talent for life" (Scheper-Hughes 2008). Hope is that which enables Nora to say "something will come; life is not all hardship." This subjectivity of hopeful and strategic waiting is a subjectivity that endures and that concretizes the coherence and durability of the women's selves. It is one that demonstrates great awareness of the risk of "defeat" or "loss" yet affirms faith in the future, a future they believe can be realized through migration. Indeed, this subjectivity might be said to emerge from the experiences of hardship faced and overcome and the positive changes that have been achieved. It might be said to have been significantly constituted by a history of overcoming difficulties. "Dumtengto latta, saan met a puro rigat ti biag" (It will come, life is not all hardship) is an expression of hope, a practice of hope in so much as it is a refusal to be defined and limited by hardship, a refusal to wallow in resignation and despair. Such hopefulness is linked to the Ilokano expression "awan rigat a di malasat" (there is no hardship that cannot be overcome), such that even if one's life is characterized by hardship, a time will come when life shall be better. International contract labor migration paves the way for it.[1]

SUBJECTIVITY, MIGRATION, AND THE NATION

Waiting game and *hopeful and strategic subjectivity* speak of the strivings of seafarers' wives and their families to survive and thrive through labor migration in a country where there are limited social possibilities and opportunities for improving life chances. They clarify the dialectic between the subjective and the social, with migration being the tie that binds them for seafarers' wives. As McNay (2004, 177) has noted, "structural forces only reveal themselves in the lived reality of social relations." Migration demonstrates how the national condition, its narrative of underdevelopment or failure to develop, is inextricably linked to the personal fortunes and individual strivings of Filipinos, a link that is made tighter by their act of crossing the country's borders. It also reveals how this relationship is fraught with conflict and tension. Filipinos migrate not with the express intention of helping improve the nation's economy but rather the lives of their families. What mediate therefore the relationship between Filipino overseas migrants and the Philippine nation are these migrants' families. Although the nation is only secondary, if not an afterthought, it is nevertheless important in bestowing a nobler purpose upon these migrants' departure. Migration is also therefore simultaneously an act of imagining in which the personal and familial horizons of Filipino migrants become meshed with the nation's narrative and horizon. Migration becomes both the means and space of convergence for the personal and the political. However, personal biography and national narrative do not become fully elided. As Aguilar (2003, 152) has pointed out, "the official policy has resulted in a substantial (but by no means exact) congruence of migrant labor and origin-state interests." It might be argued that alongside this congruence is a strong festering sense of "disaffection" understood as "emotional distance, alienation, antipathy, and isolation but also . . . disloyalty to regimes of power and authority" (Manalansan 2010, 217).

Various Philippine governments have built notions of citizenship and patriotism around the export of labor. The appellation "bagong bayani" or "modern-day national heroes" is emblematic of these attempts by the Philippine state to lay claim to these Filipinos and their earnings. The government's provision for dual citizenship has also been perceived as another way to keep the state's claim upon the "loyalty" and "patriotism" of these Filipinos. Yet overseas Filipino workers, who the former president Gloria Macapagal Arroyo (2000–2010) also referred to as overseas Filipino investors (yet another way of claiming them), see through the maneuvers of the state and have parodied, if not rejected, the status conferred on them. Two seafarer-husbands I had conversations with ridiculed the conferring on them by the state of the status of "bagong bayani." They are, they say, in reality "gagong bayani" (stupid heroes). "Gago," stupid, plays on the word "bago," new or modern-day (see also Fajardo 2011; S McKay 2007; Rupert and Solomon 2006). "Linoloko!" (what foolishness) the seafarers sum it up, thus exposing the state's attempt to fool them so that it can exploit them.

Their valorization and heroization in the instrumentalist discourse of the state and in official rituals of recognition (such as the annual rite where the Philippine president greets arriving OFWs at Manila's Ninoy Aquino International Airport (NAIA)) contrast starkly with the abuse and disrespect they routinely get from state functionaries. I have personally experienced, as well as witnessed, OFWs, being badly treated by NAIA's immigration officials and other airport, mostly security, staff. In one instance, on my return to the United Kingdom in September 2010, a male airport official (I presume this on the basis of his wearing a suit) instructed a group of female OFWs waiting for immigration checking to move to another position which previously was closed. No one moved, which incensed the official who then called the women "tanga" and "bobo" (stupid). What I saw happen at the airport must be nothing compared to the inadequate, if not lack of, support and protection from the state that OFWs suffer in their countries of work, reports of which routinely fill the pages of Philippine newspapers, online publications, and social media, especially Facebook.

To be sure, migration is a way of navigating the dire consequences of structural adjustment policies in the early 1980s and more neoliberal restructuring since then on the Philippine economy and ultimately and especially on poor Filipinos. With the devaluation of the peso, the Philippine currency, real incomes dropped making it almost impossible for most Filipinos to pay for public services such as education and health care that increasingly became privatized (Parreñas 2008; Rodriguez 2010). Migration became the single most consequential and viable way for Filipinos to afford these social services even as brokering this labor migration became the state's instrument to absolve itself from the responsibility of directly providing these social services to its citizens (Rodriguez 2010, xix). Through brokering this labor migration, the state has instituted the "responsibilization" of Filipino citizens in at least two ways. First, they become solely responsible for education, health, and other social services. Second, through the various ways it has made migrant work an act of patriotism or nationalism, the state makes Filipino citizens "directly bear the costs of neoliberal restructuring as their remittances go to debt servicing" (xix). Between 1970 and 1998, the Philippines allocated US$77.6 billion for foreign debt servicing (for principal and interest) yet by the end of 2000, its debt still amounted to US$52 billion (Diokno-Pascual 2001 cited in Parreñas 2008b). For 2016, the Philippine government allocated PhP812.1 billion for debt servicing, PhP435.9 billion for education, PhP128.4 billion for health, and PhP104.2 billion for social welfare (Republic of the Philippines 2016). With 102,965,300 Filipinos (Republic of the Philippines 2015), the amounts translate to the following expenditures per Filipino per day (at an exchange rate of PhP45 to a dollar): PhP21.61 for debt servicing, PhP11.6 for education, PhP3.42 for health, and PhP2.77 for social welfare. Compare these with 2010 figures: while the Philippine state spent the equivalent of PhP21.75 per Filipino per day for debt servicing, it only spent PhP6.85 n education, PhP1.10 for health, and PhP.16 for housing (IBON Vital Signs 2010).

Migration-dependent families might be said to be trying to address the threat of being socially and economically left behind. The wives, however, did not state an explicit link between the departure of their husbands to the failure of the Philippine state to provide for its people or their husbands' labor migration as occurring within the labor export policy of the state. All of them talked about the unavailability of opportunities for social and economic advancement in the country. The women therefore talked in terms of a lack: "awan met pagsapulan ditoy" (there are no jobs here) or "no adda man, di met umanay a pagbiag" (if there is any, it is not enough to live on). The women, their husbands, and Filipinos in general, might be argued to have become so used to striking on their own that they have come to stop expecting anything from their government, which, ironically, has increasingly come to depend on overseas contract workers for survival. The state's dependence on its migrant population is inversely proportional to the people's independence from (or non-dependence on) it.

This points to a process of subjectification in which a state actively constructs a relationship with its citizens through which it can justify its extraction of their affection and patriotism remitted as money. Filipino migrant workers do remit money but they do so more for the sake of their families and less out of a sense of nationalism as constructed by a parasitical state (see, for example, Rupert and Solomon 2006). The promotion and rationalization of the labor export policy have gone through several discursive shifts: "an unfortunate necessity (under Marcos), through being lauded as a sacrificial act (Aquino and Ramos) to being portrayed [by the Arroyo government] as the much-vaunted Filipino contribution to the global economy" (Camroux 2009, 30; also Tyner 2004, 2009). Working overseas has been cloaked in nationalist rhetoric, with Marcos claiming in the 1970s that the labor and remittances of the overseas contract workers were vital to the regime's project of building the "New Society," and beginning in 1988 during Corazon Aquino's administration (1986–1992) contract workers were cast as "bagong bayani." The "sacrifice" that workers make for their families is appropriated by the state as a sacrifice for the nation.

That the women never adverted to the state is not so much an indication of their lack of political consciousness as an indication of the insignificance of the state in terms of their economic and social well-being. Although their lives are ineluctably entwined with the nation-state in the sense that their aspirations and strategies for attaining them are both a consequence of and response to the state's failure to provide adequate social possibilities, beyond this, the state is of little real consequence to them. Whatever happens to them or to their families is their responsibility, which in itself is a ramification of the state's neoliberal policies (Rodriguez 2010). Filipino families, migrant or not, have not only borne on their own their hardships; they have also borne the state. An examination of the subjectivity and agency of Filipino seamen's wives must therefore take into account their vexed relationship with the political qua state. The state is both absent and present so that although migrants and their families turn migration into a personal and family strategy to navigate economic problems, they and their experiences cannot be completely divorced from their political qua state context. They may not be the migrants themselves but their subjectivity and agency are shaped by this absence-presence of the state. They are certainly not reducible to the workings of the state but they do engage the conditions engendered by it. Their lives, experiences and the ways they navigate (out of) the conditions of their lives speak to the presence-by-its-absence of the state.

In paying attention to the women's everyday practices, what I call "the minutiae of subjective becoming," I simultaneously demonstrated how these women moved within, or were implicated in, larger contexts and environments. My discussion of the communication practices and activities of the women and their families showed that the predominance of the mobile phone as means of communication is tied to the political economy and state of telecommunication in the Philippines. By looking at migration as a form of social navigation, I specified the role of women who stay behind in the development of cultures of migration. In the case of the women in this book, I showed how the dreams of many in San Gabriel and the Ilocos more generally might have been forged in their collective history and how in many ways their preparedness to face and endure a life without their husbands is built on what became a common experience of both men and women of staying behind when their spouses left for Hawaii or California.

An issue that has personal, familial, social, and political implications for the women is the matter of their owning and living in their own house. More than finally providing the wife with her own domicile and domain that will afford her more freedom, the house is also a concretization of how they have successfully navigated their personal, social, and economic locations. The house shows their success in improving their social possibilities and lives. With no or very little assistance from the government except by going through the state's labor export policy, the seamen and their wives have accomplished what most likely would have been impossible had their husbands not become a migrant contractual worker. The house might be seen to embody the couple's independence not only from their families but also from the Philippine state. The house is but another concretization of how the personal is political. As long as Filipino families have to strike out on their own and despite the fact they do manage to survive and even thrive, the question of where the Philippine state is and what role it plays in their lives makes the strivings of these Filipino families even more profoundly political.

CONCLUSION

The scale of Philippine migration is such that it has become part of the way Filipinos live, indeed, of how they make a living to ensure they stay alive. As strategy, migration might be said to have become routinized. Yet in contrast to routine, migration represents and embodies a purposive acting upon the world, mindful of possibilities and risks. Migration is embarked upon as an act of risk-taking (Aguilar 2014a; Rafael 2010) to secure one's prospects and future in an otherwise insecure world. For the more than three thousand Filipinos leaving the country every day for work overseas and the millions who have left before them, it is a precarious economic terrain, where the only thing certain is its uncertainty and the only thing predictable is its debilitation. Migration offers the possibility of motion, of economic and social mobility. For the women, *lung-aw* does not only embody a desired state of social and economic well-being but also the strategy of attaining it. Migration is how women and their families have navigated social and economic uncertainties in the Philippines and the very real possibility of sinking under such difficulties. The seafarer wives who stay behind are a vital part of the "migration infrastructure" (Biao and Lindquist 2014)—the array of institutions, structures, technologies, people, desires, and forces—that enable migration. As such, they have played a vital role in the "migration revolution" (Aguilar 2014b) that has slowly but irrevocably changed the Filipino nation. Their pursuit of *lung-aw,* done with the awareness that there will come a time that their husbands will no longer be able to get work, vitally shaped their subjectivity as women who stay.

ENDNOTES

CHAPTER 1. INTRODUCTION: DURABLE AND ENDURING SELVES

1. I have rearranged a little bit Nancy's narrative to minimize repetition.

2. The following is a partial list: sex workers in US military bases in South Korea (Cheng 2010); hostesses in Japanese entertainment bars (Faier 2009; Parreñas 2011); mail-order brides (Constable 2003); domestic workers in Greece (Anderson 2000), Hong Kong (Constable 1997, 2014; McKay 2012), London (Anderson 2001), Malaysia (Chin 1998), Rome and Los Angeles (Parreñas 2001, 2005, 2008a), Singapore (Cheah 2006) and Taiwan (Lan 2006); caregivers (Liebelt 2011; Pratt 2012; Willen 2007); construction workers in Saudi Arabia (Margold 2002); nurses in the USA (Choy 2003) and United Kingdom (Madianou 2012; Madianou and Miller 2012).

3. See, for example, Bloor 2012; Dacanay and Walters 2011; Fajardo 2011; Fernandez and Krootjes 2007; Lamvik 2002; S. McKay 2007, 2015; Mannov 2015; Ruggunan 2011; Sampson 2003, 2007; Swift 2010; Terry 2009; Bloor 2011; Chin 2008a, 2008b; Couper et al. 1999; George 2013; Sampson 2013.

4. Parreñas has shown that migration does not lead to the detraditionalization of gender and mothering; rather, it provides new ways of redefining the nature and practice of mothering. Indeed, she documents the intensification of mothering from a distance aided by communication technology (2005, 2008b, 2008c).

5. Pingol constructs a spectrum of masculinity built around the opposition between "malalaki" (patriarchal, traditional, macho) and "kinalalalaki" (a new masculinity that incorporates practices of care work, housework, etc.). While the conceptualization is comprehensible because of the rich empirical data that Pingol provides, the linguistic basis of the conceptualization of these two masculinities is made on the opposition constructed around a misrecognition of linguistic categories. "Malalaki" and "kinalalaki" are not oppositional terms: the former is an adjective, meaning *masculine*, the latter, a noun, meaning *masculinity*. The awkwardness of the construction

becomes apparent if we translate *malalaki* as "masculine maleness" and *kinalalaki* as "masculinity maleness."

6. Social remittances—the ideas and behaviors that migrants bring back to their home communities—can be norms, practices, identities and social capital (Levitt 1998). In revisiting the concept, Levitt acknowledges that social remittances can be positive and negative (Levitt and Lamba-Nieves 2011).

7. As Smith (1981, 12) has explained, "the Ilocos Coast had already achieved a quite high ratio of population to agricultural resources by the beginning of the twentieth century, reflecting the evolution of population in the nineteenth century and earlier. The contrast with the Philippines as a whole at that time is dramatic; remarkably, the level on the Ilocos Coast in 1903 was not achieved by the entire country until quite recently. Other census evidence corroborates this picture of substantial population pressure on land at the turn of the century." Around the beginning of the twentieth century, the national average population density (excluding Manila) was 90 people per square mile. In contrast, the figure for Ilocos Sur was 492; for La Union, 459. The two were in fact the two most densely populated provinces (España-Maram 2006, 18). The population pressure had a massive negative impact on agricultural production and land use systems and put enormous strains on social arrangements with respect to production and distribution (Smith 1981, 10): "In 1903, two-thirds of the farms on the Ilocos Coast were below one hectare in size, compared with about half the farms below that size nationwide. And the tenancy rate was near 30 percent, compared with about 20 percent nationwide" (Smith 1981, 12). It is helpful here to give an indication of the scale of the Ilokano movement. The number of Ilokanos who had moved out of the four provinces of the Ilocos Region by the end of the nineteenth century has been put at more than 290,000 or 36 percent of the population (Xenos 1998, 47). Whereas there were only about 50,000 Ilokanos in the northeastern provinces of Luzon at the beginning of the twentieth century, by 1960, they comprised 67 percent of the Northeastern Luzon population: 65 percent (or 289,340) in Cagayan, 66.7 percent (or 294,984) in Isabela and 77.7 percent (or 107,358) in Nueva Vizcaya (McLennan 1980, 114). In 1970, only 88 towns out of the 196 in Luzon where Ilokanos were the dominant ethnolinguistic group were on the Ilocos Coast itself (Smith 1981, 14).

8. The survey, called "Sons and Daughters of San Gabriel by Barangay" (2009b) was a simple enumeration of overseas migrants and where they migrated to. Although the listing was conducted village by village, it is not complete. I thank San Gabriel's Office of Development and Planning for giving me a copy of the list, which at that time had yet to be collated.

CHAPTER 2. SEAFARING LABOR AND SEAFARERS' WIVES

1. The manning industry refers to the "companies that provide employment to Filipino seafarers on board. Since the late 1980s, its purpose of recruitment slowly progressed into human resource management, since recruitment functions of training,

selection, deployment, compensation and career development can now be considered a part of standard service, depending on what the manning agent and the principal had agreed upon. As of July 2016, there are 406 manning agencies with valid licenses accredited under POEA" (Richter 2016, 1). The crewing sector, on the other hand, is responsible for employing seafarers and processing the documentation of all migrant seafarers working on ships. In January 2015, there were 421 licensed crewing agents in the Philippines" (Richter 2016, 2).

2. The education and training of seafarers is regulated by three government agencies: Commission on Higher Education (CHED), TESDA, and MARINA. Review centers, on the other hand, are wholly in the hand of the private sector and are not regulated as yet by the government (Richter 2016). The banking and finance sector is considered a key support sector of seafaring labor. Money transfers to seafarers' allottees occur through bank transactions. Richter (2016, 4) identifies the banks with the biggest share of seafarer remittances handled in 2015: BPI, 46 percent in sea-based market shares and 29 percent in the cash remittance market; BDO 26 percent sea-based market; PNB with 10 percent market share; and RCBC 3.5 percent market share.

3. The labor export policy was codified in President Ferdinand Marcos's Presidential Decree (PD) 442 or the Philippine Labor Code of 1974 and further strengthened in June 1978 with PD 1412, which amended certain provisions of PD 442. It has been argued that the Labor Code was formulated "to increase industry efficiency and responsiveness to growing international demand for temporary workers, through the provision of a legislative, political, administrative, and policy focus for the labor-export industry" (Ball 1997, 1617). In 1995, the Migrant Workers and Overseas Filipinos Act was signed into law to protect and promote the welfare of overseas Filipino workers and their families.

The overseas employment program was originally intended as a state monopoly. Two government agencies were created, namely the Overseas Employment Development Board (OEDB) and the National Seaman Board (NSB), which were tasked with market development, recruitment, and the securing of the best possible terms of employment for land-based and sea-based workers, respectively (Gonzalez 1998). Due to corruption, inefficiency, and legal challenges from the private sector (Asis 1992), the government changed its policy to give the private sector greater participation in the labor export industry. The state's policy change was also based on the realization that "conflict [with the private sector] would result in less capital accumulation for both sectors, and through a partnership, greater levels of accumulation would be possible than if either had a monopoly" (Tyner 2000, 137). Thus, in 1978, four years after the labor export program was adopted, the state reinstituted private sector participation. This state-private sector partnership resulted in a massive growth in overseas employment. From 1975 to 1982, for example, the total number of processed workers rose by 772 percent despite the fact that contract workers were being deployed to the same geographic region, the Middle East (Ball 1997; Tyner 2000). In 1982, the state's regulatory function was strengthened with the creation of the POEA to take overall responsibility for the formulation, implementation, and monitoring of the country's overseas employment program (Battistella 1999). This mandate consolidated the POEA's regulatory function which consisted mainly with regulating private recruitment agencies, and the marketing of Filipino labor. The private sector retained its role of recruitment, processing, and employment of Filipino workers (Abella 2004).

4. There are economic, demographic, and social backgrounds to Philippine labor migration, factors that needed to be present in labor-receiving countries in order for it to occur and thrive (Castles 2000, 2007). In other words, while the Philippine economy was struggling, other economies were experiencing expansion and development. The rapid economic growth and modernization in Asian economies, first by Japan, then Taiwan, Hong Kong, Singapore and South Korea, and then followed by Thailand, Malaysia and Indonesia comprises the economic background (Castles 2000, 114). This "created demand for labor," while the slower growth in the Philippines and other East Asian countries "made labor reserves available" (Castles 2000, 114). Indeed, the labor export policy took advantage of the 1970s "oil boom" in Saudi Arabia and other West Asian (or Middle East) countries which opened construction job opportunities for male Filipino workers. The demographic factor refers to the situation in which the "countries with the fastest economic growth have also had the most rapid decline in fertility" (Castles 2000, 114). The consequence has been that these economies "have run into labor shortages, while other countries have stagnant labor surpluses" (114). Because of the economic growth in labor-receiving countries, citizens have had more opportunities for educational and occupational-career advancement leading to a situation in which local workers refuse to do certain types of jobs (the 3-D: dirty, difficult and dangerous), which then get filled in by migrant workers (Castles 2000, 115). This is one of the social backgrounds of labor migration. Although the economic, demographic and social backgrounds help explain labor migration, we need to keep in mind that very little of it can occur without any political background (Castles 2000). None of this labor migration could have occurred without the state as a player.

5. Called structural adjustment loans (SALs), their availability, according to Bello et al. (1994, 27), was predicated on the following conditions: a) radically reducing government spending, in order to control inflation and reduce the demand for capital inflows from abroad, a measure that in practice translated into cutting spending in health, education, and welfare; b) cutting wages or severely constraining their rise to reduce inflation and make exports more competitive; c) liberalizing imports to make local industry more efficient and instituting incentives for producing for export markets, which were seen both as a source of much-needed foreign exchange and as a more dynamic source of growth than the domestic market; d) removing restrictions on foreign investment in industry and financial services to make the local production of goods and delivery of services more efficient, owing to the presence of foreign competition; e) devaluing the local currency relative to hard currencies like the dollar

in order to make exports more competitive; and f) privatizing state enterprises and embarking on radical deregulation in order to promote allocation of resources by the market instead of by government decree.

6. The shipping industry responded to diminishing profits by organizational restructuring and the use of technology that reduced the number of crew needed to do a certain job. There is no space here to discuss in detail these developments. See Alderton et al. (2004) and Stopford (2008) for discussions of the ramifications of the oil crisis in the 1970s and the globalization of the shipping industry.

7. Special First Division [G.R. No. 110524. July 29, 2002] Douglas Millares and Rogelio Lagda, Petitioners, vs. National Labor Relations Commission, Trans-Global Maritime Agency, Inc and Esso International Shipping Co., Ltd., Respondents.

8. An Act Protecting Seafarers Against Ambulance Chasing and Imposition of Excessive Fees, and Providing Penalties Therefor.

9. "The offense of ambulance chasing shall be committed when the following elements concur: a) That a person or his agent, solicits from seafarer or his heirs, the pursuit of any claim against the employer of the seafarer; b) that such claim is for the purpose of recovery of monetary award or benefits arising from accident, illness or death, including legal interest; and c) that the pursuit of the claim is in exchange of an amount or fee which shall be retained or deducted from the monetary award or benefit granted to or awarded to the seafarers or their heirs." DOLE 2016 IRR of RA No. 10706 otherwise known as the Seafarers Protection Act. Department no 153 series of 2016.

10. See "UK Club praises the new 'Seafarers Protection Act'." Available at: https://www.safety4sea.com/uk-club-praises-the-new-seafarers-protection-act/.

11. "The International Group of P&I Clubs has recorded 252 cases over the past eight years in which arbitration awards totaling GBP18 million have been overturned or modified in favor of the employer by the Court of Appeals or Supreme Court, yet less than US$40,000 has so far been recovered through the process of restitution. If the recent pattern of awards and appeals continues, the total to be recovered could reach over US$40 million within the next five years" (See "UK Club praises the new 'Seafarers Protection Act'").

CHAPTER 3. *LUNG-AW* AND MIGRATION SUBJECTIVITY

1. According to the "Monthly salary schedule for local government personnel in fifth class provinces and cities and third class municipalities" (effective 1 January 2010) provided to this author by the Office of the Treasurer of San Gabriel, an employee at salary grade 1 (the lowest) earns roughly PhP5,500 to PhP6,300 a month (around US$120 to US$140 at an exchange rate of PhP45 to a dollar), while someone at salary grade 30 (the highest) earns about PhP37,000 to PhP42,000 (around US$820 to US$935).

2. I use this ITF figure as a point of reference. The Philippine Overseas

Employment Agency (POEA) has its own rates, but salaries are determined by the companies or employers.

3. Length of contract also varies according to nationality (Thomas et al. 2003). The working conditions of seafarers are shaped by other factors such as labor conditions and labor policies in countries of origin. This is especially salient in the case of Chinese seafarers (see Thomas et al. 2003, 51–52). Thomas and Bailey (2009) mention employer's policies, type of trade, and routes sailed. See also Chin (2008a, 2008b).

4. I would argue, however, that because Ilokanos have been migrating in large numbers since the 1850s, the expansion of their horizons antedates the development of a culture of waged labor. Nevertheless, I agree with Bankoff's assertion that Hawaii represented a furtherance of this horizon and the possibilities it represented.

5. There are three regions where sugar plantations were located: Negros/Panay in Central Philippines; Batangas and Laguna in Southern Luzon; and Pampanga and Tarlac in Central Luzon.

6. Ilokanos dominated this recruitment mainly because the two other provinces where the recruiters went to, namely Pampanga (in Central Luzon, Philippines) and Negros (in Central Philippines), were also dependent on a sugar plantation economy. For people in these two and nearby provinces that supplied workers for these local sugar economies to go to Hawaii and work in rival sugar plantations was cast by the elites as unpatriotic, a stance that Resil Mojares (1983) has exposed for its hypocrisy.

7. Although the Ilokano migration to Hawaii is frequently cited in discussions of a Filipino culture of migration, it is to support a perspective of the concept framed at the national level. There are, however, recent works that (although it is not their explicit intention to) provide more locally contextualized and nuanced discussion of a culture of migration. In his ethnographic study of cultures of relatedness and overseas migration in a Batangas village, Aguilar provides a most cogent and insightful elucidation of this village's culture of migration (Aguilar 2009a, 2013; see also Aguilar 2009b).

CHAPTER 4. *BUKODMO AMIN*: ROUTINE, RESPONSIBILITY, AND SUBJECTIFICATION

1. It is helpful to define rhythmicity. Zerubavel (1985, 9) refers to it merely as the recurrence of activity patterns. I am partial to Barbara Adam (1988, 89), who explains that it "entails cycles, structure, and processes with variation."

2. The phraseology borrows from Zerubavel (1985, 2) who writes of a sociotemporal order that "regulates the structure and dynamics of social life." See also Zerubavel (1979).

3. Zerubavel (1985, 142) proposes a view that considers "territoriality" in time by which he means "a temporally defined *niche of inaccessibility*" (emphasis in original). For seamen's wives, "territoriality" would have to be redefined as their taking charge of responsibilities and tasks while their husband is gone. It is therefore both spatial and temporal but its spatiality refers more to domains of responsibilities than to

the physical geographies of tasks and responsibilities. My concern hence is on the territoriality and not on the inaccessibility. See also Davies' (1990, 42) critique of Zerubavel.

4. The yearly cycle is, however, less useful for the seamen's wives for although they, too, mark time in years, it is their husband's cycle of absence and presence, of departure and return that frames more their experience of longer periods of time, those that have more duration. Years are marked by either the presence or absence of their husbands which do not necessarily coincide with a January-to-December reckoning of the year or to its reckoning into twelve months.

5. Family members of those in hospital assist in looking after them. Tasks may include feeding them, giving them a wash, changing their clothes, and the like. Moreover, because hospitalization is not free, someone has to be around to make decisions such as whether tests or procedures could be done since they had to be paid for. If an expensive operation is required, someone had to be there to confirm that the family can afford to pay for it. Nothing can proceed without the family concerned being "informed" first.

6. *Nabatian,* left behind with something, was the women's humorous way of referring to their getting pregnant and then "left behind" by their husband when they had to go back to sea again. It plays on the word *nabati* (left behind), and I translate it as "left behind with something" to capture the sense in which they are not the actor but the recipient of an action done by another. "Impregnated" would be another way to translate it, capturing the sense in which the women are semantically configured as passive vessels or receptacles.

CHAPTER 5. COMMUNICATION AND IMAGINED COMMUNION

1. Salazar gives the figure of 745, but this might be a typographical error. If we deduct 844 from 1,609 (the total number of Philippine towns and cities), we get 765.

2. A *sari-sari* store (from the root word *sari* [variety] is a small store selling a variety of goods such as cooking oil, eggs, soap, soft drinks (like Coke and Pepsi Cola), cigarette, crisps, tin food, and so on. The *tingi* system is better explained by illustrating it. A seller of goods, say, a sari-sari store owner, repacks a liter of cooking oil into smaller quantities the cost of which is easier borne by buyers. Or a cigarette vendor sells cigarettes by the stick rather than by the pack.

3. Salazar (2007, 296 n. 75) explains that "US companies cited increasing global competition and the availability of cheaper options such as Voice over the Internet, callback, and international simple resale as the reasons behind this reduction in rates." Furthermore, "the collection of termination rates from international calls, a traditional source of profit and cross-subsidisation for less profitable operations such as fixed line operations, have been declining due to the US- imposed reduction on accounting rates for incoming calls from the United States and terminating in the Philippines" (Salazar 2007, 282, 284; cf. Klopfenstein 2002).

4. In using "unli-calls," wives dial an access number, followed by the mobile

number. Prepaid phone cards for unli-calls cost PhP100 and have to be used within five days. Each call lasts only for five minutes and wives would have to redial.

5. Writing and receiving letters were important to both wives and husbands but particularly more so the husbands, partly because of the dynamic in ships. The wives I interviewed and the husbands I had conversations with talked about seamen being mercilessly teased by others if they did not have a letter among the post delivered. Apparently, the delivery of letters was a "public" event as letters were "dumped" on a table by whoever was in charge. Seamen described how they would rush to fish out theirs, and whoever left empty-handed was easy to spot. Those who expected not to have one chose instead to stay in their cabin to spare themselves of the teasing. One wife, who had a period during which she rarely wrote to her husband (prompted by her discovery that her husband was having an affair with another woman, which she found out because the other woman was also at the airport to send him off), recounted how other seamen in San Gabriel, who worked with her husband on the same ship, visited her to ask her to write to her husband as he "could no longer think properly."

6. I thank Mick Bloor for providing me this clarification. Email communication, June 2016.

7. Although the focus of the discussion is on the agency of wives, this should not be taken to mean that the wives wholly determine the communication behavior of their seamen-husbands. To be sure, when they call they ask to speak to their children. My focusing on the wives is not meant to draw a link between wives and kinwork, "the work of maintaining family relations," which, as Michaela di Leonardo (1987) has demonstrated, is "generally the work of women in households" (cited in Wilding 2006, 135).

8. The discussion presented here is based on only eight interviewees who provided responses to this sort of phone conversation. However, it is safe to assume that more women have had, at one time or another, an argument with their husband over the phone.

9. I find "listen in" quite appropriate. When wives answered, and most often in narrative form, they recreated the conversations they had with their children, their husbands, or whoever was involved as though they were addressing these people and not me. In that sense, I was "transported" to those conversation events and provided with a subject position as though I was listening to them. Nevertheless, these were not the exact conversations but dramatizations of past conversations, hence inflected by the narrator. The "listening in" happens in relation to these reconstructed conversations.

10 Given the sensitivity of the matter, answers to my questions were frequently oblique. Understandably, there are personal and cultural reasons for the inability to talk openly about this matter. I provide here a composite account.

CHAPTER 6. *DIBERSYON* AND *ISU PAY*: GOSSIP AND THE MORALITY OF MOBILITY

1. Although the discussion of gossip here draws on what all the women said about it, my discussion of *dibersyon* draws only on the 29 women who were engaged in informal economic activity (farming; raising livestock; buying and selling of food items; selling cosmetics, lingerie and other clothing items; and owning a *tianggi* (small store).

CHAPTER 7. WORKING WOMEN: *ISU PAY* AND MORAL RATIONALITY

1. As an account of decision making around family responsibilities, moral rationality is developed as a theory with the capacity to bridge the gap between "the social ethics of family practices and theories of general social processes" (Duncan and Irwin 2004, 398). Duncan and Irwin (2004) conceptualize "norms, values and belief systems that have continuity with diverse social contexts" as the "middle range processes and mechanisms that shape, enable and constrain family practices" (398).

2. Duncan and Edwards (1997) construct three ideal types of gendered moral rationalities based on the domestic and employment orientations of women: one, a woman or mother who "gives primacy to the moral benefits of physically caring for their children themselves over and above any financial benefits of undertaking paid work;" two, "mother-worker integral," women who "see financial provision through employment as part of their moral responsibilities towards their children;" and three, a worker, women who "give primacy to paid work for themselves as separate to their identity as mothers" (71–72).

CHAPTER 8. *PANAGBUKBUKOD* AND RELATIONAL AUTONOMY

1. The distribution of informants according to residential arrangement is as follows: 10 wives used to live with their in-laws and now live in a separate house; 27 lived with their mothers-in-law at the time of the interview; 15 were living with their natal families at the time of the interview, and 8 women used to live with their natal families but now live in a separate house.

2. Although my research shows the rank of seafarers to be an important factor that determines a family's financial capacity to build its own house, it also shows that some women whose husbands had ratings positions were more quickly able to build their own house with the assistance of families or relatives in Hawaii or California.

3. See https://en.oxforddictionaries.com and Hau (2002).

CHAPTER 9. CONCLUSION: HOPEFUL AND STRATEGIC SUBJECTIVITY

1. I thank Lilia Quindoza Santiago for reminding me of "awan ti rigat a di malasat."

REFERENCES

Abella, Manolo. 2004. "The Role of Recruiters in Labor Migration." In *International Migration: Prospects and Policies in a Global Market,* edited by Douglas Massey and J. Edward Taylor, 201–11. Oxford: Oxford University Press.

Acosta, Pablo. 2011. "School Attendance, Child Labor, and Remittances from International Migration in El Salvador." *Journal of Development Studies* 47 (6): 913–36.

Adam, Barbara. 1988. *Time and Social Theory*. Cambridge: Polity Press.

———. 1995. *Timewatch: The Social Analysis of Time*. Cambridge: Polity Press.

Adam, Barbara, and Chris Groves. 2007. *Future Matters: Action, Knowledge, Ethics*. Leiden: Brill.

Adkins, Lisa. 2000. "Objects of Innovation: Post-occupational Reflexivity and Re-traditionalisations of Gender." In *Transformations: Thinking Through Feminism,* edited by Sarah Ahmed, Jane Kilby, Celia Lury, Maureen McNeil, and Beverley Skeggs, 259–72. London: Routledge.

Adorno, Theodor W., and Max Horkheimer. 1979. *Dialectic of Enlightenment*. London: Verso.

Aguila, Almond Pilar. 2008/2009. "Living Long-distance Relationships Through Computer-mediated Communication." *Social Science Diliman* 5 (1–2): 83–106.

Aguilar, Filomeno Jr. 1998. *Clash of Spirits: The History of Power and Sugar Planter Hegemony on a Visayan Island*. Quezon City: Ateneo de Manila University Press.

———. 1999. "Ritual Passage and the Reconstruction of Selfhood in International Labor Migration." *Sojourn* 14 (1): 98–139.

———, ed. 2002a. *Filipinos in Global Migrations: At Home in the World?*. Quezon City: Philippine Migration Research Network and Philippine Social Science Council.

———. 2002b. "Beyond Stereotypes: Human Subjectivity in the Restructuring of Global Migrations." In *Filipinos in Global Migrations: At Home in the World?,* edited by Filomeno Aguilar Jr, 1–36. Quezon City: Philippine Migration Research Network and Philippine Social Science Council.

———. 2003. "Global Migrations, Old Forms of Labor, and New Transborder Class Relations." *Southeast Asian Studies* 41 (2): 137–61.

———. 2009a. *Maalwang Buhay: Family, Overseas Migration, and Cultures of Relatedness in Barangay Paraiso*. Quezon City: Ateneo de Manila University Press.

———. 2009b. "Labor Migration and Ties of Relatedness: Diasporic Houses and Investments in Memory in a Rural Philippine Village." *Thesis Eleven* 98 (1): 88–114.

———. 2010. "The Riddle of the Alien-citizen: Filipino Migrants as US Nationals and the Anomalies of Citizenship, 1900s–1930s." *Asian and Pacific Migration Journal* 19 (2): 203–36.

———. 2013. "Brother's Keeper? Siblingship, Overseas Migration, and Centripetal Ethnography in a Philippine Village." *Ethnography* 14 (3): 346–68.

———. 2014a. "Ritual Passage and the Making of Labor Migrant Subjectivities." In *Migration Revolution: Philippine Nationhood and Class Relations in a Globalized Age*, 127–69. Quezon City: Ateneo de Manila University Press.

———. 2014b. Introduction to *Migration Revolution: Philippine Nationhood and Class Relations in a Globalized Age*, 1–23. Quezon City: Ateneo de Manila University Press.

———. 2014c. "Manilamen and Seafaring: Engaging the Maritime World Beyond the Spanish Realm." In *Migration Revolution: Philippine Nationhood and Class Relations in a Globalized Age*, 24–52. Quezon City: Ateneo de Manila University Press.

———. 2014d. "The Dialectics of Transnational Shame and Identity." In *Migration Revolution: Philippine Nationhood and Class Relations in a Globalized Age*, 83–126. Quezon City: Ateneo de Manila University Press.

Ahmad, Ali. 2008. "Dead Men Working: Time and Space in London's ('Illegal') Migrant Economy." *Work, Employment and Society* 22 (2): 301–18.

Aitken, Stuart, and Thomas Herman. 1997. "Gender, Power and Crib Geography: Transition Spaces and Potential Places." *Gender, Place and Culture* 4 (1): 63–88.

Alampay, Lianne. 2014. "Parenting in the Philippines." In *Parenting across Cultures: Childrearing, Motherhood and Fatherhood in Non-Western Cultures*, edited by Helaine Selin, 105–21. Netherlands: Springer.

Alarcon, Rafael. 1987. "Nortenizacion: Self-perpetuating Migration from a Mexican Town." In *Return to Aztlan: The Social Process of International Migration from Western Mexico*, edited by Douglas Massey, Rafael Alarcon, Jorge Durand, and Humberto Gonzalez, 302–18. Berkeley: University of California Press.

Alderton, Tony, Michael Bloor, Erol Kahveci, Tony Lane, Helen Sampson, Michelle Thomas, Nik Winchester, Bin Wu, and Minghua Zhao. 2004. *The Global Seafarer: Living and Working Conditions in a Globalized Industry*. Geneva: International Labor Organization.

Alderton, Tony, and Winchester, Nik. 2002. "Globalisation and De-regulation in the Maritime Industry." *Marine Policy* 26 (1): 35–43.

Allen, Amy. 2008. *The Politics of Our Selves: Power, Autonomy, and Gender in Contemporary Critical Theory*. New York: Columbia University Press.

Amante, Maragtas. 2004. "Industrial Democracy in the Rough Seas: The Case of Philippine Seafarers." In *Industrial Relations Research Association 56th Annual Meeting*, edited by Adrienne Eaton, 81–89. San Diego, CA: Industrial Relations Research Association.

———. 2005. "Philippine Global Seafarers: Ethnicity and Identity in Ships with Multinational Crews." *MINDAyawan Journal of Culture and Society* 2 (2): 1–23.

Amuedo-Dorantes, Catalina, and Susan Pozo. 2006. "Migration, Remittances, and Male and Female Employment Patterns." *American Economic Review* 96 (2): 222–26.

Anderson, Bridget. 2000. *Doing the Dirty Work? The Global Politics of Domestic Labor*. London: Zed.

———. 2001. "Different Roots in Common Ground: Transnationalism and Migrant Domestic Workers in London." *Journal of Ethnic and Migration Studies* 27 (4): 673–83.

———. 2007. "Battles in Time: The Relation between Global and Labor Mobilities." Working Paper 55. University of Oxford: Centre on Migration, Policy and Society.

———. 2009. "What's in a Name? Immigration Controls and Subjectivities: The Case of Au Pairs and Domestic Worker Visa Holders in the UK." *Subjectivity* 29 (1): 407–24.

———. 2010. "Migration, Immigration Controls and the Fashioning of Precarious Workers." *Work, Employment and Society* 24 (2): 300–317.

Appadurai, Arjun. 2013. "The Capacity to Aspire: Culture and the Terms of Recognition." In *The Future as Cultural Fact: Essays on the Global Condition*, 179–95. London: Verso.

Aquino, Belinda. 2000. "The Politics of Ethnicity among Ilokanos in Hawaii." In *Old Ties and New Solidarities: Studies on Philippine Communities*, edited by Charles MacDonald and Guillermo Pesigan, 100–116. Quezon City: Ateneo de Manila University Press.

Arminen, Ilkka. 2009. "New Reasons for Mobile Communication: Intensification of Time-Space Geography in the Mobile Era." In *The Reconstruction of Space and Time: Mobile Communication Practices*, edited by Rich Ling and Scott W. Campbell, 89–107. New Brunswick: Transaction Publishers.

Arnold, Fred, and Ricardo Abad. 1985. "Linkages between Internal and International Migration: The Ilocos Norte Experience." *Philippine Population Journal* 1 (2): 1–17.

Asis, Maruja. 1992. "The Overseas Employment Program Policy." In *Philippine Labour Migration: Impact and Policy*, edited by Graziano Battistella and Anthony Paganoni, 68–112. Quezon City: Scalabrini Migration Centre.

———. 1995. "Overseas Employment and Social Transformation in Source Communities: Findings from the Philippines." *Asian and Pacific Migration Journal* 4 (2–3): 327–46.

———. 2000. "Imagining the Future of Migration and Families in Asia." *Asian and Pacific Migration Journal* 9 (3): 255–72.

———. 2002. "From the Life Stories of Filipino Women: Personal and Family Agendas in Migration." *Asian and Pacific Migration Journal* 11 (1): 67–93.

———. 2006a. "Living with Migration." *Asian Population Studies* 2 (1): 45–67.

———. 2006b. "The Philippines' Culture of Migration." Migration Information Source. Washington, DC: Migration Policy Institute. http://www.migrationpolicy.org/article/philippines-culture-migration. Accessed 15 September 2014.

———. 2008. "The Social Dimensions of International Migration in the Philippines: Findings from Research." In *Moving Out, Back, and Up: International Migration and Development Prospects in the Philippines*, edited by Maruja Asis and Fabio Baggio, 77–108. Quezon City: Scalabrini Migration Center.

Asis, Maruja, and Battistella, Graziano. 2013. *The Filipino Youth and the Employment-Migration Nexus*. Quezon City: UNICEF Philippines and Scalabrini Migration Center.

Asis, Maruja, Shirlena Huang, and Brenda Yeoh. 2004. "When the Light of the Home is Abroad: Unskilled Female Migration and the Filipino Family." *Singapore Journal of Tropical Geography* 25 (2): 198–215.

Aysa, Maria, and Douglas S. Massey. 2004. "Wives Left Behind: The Labor Market Behaviour of Women in Migrant Communities." In *Crossing the Border: Research from the Mexican Migration Project*, edited by Jorge Durand and Douglas Massey, 131–44. New York: Russell Sage Foundation.

Bachelard, Gaston. 1994. *The Poetics of Space*. Boston: Beacon.

Baggio, Fabio. 2008. "The Migration-Development Disconnect in the Philippines." In *Moving Out, Back and Up*, edited by Maruja Asis and Fabio Baggio, 109–26. Quezon City: Scalabrini Migration Center.

Ball, Rochelle. 1997. "The Role of the State in the Globalization of Labor Markets: The Case of the Philippines." *Environment and Planning A* 29 (9): 1603–28.

Baltic and International Maritime Council (BIMCO), and International Chamber of Shipping (ICS). 2016. "Manpower Report: The Global Supply and Demand for Seafarers in 2015." Executive Summary. http://www.ics-shipping.org/docs/default-source/resources/safety-security-and-operations/manpower-report-2015-executive-summary.pdf?sfvrsn=16. Accessed 17 March 2017.

Bangko Sentral ng Pilipinas. 2015. "Remittances." http://www.bsp.gov.ph/statistics/keystat/ofw.htm. Accessed 19 Mar 2015.

Bankoff, Greg. 2007. "Dangers to Going It Alone: Social Capital and the Origins of Community Resilience in the Philippines." *Continuity and Change* 22 (2): 327–55.

———. 2005. "Wants, Wages, and Workers: Laboring in the American Philippines, 1899–1908." *Pacific Historical Review* 74 (1): 59–86.

———. 2004. "In the Eye of the Storm: The Social Construction of the Forces of Nature and the Climatic and Seismic Construction of God in the Philippines." *Journal of Southeast Asian Studies* 35 (1): 91–111.

Barlow, Anne, and Simon Duncan. 2000. "Supporting Families? New Labour's Communitarianism and the 'Rationality Mistake': Part I." *Journal of Social Welfare and Family Law* 22 (1): 23–42.

Battistella, Graziano. 1999. "Philippine Migration Policy: Dilemmas of a Crisis." *Sojourn: Journal of Social Issues in Southeast Asia* 14 (1): 229–48.

Beck, Ulrich. 1992. *Risk Society: Towards a New Modernity.* London: Sage.

Beck, Ulrich, and Elizabeth Beck-Gernsheim. 1995. *The Normal Chaos of Love.* Cambridge: Polity.

———. 2002. *Individualization: Institutionalized Individualism and Its Social and Political Consequences.* London: Sage.

Becker, Gary. 1996. *Accounting for Tastes.* Cambridge, MA: Harvard University Press.

Bello, Walden, David Kinley, and Elaine Elinson. 1982. *Development Debacle: The World Bank in the Philippines.* San Francisco: Institute for Food and Development Policy and Philippine Solidarity Network.

Bello, Walden, Shea Cunningham, and Bill Rain. 1994. *Dark Victory: The United States, Structural Adjustment and Global Poverty.* Quezon City: Freedom from Debt Coalition.

Bello, Walden, Herbert Docena, Marissa de Guzman, and Marylou Malig. 2009. The *Anti-Development State: The Political Economy of Permanent Crisis in the Philippines.* Manila: Anvil.

Benhabib, Seyla. 1999. "Sexual Difference and Collective Identities: The New Constellation." In *Virtual Gender: Fantasies of Subjectivity and Embodiment,* edited by Mary Ann O'Farrell and Lynne Vallone, 217–43. Ann Arbor, MI: University of Michigan Press.

Bernardo, Romeo, and Marie-Christine Tang. 2008. "The Political Economy of Reform during the Ramos Administration (1992–1998)." Commission on Growth and Development Working Paper, 39. Washington, DC: World Bank.

Bever, Sandra. 2002. "Migration and the Transformation of Gender Roles and Hierarchies in Yucatan." *Urban Anthropology* 31 (2): 199–230.

Biao, Xiang, and Johan Lindquist. 2014. "Migration Infrastructure." *International Migration Review* 48 (S1): S122–S148.

Biehl, Joao, and Peter Locke. 2010. "Deleuze and the Anthropology of Becoming." *Current Anthropology* 51 (3): 317–51.

Biehl, Joao, and Amy Moran-Thomas. 2009. "Symptom: Subjectivities, Social Ills, Technologies." *Annual Review of Anthropology* 38: 267–88.

Biehl, Joao, Byron Good, and Arthur Kleinman. 2007. "Introduction: Rethinking Subjectivity." In *Subjectivity: Ethnographic Investigations,* edited by Joao Biehl, Byron Good, and Arthur Kleinman, 1–23. Berkeley: University of California Press.

Binzel, Christine, and Ragui Assaad. 2011. "Egyptian Men Working Abroad: Labor Supply Responses by the Women Left Behind." *Labor Economics* 18 (1): 98–114.

Bittman, Michael, and Judy Wacjman. 2000. "The Rush Hour: The Character of Leisure Time and Gender Equity." *Social Forces* 79 (1): 165–89.

Bloor, Michael. 2011. "An Essay on Health Capital and the Faustian Bargains Struck by Workers in the Globalised Shipping Industry." *Sociology of Health and Illness* 33 (7): 1–14.

———. 2012. "The Rime of the Globalized Mariner: In Six Parts with Bonus Tracks from a Chorus of Greek Shippers." *Sociology* 47 (1): 30–50.

Boyce, James. 1990. *The Political Economy of External Indebtedness.* Makati: Philippine Institute for Development Studies.

Brennan, Denise. 2004. "Women Work, Men Sponge, and Everyone Gossips: Macho Men and Stigmatized/ing Women in a Sex Tourist Town." *Anthropological Quarterly* 77 (4): 705–33.

Brettell, Caroline. 1986. *Men Who Migrate, Women Who Wait: Population and History in a Portuguese Parish.* Princeton, NJ: Princeton University Press.

Broad, Robin. 1988. *Unequal Alliance, 1979–1986: The World Bank, the International Monetary Fund, and the Philippines.* Quezon City: Ateneo de Manila University Press

Brown, Claire (Vickery). 1982. "Home Production for Use in a Market Economy." In *Rethinking the Family: Some Feminist Questions,* edited by Barrie Thorne and Marilyn Yalom, 151–67. New York: Longman.

Brown, Judith. 2004. "Transitions in the Life-Course of Women." In *Encyclopedia of Sex and Gender,* edited by Carol R. Ember and Melvin Ember, 163–74. New York: Kluwer Academic–Plenum.

Bryant, Joanne, and Toni Schofield. 2007. "Feminine Sexual Subjectivities: Bodies, Agency and Life History." *Sexualities* 10 (3): 321–40.

Burkitt, Ian. 2008. "Subjectivity, Self, and Everyday Life in Contemporary Capitalism." *Subjectivity* 23 (1): 236–45.

Busby, Cecilia. 2000. *The Performance of Gender: An Anthropology of Everyday Life in a South Indian Fishing Village.* London: Athlone Press.

Cabegin, Emily Christi. 2006. *The Effect of Filipino Overseas Migration on the Non-Migrant Spouse's Market Participation and Labor Supply Behavior.* Bonn, Germany: Institute for the Study of Labor IZA Discussion Paper No. 2240. http://ftp.iza.org/dp2240.pdf. Accessed 15 January 2016.

Campbell, Scott, and Rich Ling. 2009. "Conclusion: Mobile Communication in Space and Time—Furthering the Theoretical Dialogue." In *The Reconstruction of Space and Time: Mobile Communication Practices,* edited by Rich Ling and Scott W. Campbell, 251–60. New Brunswick, NJ: Transaction Publishers.

Camroux, Stephen. 2009. "Nationalizing a 'Transnational' Diaspora?: The Philippine State and Filipino Emigration." In *The Changing Dynamics of Filipino Overseas Migration: The State in the Context of Nationalism, Regionalism, and Transnationalism,* edited by Jorge V. Tigno, 1–59. Quezon City: Philippine Migration Research Network and Philippine Social Sciences Council.

Carino, Benjamin. 1987. "The Philippines and Southeast Asia: Historical Roots and Contemporary Linkages." In *Pacific Bridges: The New Immigration from Asia and the Pacific Islands,* edited by James Fawcett and Benjamin Carino, 305–25. New York: Center for Migration Studies.

Carling, Jorgen, Cecilia Menjivar, and Leah Schmalzbauer. 2012. "Central Themes in the Study of Transnational Parenthood." *Journal of Ethnic and Migration Studies* 38 (2): 191–217.

Carsten, Janet. 1995. "Houses in Langkawi: Stable Structures or Mobile Homes." In *About the House: Levi-Strauss and Beyond,* edited by Janet Carsten and Stephen Hugh-Jones, 105–28. Cambridge: Cambridge University Press.

———. 2000. "Introduction: Cultures of Relatedness." In *Cultures of relatedness: New Approaches to the Study of Kinship*, edited by Janet Carsten, 1–36. Cambridge: Cambridge University Press.

———. 2007. "Introduction: Ghosts of Memory." In *Ghosts of Memory: Essays on Remembrance and Relatedness*, edited by Janet Carsten, 1–35. Oxford: Blackwell.

______. 2013. "What Kinship Does—and How." *HAU: Journal of Ethnographic Theory* 3 (2): 245–51.

Carsten, Janet, and Stephen Hugh-Jones. 1995. "Introduction: About the House – Levi-Strauss and Beyond." In *About the House: Levi-Strauss and Beyond*, edited by Janet Carsten and Stephen Hugh-Jones, 1–46. Cambridge: Cambridge University Press.

Castells, Manuel, Mireia Fernandez-Ardevol, Jack Linchuan Qiu, and Araba Sey. 2007. *Mobile Communication and Society: A Global Perspective*. Cambridge, MA: MIT Press.

Castles, Stephen. 2000. "Migration as a Factor in Social Transformation in East Asia." Paper Presented to a Conference on Migration and Development. Princeton University. http://prami.ibero.mx/wp-content/ uploads/2012/03/ Castles-Migracion-Asia-Revisado.pdf. Accessed 15 September 2010.

Castles, Stephen. 2007. "*Comparing the Experience of Five Major Emigration Countries*." Working Paper 7. Oxford: Oxford University International Migration Institute.

Chant, Sylvia. 1992a. "Migration at the Margins: Gender, Poverty and Population Movement on the Costa Rican Periphery." In *Gender and Migration in Developing Countries*, edited by Sylvia Chant, 49–72. London: Belhaven Press.

———. 1992b. "Conclusion: Towards a Framework for the Analysis of Gender-Selective Migration." In *Gender and Migration in Developing Countries*, edited by Sylvia Chant, 197–206. London: Belhaven Press.

———, ed. 1992c. *Gender and Migration in Developing Countries*. London: Belhaven Press.

———. 1997. *Women-Headed Households*. Basingstoke: Macmillan.

———. 2003. *Gender in Latin America*. London: Latin American Bureau.

———. 2006. *Re-visiting the 'Feminisation of Poverty' and the UNDP Gender Indices: What Case for a Gendered Poverty Index?* Working Papers Series 18. London: London School of Economics Gender Institute.

Chant, Sylvia, and Cathy McIlwaine. 1995. *Women of a Lesser Cost: Female Labour, Foreign Exchange, and Philippine Development*. London: Pluto Press.

Chao, Ruth, and Vivienne Tseng. 2002. "Parenting of Asians." In *Handbook of Parenting*, Volume 1: Children and Parenting, edited by Marc Bornstein, 59–93. Mahwah, NJ: Lawrence Erlbaum Associates.

Cheah, Pheng. 2006. *Inhuman Conditions: On Cosmopolitanism and Human Rights*. Cambridge, MA: Harvard University Press.

Cheng, Sealing. 2010. *On the Move for Love: Migrant Entertainers and the U.S. Military in South Korea*. Philadelphia, PA: University of Pennsylvania Press.

Chin, Christine. 1998. *In Service and Servitude: Foreign Female Domestic Workers and the Malaysian "Modernity" Project*. New York: Columbia University Press.

———. 2008a. "Labour Flexibilization at Sea." *International Feminist Journal of Politics* 10 (1): 1–18.

———. 2008b. *Cruising in the Global Economy: Profits, Pleasure and Work at Sea.* Aldershot, Hampshire: Ashgate.

Choy, Catherine Ceniza. 2003. *Empire of Care: Nursing and Migration in Filipino American History.* Durham, NC: Duke University Press.

Christensen, Toke Haunstrup. 2009. "'Connected Presence' in Distributed Family Life." *New Media and Society* 11 (3): 433–51.

Clarke, John, and Chas Critcher. 1985. *Devil Makes Work: Leisure in Capitalist Britain.* Basingstoke: Macmillan Press.

Cole, Sally. 1991. *Women of the Praia: Work and Lives in a Portuguese Coastal Community.* Princeton, NJ: Princeton University Press.

Coltrane, Scott. 1998. "Changing Patterns of Family Work: Chicano Men and Housework." In *Shifting the Center: Understanding Contemporary Families,* edited by Susan Ferguson, 547–62. Mountain View, CA: Mayfield Publishing.

———. 1989. "Household Labor and the Routine Production of Gender." *Social Problems* 36: 473–90.

Commission on Filipinos Overseas (CFO). 2013. "Number of Registered Filipino Emigrants by Major Country of Destination: 1981–2013." www.cfo. gov.ph/images/stories/pdf/bymajoritycountry2013.pdf. Accessed 15 January 2015.

Connel, Raewyn. 1995. *Masculinities.* Cambridge: Polity Press.

Constable, Nicole. 2014. *Born Out of Place: Migrant Mothers and the Politics of International Labor.* Berkeley and Los Angeles, CA: University of California Press.

———. 2003. *Romance on a Global Stage: Pen Pals, Virtual Ethnography, and "Mail Order" Marriages.* Berkeley: University of California Press.

———. 1997. *Maid to Order in Hong Kong: Stories of Filipino Workers.* Ithaca, NY: Cornell University Press.

Couper, Alastair, Chris Walsh, Ben Stanberry, Geoff Boerne. 1999. *Voyages of Abuse: Seafarers, Human Rights and International Shipping.* London: Pluto Press.

Craig, Lyn. 2006. "Does Father Care Mean Fathers Share?: A Comparison of How Mothers and Fathers in Intact Families Spend Time with Children." *Gender & Society* 20 (2): 259–81.

Cruz, Victoria. 1990. "Solo Parenting for Land-Based Workers' and Seamen's Wives." *Asian Migrant* 3 (1): 19–20.

Cruz, Victoria, and Anthony Paganoni. 1989. *Filipinas in Migration: Big Bills and Small Change.* Quezon City: Scalabrini Migration Center.

Cunningham-Burley, Sarah, Kathryn Backett-Milburn, and Debbie Kemmer. 2005. "Balancing Work and Family Life: Mothers' Views." In *Families in Society: Boundaries and Relationships,* edited by Linda McKie and Sarah Cunningham-Burley, 23–56. Bristol: Policy Press.

Cunningham-Burley, Sarah, and Lynn Jamieson, eds. 2003. *Families and the State: Changing Relationships.* Basingstoke: Palgrave Macmillan.

Cwerner, Saulo. 2001. "The Times of Migration." *Journal of Ethnic and Migration Studies* 27 (1): 7–36.

Dacanay, Jabeth. Ongoing. "Regulating Occupational Health and Safety in the Global Maritime Industry: A Case Study of the Philippines." PhD research, Cardiff University.

Dacanay, Jabeth, and David Walters. 2011. "Protecting Precarious Workers in the Global Maritime Industry: A Case of Regulatory Failure?" *Policy and Practice in Health and Safety* 9 (2): 47–68.

Dalisay, Grace Aguiling, Roberto Mendoza, John Benedict Santos, and Anita Echevaria. 1996. *Luto ng Diyos: Mga Kuwento ng Buhay Mag-asawa.* Manila: De La Salle University Press.

Daly, Kerry. 2001. "Deconstructing Family Time: From Ideology to Lived Experience." *Journal of Marriage and Family* 63 (2): 283–94.

———. 1996. *Families and Time: Keeping Pace in a Hurried Culture.* Thousand Oaks, CA: Sage.

Davies, Karen. 1990. *Women, Time and the Weaving of the Strands of Everyday Life.* Aldershot: Avebury.

———. 2001. "Responsibility and Daily Life: Reflections over Timespace." In *Timespace: Geographies of Temporality,* edited by Jon May and Nigel Thrift, 133–48. London: Routledge.

De Haas, Hein. 2007a. "Remittances, Migration and Social Development: A Conceptual Review of the Literature." Social Policy and Development Programme Paper 34. Geneva: United Nations Research Institute for Social Development.

———. 2007b. "The Complex Role of Migration in Shifting Rural Livelihoods: A Moroccan Case Study." In *Global Migration and Development,* edited by Ton van Naerssen, Ernst Spaan and Annelies Zoomers, 21–42. New York: Routledge.

De Haas, Hein, and Aleida Van Rooij. 2010, "Migration as Emancipation? The Impact of Internal and International Migration on the Position of Women Left Behind in Rural Morocco." *Oxford Development Studies* 38 (1): 43–62.

De Jesus, Edilberto. 1980. *The Tobacco Monopoly in the Philippines: Bureaucratic Enterprise and Social Change, 1766–1880.* Quezon City: Ateneo de Manila University Press.

Desai, Sonalde, and Manjistha Banerji. 2008. "Negotiated Identities: Male Migration and Left-Behind Wives in India." *Journal of Population Research* 25 (3): 337–55.

Desjarlais, Robert, and Jason C. Throop. 2011. "Phenomenological Approaches in Anthropology." *Annual Review of Anthropology* 40: 87–102.

Desmond, Matthew. 2016. *Evicted: Poverty and Profit in the American City.* London: Allen Lane.

Deutsch, Francine. 2007. "Undoing Gender." *Gender & Society* 24 (1): 31–55.

Deutscher, Penelope. 2006. "Repetition Facility: Beauvoir on Women's Time." *Australian Feminist Studies* 21 (51): 335–51.

DeVault, Marjorie. 1991. *Feeding the Family: The Social Organization of Caring as Gendered Work.* Chicago: University of Chicago Press.

Di Leonardo, Michaela. 1987. "The Female Worlds of Cards and Holidays: Women, Families and the Work of Kinship." *Signs: Journal of Women in Culture and Society* 12: 440–53.

Dreby, Joanna. 2009. "Gender and Transnational Gossip." *Qualitative Sociology* 32 (1): 33–52.

Drothbom, Heike. 2010. "Gossip and Social Control Across the Seas: Targeting Gender, Resource Inequalities and Support in Cape Verdean Transnational Families." *African and Black Diaspora* 3 (1): 51–68.

Duncan, Simon, and Rosalind Edwards. 1997. "Lone Mothers and Paid Work – Rational Economic Man or Gendered Moral Rationalities?" *Feminist Economics* 3 (2): 29–61.

———. 1999. *Lone Mothers, Paid Work and Gendered Moral Rationalities*. Basingstoke, UK: Macmillan Press.

Duncan, Simon, Rosalind Edwards, Tracey Reynolds, and Pam Alldred. 2003. "Motherhood, Paid Work and Partnering: Values and Theories." *Work, Employment and Society* 17 (2): 309–30.

———. 2004. "Mothers and Child Care: Policies, Values and Theories." *Children and Society* 18 (4): 254–65.

Duncan, Simon, and Sara Irwin. 2004. "The Social Patterning of Values and Rationalities: Mother's Choices in Combining Caring and Employment." *Social Policy and Society* 3 (4): 391–99.

Dungo, Nanette. 2007. *Negotiating from the Margins: Dynamics of Women's Work in a Globalized Economy*. Quezon City: University of the Philippines Press.

Ehn, Billy, and Orvar Lofgren. 2009. "Routines—Made and Unmade." In *Time, Consumption and Everyday Life: Practice, Materiality, and Culture*, edited by Elizabeth Shove, Frank Trentmann, and Richard Wilk, 99–112. London: Bloomsbury.

Elrick, Tim. 2008. "The Influence of Migration on Origin Communities. Insights from Polish Migrations to the West." *Europe-Asia Studies* 60 (9): 1503–17.

England, Kim, and Victoria Lawson. 2005. "Feminist Analyses of Work: Rethinking the Boundaries, Gendering, and Spatiality of work." In *A Companion to Feminist Geography*, edited by Lise Nelson and Joni Seager, 77–92. Oxford: Blackwell.

Ennaji, Moha, and Fatima Sadiqi. 2008. *Migration and Gender in Morocco: The Impact of Migration on the Women Left Behind*. Trenton, NJ: The Red Sea Press.

Enriquez, Virgilio. 1992. *From Colonial to Liberation Psychology: The Philippine Experience*. Quezon City: University of the Philippines Press.

Ermisch John. 2003. *An Economic Analysis of the Family*. Princeton, NJ: Princeton University Press.

España-Maram, Linda. 2006. *Creating Masculinity in Los Angeles's Little Manila: Working-Class Filipinos and Popular Culture, 1920s–1950s*. New York: Columbia University Press.

Espiritu, Yen Le. 2002. "Filipino Navy Stewards and Filipina Health Care Professionals: Immigration, Work and Family Relations." *Asian and Pacific Migration Journal* 11 (1): 47–66.

Eviota, Elizabeth. 1982. "Time Use and the Sex Division of Labor." *Philippine Journal of Industrial Relations* 4 (1–2): 116–33.

Fagan, Colette. 2001. "The Temporal Reorganization of Employment and the Household Rhythm of Work Schedules: The Implications for Gender and Class Relations." *American Behavioral Scientist* 44 (7): 1199–212.

Faier, Lieba. 2009. *Intimate Encounters: Filipina Women and the Remaking of Rural Japan.* Berkeley: University of California Press.

Fajardo, Kale Bantigue. *Filipino Crosscurrents: Oceanographies of Seafaring, Masculinities, and Globalization.* Minneapolis, MN: University of Minnesota Press.

Feldman, Martha, and Brian Pentland. 2003. "Reconceptualizing Organizational Routines as a Source of Flexibility and Change." *Administrative Science Quarterly* 48: 94–118.

Feeley, Kathleen, and Jennifer Frost. 2014. "Introduction." In *When Private Talk Goes Public,* ed. Kathleen Feeley and Jennifer Frost, 1–16. New York: Palgrave Macmillan.

Fernandez, Basco, and Roos Krootjes. 2007. "Seafarers—Invisible Part of the Filipino Diaspora in Europe: Scenarios from Onboard Research." In *In De Olde Worlde: Views of Filipino Migrants in Europe,* edited by Filomenita Mongaya Hoegsholm, 56–82. Quezon City: Philippine Social Science Council.

Finch, Janet, 1989, *Family Obligations and Social Change.* Cambridge: Polity Press.

———. 2003. "The State and the Family." In *Families and the State: Changing Relationships,* edited by Sarah Cunningham-Burley and Lynn Jamieson, 29–44. Basingstoke: Palgrave Macmillan.

Finch, Janet, and Jennifer Mason. 2000. *Passing On: Kinship and Inheritance in England.* London: Routledge.

Findley, Sally, and Gordon de Jong. 1985. "Community and Family Factors Influencing Family Migration in Ilocos Norte." *Philippine Population Journal* 1 (2): 18–44.

Forman, Friedah Johles. 1989. "Feminizing Time: An Introduction." In *Taking Our Time: Feminist Perspectives on Temporality,* edited by Friedah Johles Forman and Caoran Sowton, 1–9. Oxford: Pergamon Press.

Fortunati, Leopoldina. 2002. "Italy: Stereotypes, True and False." In *Perpetual Contact: Mobile Communication, Private Talk, Public Performance,* edited by James Katz and Mark Aakhus, 42–62. Cambridge: Cambridge University Press.

———. 2005. "Is Body to Body Communication Still the Prototype?" *The Information Society* 21 (1): 53–61.

Frederiksen, Martin. 2013. *Global Youth: Young Men, Time, and Boredom in the Republic of Georgia.* Philadelphia, PA: Temple University Press.

Freedom House. 2015. "Freedom on the Net 2015: Philippines." https://freedomhouse.org/sites/default/files/resources/FOTN%202015_Philippines.pdf. Accessed 15 March 2016.

Gardner, Katy. 1995. *Global Migrants, Local Lives: Travel and Transformation in Rural Bangladesh.* Oxford: Clarendon Press.

Garey, Anita. 1999. *Weaving Work and Moherhood.* Philadelphia, PA: Temple University Press.

George, Rose. 2013. *Deep Sea and Foreign Going*. London: Portobello.

George, Sheba. 2005. *When Women Come First: Gender and Class in Transnational Migration*. Berkeley, CA: University of California Press.

Gergen, Kenneth. 2002. "The Challenge of Absent Presence." In *Perpetual Contact: Mobile Communication, Private Talk, Public Performance*, edited by James Katz and Mark Aakhus, 227–41. Cambridge: Cambridge University Press.

Gerson Kathleen. 2002. "Moral Dilemmas, Moral Strategies and the Transformation of Gender: Lessons from Two Generations of Work and Family Change." *Gender & Society* 16 (1): 8–28.

Giddens, Anthony. 1990. *The Consequences of Modernity*. Cambridge: Polity Press.

———. 1992. *The Transformation of Intimacy*. Cambridge: Polity Press.

Gluckman, Max. 1963. "Gossip and Scandal." *Current Anthropology* 4 (3): 307–16.

Glucksmann, Miriam. 2000. *Cottons and Casuals: The Gendered Organisation of Labour in Time and Space*. Durham: Sociology Press.

Go, Stella. 1993. *The Filipino Family in the Eighties*. Manila: DLSU Social Development Research Centre.

Gonzalez, Joaquin. 1998. *Philippine Labor Migration: Critical Dimensions of Public Policy*. Singapore: Institute of Southeast Asian Studies.

Griffiths, Stephen. 1988. *Emigrants, Entrepreneurs and Evil Spirits: Life in a Philippine Village*. Honolulu, HI: University of Hawaii Press.

Grigolini, Silvia. 2005. "When Houses Provide More Than Shelter: Analyzing the Uses of Remittances within Their Sociocultural Context." In *Migration and Economy: Global and Local Dynamics*, edited by Lillian Trager, 193–223. Lanham, MD: Altamira Press.

GSMA Intelligence. 2014. "Country Overview. Philippines: Growth through Innovation." https://www.gsmaintelligence.com/research/ ?file=141201-philippines.pdf&download. Accessed 25 April 2015.

Guevarra, Ana Romina. 2009. *Marketing Dreams, Manufacturing Heroes: The Transnational Labor Brokering of Filipino Workers*. New Brunswick, NJ: Rutgers University Press.

Guillermo, Ramon. 2013. *Ang Makina ni Mang Turing*. Quezon City: University of the Philippines Press.

———. *Translation and Revolution: A Study of Jose Rizal's Guillermo Tell*. Quezon City: Ateneo de Manila University Press.

Gulati, Leela. 1993. *In the Absence of Their Men: The Impact of Male Migration on Women*. New Delhi: Sage.

Gutmann, Matthew. 1996. *The Meanings of Macho: Being a Man in Mexico City*. Berkeley: University of California Press.

———. 2002. *The Romance of Democracy: Compliant Defiance in Contemporary Mexico*. Berkeley: University of California Press.

Hadi, Abdullahel. 2001. "International Migration and the Change of Women's Position among the Left-Behind in Rural Bangladesh." *International Journal of Population Geography* 7 (1): 53–61.

Hassard, John. 1990. "Introduction: The Sociological Study of Time." In *The Sociology of Time,* edited by John Hassard, 1–18. Basingstoke: Macmillan.

Hau, Caroline. 2002. "Postscript." In *Suddenly Stateside: Funny Essays on Pinoy Life in America,* by Marivi Soliven Blanco, 177–81. Quezon City: Milflores Publishing.

Hegland, Mary Elaine. 2010. "Tajik Male Labor Migration and Women Left Behind: Can They Resist Gender and Generational Hierarchies?" *Anthropology of the Middle East* 5 (2): 16–35.

Henriques, Julian, Wendy Hollway, Cathy Urwin, Couze Venn, and Valerie Walkerdine. 1998. *Changing the Subject: Psychology, Social Regulation, and Subjectivity.* London: Routledge.

Herd, Pamela, and Madonna Harrington Meyer. 2002. "Care Work: Invisible Civic Engagement." *Gender & Society* 16 (5): 665–88.

Herriman, Nicholas. 2010. "The Great Rumor Mill: Gossip, Mass Media, and the Ninja Fear." *Journal of Asian Studies* 69 (3): 723–48.

Ho, David. 1993. "Relational Orientation in Asian Social Psychology." In *Indigenous Psychologies: Research and Experience in Cultural Context,* edited by Uichol Kim and John Berry, 240–59. Thousand Oaks: Sage.

Hochschild, Arlie. 1983. *The Managed Heart: Commercialization of Human Feeling.* Berkeley: University of California Press.

———. 1989. *The Second Shift: Working Papers and the Revolution at Home.* New York: Viking.

———. 1997. *The Time Bind: When Work Becomes Home and Home Becomes Work.* New York: Metropolitan Books.

———. 2003. *The Commercialization of Intimate Life: Notes from Home and Work.* Berkeley: University of California Press.

Holland, Dorothy, and Kevin Leander. 2004. "Ethnographic Studies of Positioning and Subjectivity: An Introduction." *Ethos* 32 (2): 127–39.

Holland, Dorothy, William Lachiotte Jr., Debra Skinner, and Carol Cain. 1998. *Identity and Agency in Cultural Worlds.* Cambridge, MA: Harvard University Press.

Hoodfar, Homa. 1997. "The Impact of Male Migration on Domestic Budgeting: Egyptian Women Striving for an Islamic Budgeting Pattern." *Journal of Comparative Family Studies* 28 (2): 73–98.

Horst, Heather, and Daniel Miller. 2006. *The Cell Phone: An Anthropology of Communication.* Oxford: Berg.

Horst, Heather. 2006. "The Blessings and Burdens of Communication: Cell Phones in Jamaican Transnational Social Fields." *Global Networks* 6 (2): 143–59.

Horvath, Istvan. 2008. "The Culture of Migration of Rural Romanian Youth." *Journal of Ethnic and Migration Studies* 3 (6): 771–86.

Hugo, Graeme. 1992. "Women on the Move: Changing Patterns of Population Movement of Women in Indonesia." In *Gender and Migration in Developing Countries,* edited by Sylvia Chant, 174–96. London: Belhaven Press.

———. 1995. "International Labor Migration and the Family: Some Observations from Indonesia." *Asian and Pacific Migration Journal* 4 (2–3): 273–301.

———. 2008. "International Migration in Indonesia and its Impacts on Regional Development." In *Global Migration and Development,* edited by Ton van Naerssen, Ernst Spaan and Annelies Zoomers, 43–65. New York: Routledge.

Hutchcroft, Paul. 1998. *Booty Capitalism: The Politics of Banking in the Philippines.* Quezon City: Ateneo de Manila University Press.

Hutchison, Jane. 1997. "Pressure on Policy in the Philippines." In *The Political Economy of Southeast Asia: An Introduction,* ed. Garry Rodan, Kevin Hewison, and Richard Robison, 64–92. Melbourne: Oxford University Press.

IBON Foundation. 2010. "Vital Signs: National Government Debt, Deficit and Social Services Spending." http://www.ibon.org/ibon_vitalsigns.php? page=gov-debt. Accessed 18 May 2011.

Ikuomola Adediran Daniel. 2015. "An Exploration of Life Experiences of Left Behind Wives in Edo State, Nigeria." *Journal of Comparative Research in Anthropology and Sociology* 6 (1): 289–307.

Ileto, Reynaldo. 1979. *Pasyon and Revolution: Popular Movements in the Philippines, 1840–1910.* Quezon City: Ateneo de Manila University Press.

International Transport Workers' Federation (ITF). 2014. ITF uniform "TCC" Collective Agreement for Crews on Flag of Convenience Ships 1 January 2012–14. Annex 1 to ITF Circular No. 258/S.104/D.87/ SS.12/2011. Available at: www.sur.ru/sites/default/files/mft/dogovor/11en258s104d87ss12uniformtcc2012-2014ax1_3.docx.

Irwin, Sara, and Wendy Bottero. 2000. "Market Returns? Gender and Theories of Change in Employment Relations." *British Journal of Sociology* 51 (2): 261–80.

Ito, Mizuko, Daisuke Okabe, and Misa Matsuda, eds. 2005. *Personal, Portable, Pedestrian: Mobile Phones in Japanese Life.* Cambridge, MA: MIT Press.

Jackson, Michael. 2008. "The Shock of the New: On Migrant Imaginaries and Critical Transitions." *Ethnos* 73 (1): 57–72.

Jamieson, Lynn. 2005. "Boundaries of Intimacy." In *Families in Society: Boundaries and Relationships,* edited by Linda McKie and Sarah Cunningham-Burley, 189–206. Bristol: Policy Press.

Jamieson, Lynn, and Sarah Cunningham-Burley. 2003. "The Family and the State: An Introduction." In *Families and the State: Changing Relationships,* edited by Sarah Cunningham-Burley and Lynn Jamieson, 1–26. Basingstoke: Palgrave Macmillan.

Jocano, Felipe Landa. 1982. *The Ilocanos: An Ethnography of Family and Community Life in the Ilocos Region.* Quezon City: University of the Philippines Asian Center.

———. 1995. "Filipino Family Values." In *The Filipino Family: A Spectrum of Views and Issues,* edited by Aurora Perez, 1–11. Quezon City: University of the Philippines Office of Research Coordination.

Kabamalan, Midea. 2004. "New Path to Marriage: The Significance of Increasing Cohabitation in the Philippines." *Philippine Population Review* 3: 111–27.

Kanaiaupuni, Shawn Malia. 2000. "Sustaining Families and Communities: Nonmigrant

Women and Mexico-U.S. Migration Processes." CDE Working Paper No. 2000–13. University of Wisconsin Madison Center for Demography and Ecology.

Kandell, William, and Douglas Massey. 2002. "The Culture of Mexican Migration: A Theoretical and Empirical Analysis." *Social Forces* 80 (3): 981–1004.

Kandiyoti, Deniz. 1988. "Bargaining with Patriarchy." *Gender & Society* 2 (3): 274–90.

Kelly, Philip. 2000. *Landscapes of Globalization: Human Geographies of Economic Change in the Philippines.* New York: Routledge.

Kirby, Kathleen. 1996. *Indifferent Boundaries: Spatial Concepts of Human Subjectivity.* New York: Guilford Press.

Kleinman, Arthur, and Erin Fitz-Henry. 2007. "The Experiential Basis of Subjectivity: How Individuals Change in the Context of Societal Transformation." In *Subjectivity: Ethnographic Investigations,* edited by Joao Biehl, Byron Good, and Arthur Kleinman, 52–65. Berkeley: University of California Press.

Klopfenstein, Bruce. 2002. "The Role of the United States in the Global Internet Innovation and Diffusion." In *Cyberpath to Development in Asia: Issues and Challenges,* edited by Sandhya Rao and Bruce Klopfenstein, 17–35. Westport, CT: Praeger.

Kothari, Uma. 2003. "Staying Put and Staying Poor?" *Journal of International Development* 15: 645–57.

Krinks, Peter. 2002. *The Economy of the Philippines: Elites, Inequalities and Economic Restructuring.* London: Routledge.

Laliotou, Ioanna. 2004. *Translating Subjects: Acts of Immigration and Cultures of Transnationalism between Greece and America.* Chicago, IL: University of Chicago Press.

Lamvik, Gunnar. 2002. *The Filipino Seafarer: A Life between Sacrifice and Shopping.* Dr. Art., Norwegian University of Science and Technology, Trondheim.

Lan, Pei-Chia. 2006. *Global Cinderellas: Migrant Domestics and Newly Rich Employers in Taiwan.* Durham, NC: Duke University Press.

Lane, Tony, Bernardo Obando-Rojas, Bin Wu, and Ali Tasiran. 2002. *Crewing the International Merchant Fleet.* London: Lloyds Register-Fairplay.

Lang, Graeme, and Josephine Smart. 2002. "Migration and the 'Second Wife' in China." *International Migration Review* 36 (2): 546–69.

Larson, Elizabeth, and Ruth Zemke. 2003. "Shaping the Temporal Patterns of Our Lives: The Social Coordination of Occupation." *Journal of Occupational Science* 10 (2): 80–89.

Lasker, Bruno. 1931. *Filipino Immigration to Continental United States and to Hawaii.* Chicago: University of Chicago Press.

Levitt, Peggy. 1998. "Social Remittances: Migration-Driven Local-level Forms of Cultural Diffusion." *International Migration Review* 32 (4): 926–48.

Levitt, Peggy, and Deepak Lamba-Nieves. 2011. "Social Remittances Revisited." *Journal of Ethnic and Migration Studies* 37 (1): 1–22.

Lewin, Ellen. 1997. "This Permanent Roommate." In *Situated Lives: Gender and Culture in Everyday Life,* edited by Louise Lamphere, Helena Ragone and Patricia Zavella, 192–207. New York: Routledge.

Lewis, Henry. 1971. *Ilocano Rice Farmers: A Comparative Study of Two Philippine Barrios.* Honolulu: University of Hawaii Press.

Lewis, J. David, and Andrew Weigart. 1990. "The Structures and Meanings of Social Time." In *The Sociology of Time,* edited by John Hassard, 77–101. Basingstoke: Macmillan.

Licoppe, Christian. 2004. "'Connected' Presence: The Emergence of a New Repertoire for Managing Social Relationships in a Changing Communication Technoscape." *Environment and Planning D: Society and Space* 22: 135–56.

Liebelt, Claudia. 2011. *Caring for the Holy Land: Filipino Domestic Workers in Israel.* New York & Oxford: Berghahn.

Liu, John, Paul Ong, and Carolyn Rosenstein. 1991. "Dual Chain Migration: Post-1965 Immigration to the United States." *International Migration Review* 25 (3): 487–513.

Lois, Jennifer. 2010. "The Temporal Emotion Work of Motherhood: Homeschoolers' Strategies for Managing Time Shortage." *Gender & Society* 24 (4): 421–46.

Lokshin, Michael, and Elena Glinskaya. 2009. "The Effect of Male Migration on Employment Patterns of Women in Nepal." *World Bank Economic Review* 23 (3): 481–507.

Lucht, Hans. 2012. *Darkness before Daybreak: African Migrants Living on the Margins in Southern Italy Today.* Berkeley, CA: University of California Press.

Luhrmann, Tania. 2006. "Subjectivity." *Anthropological Theory* 6 (3): 345–61.

McCarty, Dawn, and Rick Altemose. 2010. "The Voices of Mexican Women Left-Behind: Responses to Their Challenges." *Journal of Immigrant and Refugee Studies* 8 (3): 284–300.

McDowell, Linda. 2003. *Redundant Masculinities: Employment Change and White Working Class Youth.* Oxford: Blackwell.

———. 2012. "Post-Crisis, Post-Ford, and Post-Gender? Youth Identities in an Era of Austerity." *Journal of Youth Studies* 15 (5): 573–90.

McDowell, Linda, Kath Ray, Diane Perrons, Collette Fagan, and Kevin Ward. 2005. "Women's Paid Work and Moral Economies of Care." *Social and Cultural Geography* 6 (2): 219–35.

McEvoy, Jamie, Peggy Petrzelka, Cecilia Radel, and Birgit Schmook. 2012. "Gendered Mobility and Morality in a South-Eastern Mexican Community: Impacts of Male Labor Migration on the Women Left behind." *Mobilities* 7 (3): 369–88.

McKay, Deirdre. 2007. "'Sending Dollars Shows Feeling:' Emotions and Economies in Filipino Migration." *Mobilities* 2 (2): 175–94.

———. 2012. *Global Filipinos: Migrants' Lives in the Virtual Village.* Bloomington, IN: Indiana University Press.

McKay, Steven. 2007. "Filipino Sea Men: Identity and Masculinity in a Global Labor Niche." In *Asian Diasporas: New Formations, New Conceptions,* edited by Rhacel Parreñas and Lok C. D. Siu, 61–83. Stanford: Stanford University Press.

———. 2015. "'So They Remember Me When I'm Gone:' Remittances, Fatherhood, and Gender Relations in Filipino Migrant Men." In *Transnational Labor Migrations, Remittances, and the Changing Family in Asia*, edited by Lan Anh and Brenda Yeoh, 111–35. London: Palgrave Macmillan.

McKie, Linda, Sophia Bowlby, and Susan Gregory. 1999. "Connecting Gender, Power and the Household." In *Gender, Power and the Household*, edited by Linda McKie, Sophia Bowlby, and Susan Gregory, 3–21. Basingstoke: Macmillan.

McKie, Linda, Sarah Cunningham-Burley, and John McKendrick. 2005. "Families and Relationships: Boundaries and Bridges." In *Families in Society: Boundaries and Relationships*, edited by Linda McKie and Sarah Cunningham-Burley, 3–18. Bristol: Policy Press.

McLennan, Marshall. 1980. *The Central Luzon Plain: Land and Society on the Inland Frontier.* Quezon City: Alemar-Phoenix Publishing.

McMichael, Philip. 1996. *Development and Social Change: A Global Perspective.* London: Pine Forge Press.

McNay, Lois. 1992. *Foucault and Feminism: Power, Gender and the Self.* Cambridge: Polity Press.

———. 2000. *Gender and Agency: Reconfiguring the Subject in Social and Feminist Theory.* Cambridge: Polity Press.

———. 2003a. "Agency, Anticipation, and Indeterminacy in Feminist Theory." *Feminist Theory* 4 (2): 139–48.

———. 2003b. "Having It Both Ways: The Incompatibility of Narrative Identity and Communicative Ethics in Feminist Thought." *Theory, Culture & Society* 20 (6): 1–20.

———. 2004. "Agency and Experience: Gender as a Lived Relation." *Sociological Review* 52 (2): 173–90.

———. 2008. *Against Recognition.* Cambridge: Polity.

Madianou, Mirca. 2012. "Migration and the Accentuated Ambivalence of Motherhood: The Role of ICTs in Filipino Transnational Families." *Global Networks* 12 (3): 277–95.

Madianou, Mirca, and Daniel Miller. 2012. *Migration and New Media: Transnational Families and Polymedia.* London: Routledge.

Maher, Janemaree. 2009. "Accumulating Care: Mothers Beyond the Conflicting Temporalities of Caring and Work." *Time and Society* 18 (2–3): 231–45.

———. 2005. "A Mother by Trade: Australian Women Reflecting Mothering as Activity, Not Identity." *Australian Feminist Studies* 20 (46): 17–29.

Mahler, Sarah. 2001. "Transnational Relationships: The Struggle to Communicate across Borders." *Identities* 7 (4): 583–619.

Mahler, Sarah, and Patricia Pessar. 2006. "Gender Matters: Ethnographers Bring Gender from the Periphery toward the Core of Migration Studies." *International Migration Review* 40 (1): 27–63.

Manalansan, Martin IV. 2010. "Servicing the World: Flexible Filipinos and the

Unsecured Life." In *Political Emotions: New Agendas in Communication*, edited by Janet Staiger, Ann Cvetkovich, and Ann Reynolds, 215–28. New York: Routledge.

Mannov, Adrienne. 2015. "Economies of Security." PhD Dissertation. University of Copenhagen, Denmark.

Manohar, Namita, and Erika Busse-Cardenas. 2011. "Valuing 'Good' Motherhood in Migration: The Experiences of Indian Professional Wives in America and Peruvian Working-Class Wives Left Behind in Peru." *Journal of the Motherhood Initiative* 2 (2): 175–95.

Maram-España, Linda. 2006. *Creating Masculinity in Los Angeles's Little Manila: Working-Class Filipinos and Popular Culture, 1920s–1950s*. New York: Columbia University Press.

Margold, Jane. 1999. "From 'Cultures of Fear and Terror' to the Normalization of Violence." *Critique of Anthropology* 19 (1): 63–88.

Mason, Jennifer. 2004. "Personal Narratives, Relational Selves: Residential Histories in the Living and Telling." *Sociological Review* 52 (2): 162–79.

Massey, Doreen. 1994. "*Space, Place and Gender*." Minneapolis: University of Minnesota Press.

Massey Douglas, Joaquin Arango, Graeme Hugo, Ali Kouaouci, Adela Pellegrino, and J. Edward Taylor. 1998. *Worlds in Motion: Understanding International Migration at the End of the Millennium*. New York: Oxford University Press.

Matejowsky, Ty. 2007. "Convenience Store Pinoy: Sari-Sari, 7-Eleven, and Retail Localization in the Contemporary Philippines." *Philippine Quarterly of Culture and Society* 35 (4): 247–77.

Meah, Angela. 2014. "Conceptualizing Power and Gendered Subjectivities in Domestic Cooking Spaces." *Progress in Human Geography* 38 (5): 671–90.

Meah, Angela, and Peter Jackson. 2013. "Crowded Kitchens: The 'Democratisation' of Domesticity?" *Gender, Place & Culture* 20 (5): 578–96.

Medina, Belen. 2001. *The Filipino Family*. Quezon City: University of the Philippines Press.

Mendez, Paz Policarpio, and Felipe Landa Jocano. 1974. *The Filipino Family in Its Rural and Urban Orientation: Two Case Studies*. Manila: Centro Escolar University Research and Development Center.

Mendola, Mariapia, and Calogero Carletto. 2012. "Migration and Gender Differences in the Home Labor Market: Evidence from Albania." *Labour Economics* 19 (6): 870–80.

Menjivar, Cecilia, and Victor Agadjanian. 2007. "Men's Migration and Women's Lives: Views from Rural Armenia and Guatemala." *Social Science Quarterly* 88 (5): 1243–62.

Migration Policy Institute (MPI). 2014. "RAD Diaspora Profile Series: The Filipino Diaspora in the United States. www.migrationpolicy.org/ research/select-diaspora-populations-united-states." Accessed 15 January 2015.

Miller, Daniel. 2007. "What is a Relationship? Is Kinship Negotiated Experience?" *Ethnos* 72 (4): 535–54.

Miller, Daniel, and Don Slater. 2000. *The Internet: An Ethnographic Approach.* Oxford: Berg.

Mintz, Jerome. 1997. *Carnival Song and Society: Gossip, Sexuality, and Creativity in Andalusia.* Oxford: Berg.

Mohl, Perle. 1997. *Village Voices: Coexistence and Communication in a Rural Community in Central France.* Copenhagen: Museum Tusculanum Press, University of Copenhagen.

Mojares, Resil. 1983. "Cebuano Perceptions of the Hawaii Migration, 1909–1934." *Philippine Quarterly of Culture and Society* 11: 79–92.

Montes, Manuel. 1992. "The Effects of External Adjustment on the Population." In *Of Bonds and Bondage: A Reader on Philippine Debt,* edited by Emmanuel S. de Dios and Joel Rocamora, 48–58. Quezon City: Transnational Institute, Philippine Center for Policy Studies, and Freedom from Debt Coalition

Morrison, Carey-Ann. 2013. "Homemaking in New Zealand: Thinking through the Mutually Constitutive Relationship between Domestic Material Objects, Heterosexuality and Home." *Gender, Place & Culture* 20 (4): 413–31.

Municipality of San Gabriel. 2009a. *Annual State of Local Government Report.* San Gabriel: Office of the Municipal Mayor.

———. 2009b. *Sons and Daughters of San Gabriel by Barangay.* San Gabriel: Office of Municipal Planning and Coordination.

Nagasaka, Itaru. 1999. "Bringing Up the Children of Migrants: Continuity and Change of Ilocano Child Fosterage." *Asian Studies: Journal of Critical Perspectives on Asia* 35: 28–43.

———. 2007. "Cellphones in the Rural Philippines." In *The Social Construction and Usage of Communication Technologies: Asian and European Experiences,* edited by Raul Pertierra, 100–125. Quezon City: University of the Philippines Press.

———. 2015. "Growing Up in a Transnational Family: Experiences of Family Separation and Reunification of Filipino Migrants' Children in Italy." In *Southeast Asian Migration: People on the Move in Search of Work, Marriage and Refuge,* edited by Katharya Um and Sofia Gaspar, 8–39. Brighton: Sussex Academic Press.

Nansen, Bjorn, Michael Arnold, Martin Gibbs, and Hilary Davis. 2009. "Domestic Orchestration: Rhythms in the Mediated Home." *Time and Society* 18 (2–3): 181–207.

National Telecommunications Commission (NTC). 2007. "Consumer Information Statistical Data 2007." http://www.ntc.gov.ph/ consumerframe.html. Accessed 20 Feb. 2011.

Neysmith, Sheila, and Marge Reitsma-Street. 2005. "'Provisioning': Conceptualizing the Work of Women for 21st Century Social Policy." *Women's Studies International Forum* 28: 381–91.

———. 2009. "The Provisioning Responsibilities of Older Women." *Journal of Aging Studies* 23: 236–44.

Ngai, Mae. 2004. *Impossible Subjects: Illegal Aliens and the Making of Modern America.* Princeton: Princeton University Press.

Nielsen, Morten. 2011. "Futures Within: Reversible Time and House-Building in Maputo, Mozambique." *Anthropological Theory* 11 (4): 397–423.

Nippert-Eng, Christena. 1996. *Home and Work: Negotiating Boundaries through Everyday Life.* Chicago: University of Chicago Press.

Nowotny, Helga. 1994. *Time: The Modern and Postmodern Experience.* Cambridge: Polity Press.

Nydegger, Corinne. 1986. "Asymmetrical Kin and the Problematic Son-in-Law." In *Life-span Developmental Psychology: Intergenerational Relations,* edited by N. Datan, A. Greene and H. Reese, 99–123. Hillsdale, NJ: Lawrence Erlbaum Associates.

Nydegger, William, and Nydegger, Corinne. 1966. *Tarong: An Ilocos Barrio in the Philippines,* New York, NY: Wiley.

Oishi, Nana. 2005. *Women in Motion: Globalization, State Policies, and Labor Migration in Asia.* Palo Alto, CA: Stanford University Press.

Ortner, Sherry. 2006. *Anthropology and Social Theory: Culture, Power, and the Acting Subject.* Durham, NC: Duke University Press.

Paine, Robert. 1967. "What is Gossip About? An Alternative Hypothesis." *Man* 2 (2): 278–85.

Pangalangan, Elizabeth. 1995. "The Family under Philippine Law." In *The Filipino Family: A Spectrum of Views and Issues,* edited by Aurora Perez, 12–26. Quezon City: University of the Philippines Office of Research Coordination.

Paragas, Fernando. 2009. "Migrant Workers and Mobile Phones: Technological, Temporal, and Spatial Simultaneity." In *The Reconstruction of Space and Time: Mobile Communication Practices,* edited by Rich Ling and Scott W. Campbell, 39–65. New Brunswick: Transaction Publishers.

Parreñas, Rhacel. 2001. *Servants of Globalization: Women, Migration, and Domestic Work.* Palo Alto, CA: Stanford University Press.

———. 2005. *Children of Global Migration: Transnational Families and Gendered Woes.* Palo Alto, CA: Stanford University Press.

———. 2008a. *The Force of Domesticity: Filipina Migrants and Globalization.* New York: New York University Press.

———. 2008b. "Gender and Communication in Transnational Migrant Families." In *The Force of Domesticity: Filipina Migrants and Globalization,* 62–86. New York: New York University Press.

———. 2008c. "Transnational Fathering: Gendered Conflicts, Distant Disciplining and Emotional Gaps." *Journal of Ethnic and Migration Studies* 34 (7): 1057–72.

———. 2011. *Illicit Flirtations: Labor, Migration, and Sex Trafficking in Tokyo.* Palo Alto, CA: Stanford University Press.

———. 2015. *Servants of Globalization: Migration and Domestic Work.* 2nd edition. Palo Alto, CA: Stanford University Press.

Pauli, Julia. 2008. "A House of One's Own: Gender, Migration, and Residence in Rural Mexico." *American Ethnologist* 35 (1): 171–87.

Pe-Pua, Rogelia. 1991. "Ang Mga Balikbayang Hawayano ng Ilocos Norte: Pandarayuhan at Pagbabalik." In *Pilipinolohiya: Kasaysayan, Pilosopiya, at Pananaliksik,* edited by Violeta Bautista and Rogelia Pe-Pua, 171–73. Manila: Kalikasan Press.

Pertierra, Raul. 1997. "Trust and Time in a Philippine Village." In *Explorations in Social Theory and Philippine Ethnography*, 225–62. Quezon City: University of the Philippines Press.

———. 2005. "Mobile Phones, Identity and Discursive Intimacy." *Human Technology* I (1): 23–44.

———. 2006. *Transforming Technologies: Altered Selves.* Manila: De la Salle University.

———. 2007. "Introduction." In *The Social Construction and Usage of Communication Technologies: Asian and European Experiences*, edited by Raul Pertierra, xiii–xxxiv. Quezon City: University of the Philippines Press.

———. 2008. "The New Media and Heterotopic Technologies in the Philippines." *Human Technology* 4 (2): 169–85.

———. 2010. *The Anthropology of New Media in the Philippines.* Quezon City: Institute of Philippine Culture, Ateneo de Manila University.

———. ed. 1992. *Remittances and Returnees: The Cultural Economy of Migration in Ilocos.* Quezon City: New Day Publishers.

Pesquera, Beatriz. 1997. "'In the Beginning He Wouldn't Lift Even a Spoon': The Division of Household Labor." In *Situated Lives: Gender and Culture in Everyday Life*, edited by Louise Lamphere, Helena Ragone and Patricia Zavella, 208–22. New York: Routledge.

Philippine Overseas Employment Agency (POEA). 2015. "Overseas Employment Statistics." http://www.poea.gov.ph/stats/ 2014%20POEA%20Stats.pdf. Accessed 19 March 2016.

———. 2002. "POEA Rules and Regulations Governing the Recruitment and Employment of Seafarers." http://www.poea.gov.ph/laws&rules/files/ 2003%20 POEA%20Rules%20on%20Overseas%20Employment%20of%20Seafarers.pdf.

Pia, Jean. 2017. "'Nangangamuhan': An Analysis of the Standard Employment Contract (POEA-SEC) for Filipino Seafarers." Unpublished PhD thesis, Cardiff University.

Pingol, Alicia. 2001. *Remaking Masculinities: Identity, Power, and Gender Dynamics in Families with Migrant Wives and Househusbands.* Quezon City: University of the Philippines Center for Women's Studies.

Power, Marilyn. 2004. "Social Provisioning as a Starting Point for Feminist Economics." *Feminist Economics* 10 (3): 3–19.

Pratt, Geraldine. 2002. "From Registered Nurse to Registered Nanny: Discursive Geographies of Filipina Domestic Workers in Vancouver, B.C." In *Filipinos in Global Migrations: At Home in the World?*, edited by Filomeno Aguilar, Jr., 111–43. Quezon City: Philippine Migration Research Network and Philippine Social Science Council.

———. *Working Feminism.* Edinburgh: Edinburgh University Press.

———. 2012. *Families Apart: Migrant Mothers and the Conflicts of Labor and Love.* Minneapolis, MN: University of Minnesota Press.

Rafael, Vicente. 2010. "Welcoming What Comes: Sovereignty and Revolution in the Colonial Philippines." *Comparative Studies in Society and History* 52 (1): 157–79.

Ramones, Ronelyn. 2013. "Ina." *Bannawag.* Hunio 17.

Reeves, Madeleine. 2011. "Staying Put?: Towards a Relational Politics of Mobility at a Time of Migration." *Central Asian Survey* 30 (3–4): 555–76.

Republic of the Philippines. 2016. "National Expenditure Program (Volume I) Fiscal Year 2016." http://www.dbm.gov.ph/wp-content/uploads/ NEP2016/ NEP-VOLUME%20I.pdf. Accessed 24 Mar 2016.

———. 2015. "Population Projections." Philippine Statistics Authority. http://www.nscb.gov.ph/secstat/d_popnProj.asp. Accessed 24 Mar 2016.

Richter, Lara. 2016. "The Impact of the Maritime Industry on the Philippine Economy." Makati: German-Philippine Chamber of Commerce and Industry. http://philippinen.ahk.de/fileadmin/ahk_philippinen/ Committees/ Maritime_Industry_in_the_Philippines__GPCCI_2016_.pdf. Accessed 17 March 2017.

Roberts, Ken. 2002. "Are Long or Unsocial Hours of Work Bad for Leisure?" In *Social Conceptions of Time: Structure and Process in Work and Everyday Life,* edited by Graham Crow and Sue Heath, 165–78. Basingstoke: Palgrave Macmillan.

Rodriguez, Robyn. 2010. *Migrants for Export: How the Philippine State Brokers Labor to the World.* Minneapolis: University of Minnesota Press.

Rodriguez, Edgar, and Erwin Tiongson. 2001. "Temporary Migration Overseas and Household Labor Supply: Evidence from Urban Philippines." *International Migration Review* 35 (3): 709–25.

Rogaly, Ben. 2009. "Spaces of Work and Everyday Life: Labour Geographies and the Agency of Unorganised Temporary Migrant Workers." *Geography Compass* 3 (6): 1975–87.

Rollins, Judith. 1997. "Invisibility, Consciousness of the Other, *Ressentiment.*" In *Situated Lives: Gender and Culture in Everyday Life,* edited by Louise Lamphere, Helena Ragone and Patricia Zavella, 255–70. New York: Routledge.

Roy, Kevin, Carolyn Tubbs, and Linda Burton. 2004. "Don't Have No Time: Daily Rhythms and the Organization of Time for Low-Income Families." *Family Relations* 53 (2): 168–78.

Ruggunan, Shawn. 2009. "Global Transformation of the Contemporary Labor Market for Merchant Navy Seafarers: Case Studies of Filipino, South African and British Seafaring Labor Markets." PhD thesis, University of KwaZulu-Natal, Durban.

———. 2011. "The Global Labor Market for Filipino and South African Seafarers in the Merchant Navy." *South African Review of Sociology* 42 (1): 78–96.

Rupert, Mark, and M. Scott Solomon. 2006. *Globalization and International Political Economy: The Politics of Alternative Futures.* Lanham, MD: Rowman and Littlefield Publishers.

Sahlstein, Erin. 2004. "Relating at a Distance: Negotiating Being Together and Being Apart in Long-Distance Relationships." *Journal of Social and Personal Relationships* 21 (5): 689–710.

Salazar, Lorraine. 2007. *Getting a Dial Tone: Telecommunications Liberalization in Malaysia and the Philippines.* Singapore: Institute of Southeast Asian Studies.

Salgado de Snyder, V. Neily. 1993. "Family Life across the Border: Mexican Wives Left Behind." *Hispanic Journal of Behavioural Sciences* 15 (3): 391–401.

Sampson, Helen. 2003. "Transnational Drifters or Hyperspace Dwellers: An Exploration of the Lives of Filipino Seafarers Aboard and Ashore." *Ethnic and Racial Studies* 26 (2): 253–77.

———. 2005. "Left High and Dry?: The Lives of Women Married to Seafarers in Goa and Mumbai." *Ethnography* 6 (1): 61–85.

———. 2013. *International Seafarers and Transnationalism in the Twenty-first Century*. Manchester: University of Manchester Press.

Sampson, Helen, and Torsten Schroeder. 2006. "In the Wake of the Wave: Globalization, Networks, and the Experiences of Transmigrant Seafarers in Northern Germany." *Global Networks* 6 (1): 61–80.

Schatzki, Ted. 2009. "Timespace and the Organization of Social Life." In *Time, Consumption, and Everyday Life: Practice, Materiality, and Culture*, edited by Elizabeth Shove, Frank Trentmann, and Richard Wilk, 35–48. London: Bloomsbury.

Scheper-Hughes, Nancy. 2008. "A Talent for Life: Reflections on Human Vulnerability and Resilience." *Ethnos* 73 (1): 25–56.

Schneider, David. 1980. *American Kinship: A Cultural Account*. 2nd edition, Chicago: University of Chicago Press

Sennett, Richard. 1998. *The Corrosion of Character: The Personal Consequences of Work in the New Capitalism*. New York: W.W. Norton.

Sharma, Miriam. 1987. "Towards a Political Economy of Emigration from the Philippines: The 1906 to 1946 Ilocano Movement to Hawaii in Historical Perspective." *Philippine Sociological Review* 35 (3–4): 15–33.

Shih, Kristy, and Karen Diane Pyke. 2009. "Power, Resistance and Emotional Economies in Women's Relationships with Mothers-in-law in Chinese Immigrant Families." *Journal of Family Issues* 31 (3): 333–57.

Sillars, Stuart. 2010. "Illustrated Shakespeare and the Limits of Interpretation." Public Lecture. Cardiff: Centre for Editorial and Intertextual Research, Cardiff University, 14 December.

Sills, Stephen. 2007. "Philippine Labour Migration to Taiwan: Social, Political, Demographic, and Economic Dimensions." *Migration Letters* 4 (1): 1–14.

Sills, Stephen, and Natassaja Chowthi. 2008. "Becoming an OFW: Renegotiations in Self-concept among Filipino Factory Workers in Taiwan." *Asian and Pacific Migration Journal* 17 (2): 189–220.

Silva, Elizabeth, and Carol Smart. 1999. "The 'New' Practices and Politics of Family Life." In *The New Family?* edited by Elizabeth Silva and Carol Smart, 1–12. London: Sage.

Silva, Elizabeth. 2002. "Routine Matters: Narratives of Everyday Life in Families." In *Social Conceptions of Time: Structure and Process in Work and Everyday Life*, edited by Graham Crow and Sue Heath, 179–94. Basingstoke: Palgrave Macmillan.

Silverstein, Judith. 1990. "The Problem with In-laws." *Journal of Family Therapy* 14 (4): 399–412.

Simon, Gregory. 2014. *Caged in on the Outside: Moral Subjectivity, Selfhood, and Islam in Minangkabau, Indonesia*. Honolulu, HI: University of Hawaii Press.

Skolnik, Jocelyn, Sandra Lazo de la Vega, and Timothy Steigenga. 2012. "*Chisme* across Borders: The Impact of Gossip in a Guatemalan Transnational Community." *Migraciones Internacionales* 6 (3): 9–38.

Slater, Don. 2009. "The Ethics of Routine: Consciousness, Tedium, and Value." In *Time, Consumption, and Everyday Life: Practice, Materiality, and Culture*, edited by Elizabeth Shove, Frank Trentmann, and Richard Wilk, 217–30. London: Bloomsbury.

Smart, Carol and Neale, Bren. 1999. *Family Fragments?* Cambridge: Polity Press.

Smith, Dorothy. 1987. *The Everyday World as Problematic: A Feminist Sociology*. Boston: Northeastern University Press.

Smith, Peter. 1977. "The Evolving Pattern of Interregional Migration in the Philippines." *Philippine Economic Journal* 16 (1–2): 121–59.

———. 1981. "Population Pressure and Social Response on the Ilocos Coast in the Philippines." Working Papers: A Prepublication Series Reporting on Research in Progress No. 2. Honolulu, HI: East-West Population Institute.

Somers, Margaret. 1994. "The Narrative Constitution of Identity: A Relational and Network Approach." *Theory and Society* 23 (5): 605–49.

Somers, Margaret, and Gloria Gibson. 1994. "Reclaiming the Epistemological 'Other': Narrative and the Social Constitution of Identity." In *Social Theory and the Politics of Identity*, edited by Craig Calhoun, 37–99. Oxford: Basil Blackwell.

Southerton, Dale. 2009. "Re-ordering Temporal Rhythms: Coordinating Daily Practices in the UK in 1937 and 2000." In *Time, Consumption, and Everyday Life: Practice, Materiality, and Culture*, edited by Elizabeth Shove, Frank Trentmann, and Richard Wilk, 49–63. London: Bloomsbury.

———. 2006. "Analysing the Temporal Organization of Daily Life: Social Constraints, Practices and Their Allocation." *Sociology* 40 (3): 435–54.

Starrels, Marjorie. 1994. "Husbands' Involvement in Female Gender-Typed Household Chores." *Sex Roles* 31 (7–8): 473–91.

Stewart, Pamela, and Andrew Strathern. 2004. *Witchcraft, Sorcery, Rumors and Gossip*. Cambridge: Cambridge University Press.

Stopford, Martin. 2008. *Maritime Economics*. 3rd ed. London: Routledge.

Strathern, Marilyn. 1988. *The Gender of the Gift: Problems with Women and Problems with Society in Melanesia*. Berkeley: University of California Press.

Sullivan, Oriel. 2004. "Changing Gender Practices within the Household: A Theoretical Perspective." *Gender & Society* 18 (2): 207–22.

Swift, Olivia. 2007. "'Natural-Born' Sailors?: Reconsidering Stereotypes of Filipino Global Seafarers." *AghamTao* 16: 1–28.

_______. 2010. "Making a Model Union Village in the Philippines: Labor, Gender, and Global Shipping." PhD thesis, Goldsmiths, University of London.

Teodoro, Luis, ed. 1981. *Out of This Struggle: The Filipinos in Hawaii*. Honolulu: University of Hawaii Press.

Terry, William. 2009. "Working on the Water: On Legal Space and Seafarer Protection in the Cruise Industry." *Economic Geography* 854: 463–82.

Thomas, Michelle, and Nicholas Bailey. 2006. "Square Pegs in Round Holes?: Leave Periods and Role Displacement in UK-Based Seafaring Families." *Work, Employment and Society* 20 (1): 129–49.

———. 2009. "Out of Time: Work, Temporal Synchrony and Families." *Sociology* 43 (4): 613–30.

Thomas, Michelle, Helen Sampson, and Minghua Zhao. 2003. "Finding a Balance: Companies, Seafarers, and Family Life." *Maritime Policy and Management* 30 (1): 59–76.

Thorne, Barrie. 1999. "Pick-up Time at Oakdale Elementary School: Work and Family from the Vantage Points of Children." Working Paper No. 2. Berkeley, CA: Centre for Working Families, University of California.

Tiglao, Rigoberto. 1993. "Into a Corner: Philippine Phone Monopoly Assailed by Critics." *Far Eastern Economic Review*, 11 Feb.: 55–56.

Torres-Mejia, Patricia. 2000. *Peasants, Merchants, and Politicians in Tobacco Production: Philippine Social Relations in a Global Economy*. Quezon City: Ateneo de Manila University Press.

Toundjis, Peter. 1975. *The Philippine Crewing Industry: Jobs and Dollars the Philippines Might Lose.* Quezon City: Peter Toundjis.

Toyota, Mika, Brenda Yeoh, and Liem Nguyen. 2007. "Bringing the 'Left Behind' Back into View in Asia: A Framework for Understanding the 'Migration-Left Behind Nexus.'" *Population, Space and Place* 13 (3): 157–61.

Trager, Lillian. 1988. *The City Connection: Migration and Family Interdependence in the Philippines.* Ann Arbor, MI: University of Michigan Press.

Tronto, Joan. 2003. "Time's Place." *Feminist Theory* 4 (2): 119–38.

Tsing, Anna. 1993. *In the Realm of the Diamond Queen: Marginality in an Out-of-the-way Place.* Princeton, NJ: Princeton University Press.

Tyner, James. 2004. *Made in the Philippines: Gendered Discourses and the Making of Migrants.* London: Routledge.

———. 2009. *The Philippines: Mobilities, Identities, Globalization.* London: Routledge.

Van den Broek, Andries, Koe Breedveld, and Wim Knulst. 2002. "Roles, Rhythms and Routines: Towards a New Script of Daily Life in the Netherlands?" In *Social Conceptions of Time: Structure and Process in Work and Everyday Life*, edited by Graham Crow and Sue Heath, 195–214. Basingstoke: Palgrave Macmillan.

Van Vleet, Krista, 2002. "The Intimacies of Power: Rethinking Violence and Affinity in the Bolivian Andes." *American Ethnologist* 29 (3): 567–601.

———. 2003. "Partial Theories: On Gossip, Envy, and Ethnography in the Andes." *Ethnography* 4 (4): 491–591.

Vera-Sanso, Penny. 1999. "Dominant Daughters-in-law and Submissive Mothers-in-law? Cooperation and Conflict in South India." *Journal of the Royal Anthropological Institute* 5 (4): 577–93.

Vertovec, Steven. 2004. "Cheap Calls: The Social Glue of Migrant Transnationalism." *Global Networks* 4 (2): 219–24.

Vlahoutsikou, Christina. 1997. "Mothers-in-law and Daughters-in-law: Politicizing Confrontations." *Journal of Modern Greek Studies* 15 (2): 283–302.

Vigh, Henrik. 2006. *Navigating Terrains of War: Youth and Soldiering in Guinea-Bissau.* Oxford: Berghahn Books.

———. 2008. "Crisis and Chronicity: Anthropological Perspectives on Continuous Conflict and Decline." *Ethnos* 73 (1): 5–24.

———. 2009. "Wayward Migration: On Imagined Futures and Technological Voids." *Ethnos* 74 (1): 91–109.

Walker, Jim. 2016. "Seafarer 'Protection Act' Shields Ship Owners, not Seafarers." 20 August. http://globalnation.inquirer.net/143023/seafarer-protection-act-shields-cruise-line-owners-not-seafarers. Accessed 17 March 2017.

Walkerdine, Valerie. 2010. "Communal Beingness and Affect: An Exploration of Trauma in an Ex Industrial Community." *Body and Society* 16 (1): 91–116.

Wang, Qing. 2013. "Male Migration and Female Labour Force Participation: New Evidence from the Mexican Family Life Survey." SSRN: https://ssrn.com/abstract=2232117 or http://dx.doi.org/10.2139/ssrn.2232117. Accessed 23 December 2015.

Wasoff, Fran, and Sarah Cunningham-Burley. 2005. "Perspectives on Social Policies and Families." In *Families in Society: Boundaries and Relationships,* edited by Linda McKie and Sarah Cunningham-Burley, 261–70. Bristol: Policy Press.

Wert, Sarah, and Peter Salovey. 2004. "A Social Comparison Account of Gossip." *Review of General Psychology* 8 (2): 122–37.

West, Candace, and Don Zimmerman. 1987. "Doing Gender." *Gender & Society* 1: 125–51.

White Anne. 2010. *Polish Families and Migration since EU Accession.* Bristol, UK: Policy Press.

Wilding, Raelene. 2006. "'Virtual' Intimacies? Families Communicating across Transnational Contexts." *Global Networks* 6 (2): 125–42.

Willen, Sarah. 2007. "Toward a Critical Phenomenology of 'Illegality': State, Power, Criminalization, and Abjectivity among Undocumented Migrant Workers in Tel Aviv, Israel." *International Migration* 45 (3): 8–38.

Williams, Lindy, Midea Kabamalan, and Nimfa Ogena. 2007. "Cohabitation in the Philippines: Attitudes and Behaviours among Young Women and Men." *Journal of Marriage and Family* 69 (5): 1244–56.

Wolf, Margery. 1972. *Women and the Family in Rural Taiwan.* Stanford: Stanford University Press.

Wu, Bin. 2005. *The World Cruise Industry: A Profile of the Global Labour Market.* Cardiff, Wales: Seafarers International Research Centre.

Wu, Huifang, and Jingzhong Ye. 2016. "Hollow Lives: Women Left Behind in Rural China." *Journal of Agrarian Change* 16 (1): 50–69.

Xenos, Peter. 1998. "The Ilocos Coast since the 1800: Population Pressure, the Ilocano Diaspora, and Multiphasic Response." In *Population and History: The*

Demographic Origins of the Modern Philippines, edited by Daniel Doeppers and Peter Xenos, 39–70. Quezon City: Ateneo de Manila University Press.

Yabiku, Scott, Victor Agadjanian, and Arusyak Sevoyan. 2010. "Husbands' Labor Migration and Wives' Autonomy, Mozambique 2000–2006." *Population Studies* 64 (3): 293–306.

Yeoh, Brenda, Elspeth Graham, and Paul Boyle. 2002. "Migrations and Family Relations in the Asia Pacific Region." *Asian and Pacific Migration Journal* 11 (1): 1–11.

Young, Iris Marion. 1998. "House and Home: Feminist Variations on a Theme." In *Intersecting Voices: Dilemmas of Gender, Political Philosophy, and Policy,* 134–64. Princeton, NJ: Princeton University Press.

Young, James. 1982. "Intimate Allies in Migration: Education and Propaganda in a Philippine Village." *Comparative Education Review* 26 (2): 218–34.

Young, Michael. 1988. *The Metronomic Society: Natural Rhythms and Human Timetables.* London: Thames and Hudson.

Zerubavel, Eviatar. 1979. *Patterns of Time in Hospital Life: A Sociological Perspective.* Chicago: University of Chicago Press.

———. 1985a. *Hidden Rhythms.* Berkeley: University of California Press.

———. 1985b. *The Seven-Day Circle.* Berkeley: University of California Press.

INDEX

T

U

W